AFTER THE VERSAILLES TREATY

Designed to secure a lasting peace between the Allies and Germany, the Versailles Settlement soon came apart at the seams. In *After The Versailles Treaty* an international team of historians examines the almost insuperable challenges facing victors and vanquished alike after the ravages of WW1.

This is not another diplomatic history, instead focusing on the practicalities of treaty enforcement and compliance as western Germany came under Allied occupation and as the reparations bill was presented to the defeated and bankrupt Germans. It covers issues such as:

- How did the Allied occupiers conduct themselves and how did the Germans respond?
- Were reparations really affordable and how did the reparations regime affect ordinary Germans?
- What lessons did post-WW2 policymakers learn from this earlier reparations settlement?
- The fraught debates over disarmament as German big business struggled to adjust to the sudden disappearance of arms contracts and as efforts were made on the international stage to achieve a measure of global disarmament.
- The price exacted by the redrawing of frontiers on Germany's eastern and western margins, as well as the (gentler) impact of the peace settlement on identity in French Flanders.

This book was previously published as a special issue of *Diplomacy and Statecraft*.

Conan Fischer is Professor of European History at the University of Strathclyde in Glasgow.

Alan Sharp is Professor of International Relations and Provost of the Coleraine campus of the University of Ulster.

AFTER THE VERSAILLES TREATY

Enforcement, Compliance, Contested Identities

*Edited by Conan Fischer and
Alan Sharp*

Routledge
Taylor & Francis Group

LONDON AND NEW YORK

First published 2008
by Routledge
2 Park Square, Milton Park, Abingdon, Oxon, OX14 4RN

Simultaneously published in the USA and Canada
by Routledge
270 Madison Avenue, New York, NY 10016

Routledge is an imprint of the Taylor & Francis Group

Transferred to Digital Printing 2009

© 2007 Edited by Conan Fischer and Alan Sharp

Typeset in Times by RefineCatch Ltd, Bungay, Suffolk NR35 1EF

British Library Cataloguing in Publication Data
A catalogue record for this book is available from the British Library

Library of Congress Cataloguing in Publication Data

ISBN10: 0–415–44585–X (hbk)
ISBN10: 0–415–49496–6 (pbk)

ISBN13: 978–0–415–44585–6 (hbk)
ISBN13: 978–0–415–49496–0 (pbk)

CONTENTS

Notes on contributors   **vii**

Introduction   **1**
ALAN SHARP AND CONAN FISCHER

1   **The Enforcement of the Treaty of Versailles, 1919–1923**   **5**
ALAN SHARP

2   **The British Zone of Occupation in the Rhineland**   **21**
ELSPETH O'RIORDAN

3   **"Hut ab," "Promenade with Kamerade for Schokolade," and
the *Flying Dutchman*: British Soldiers in the Rhineland, 1918–1929**   **37**
KEITH JEFFERY

4   **French Policy in the Rhineland 1919–1924**   **57**
STANISLAS JEANNESSON

5   **The Reparations Debate**   **69**
GERALD FELDMAN

6   **The Human Price of Reparations**   **81**
CONAN FISCHER

7   **Reparations in the Long Run: Studying the Lessons of History**   **97**
PATRICIA CLAVIN

8   **Disarmament and Big Business: The Case of Krupp, 1918–1925**   **113**
KLAUS TENFELDE

9   **Making Disarmament Work: The Implementation of the
    International Disarmament Provisions in the League of
    Nations Covenant, 1919–1925**   **133**
    ANDREW WEBSTER

10 **From Lothringen to Lorraine: Expulsion and Voluntary Repatriation** **153**
    CAROLYN GROHMANN

11 **The Versailles Settlement and Identity in French Flanders**   **171**
    TIMOTHY BAYCROFT

12 **"The Sore That Would Never Heal": The Genesis of the
    Polish Corridor**   **185**
    ROGER MOORHOUSE

    Conclusion   197
    Index   201

NOTES ON CONTRIBUTORS

Timothy Baycroft is Senior Lecturer in Modern History at the University of Sheffield. He is the author of *Nationalism in Europe 1789–1945* (1998), *Culture, Identity and Nationalism: French Flanders in the Nineteenth and Twentieth Centuries* (2004) and joint editor with Mark Hewitson of *What is a Nation? Europe 1789–1914* (2006). He is currently completing a book entitled *France: Inventing the Nation*.

Patricia Clavin is Fellow and Tutor in History at Jesus College, Oxford. She is the author of *The Failure of Economic Diplomacy. Britain, France and the United States, 1931–1936* (1996), *The Great Depression in Europe, 1929–1939* (2000), (with Asa Briggs) *Modern Europe, 1789–1989* (1996, 2003) and editor of *Transnational Communities in European History, 1920–1960* (2005). She is currently completing a history of the Economic and Financial Organisation of the League of Nations.

Gerald Feldman is Jane K Sather Professor of History and Director of the Institute of European Studies at the University of California, Berkeley. His major works include *Army, Industry and Labor in Germany, 1914–1918* (1966), *Iron and Steel in the German Inflation, 1916–1924* (1977), *Vom Weltkrieg zur Weltwirtschaftskrise* (1984), *The Great Disorder: Politics, Economics and Society in the German Inflation, 1914–1924* (1993), *Hugo Stinnes: Biographie eines Industriellen 1870–1924* (1998), and *Allianz and the German Insurance Business, 1933–1945* (2001). He is currently completing a study of the Austrian banks under National Socialism. He is also the editor/joint editor of some fifteen further volumes.

Conan Fischer is Professor of European History, University of Strathclyde, Glasgow. He is the author of *Stormtroopers: A Social, Economic and Ideological Analysis 1929–35* (1983), *The German Communists and the Rise of Nazism* (1991), *The Rise of the Nazis* (1995, 2002), *The Ruhr Crisis, 1923–1924* (2003) and editor of *The Rise of National Socialism and the Working Classes in Weimar Germany* (1996). He is currently completing a book entitled *Europe between Democracy and Dictatorship, 1900–1945*.

Carolyn Grohmann has taught history at the Universities of Stirling and Edinburgh. She completed her doctorate at the University of Stirling in 2000 and is the author of several articles on the history and identity of interwar Lorraine.

Stanislas Jeannesson is *maître de conferences* at the Sorbonne. He is a member of the IRICE (CRNS). He is author of *Poincaré, la France et la Ruhr (1922–1924)* (1998) and *La Guerre froide* (2002). He is joint editor with Laurence Badel of *Les administrations nationals et la construction européene* (2005) and is currently completing a biography of the French diplomat Jacques Seydoux.

Keith Jeffery is Professor of British History at Queen's University, Belfast. He is author of *States of Emergency: British Governments and Strikebreaking since 1919* (with Peter Hennessey) (1983), *The British Army and the Crisis of Empire, 1918–1922* (1984), *Northern Ireland since 1968* (with Paul Arthur) (1988, 1996), *Ireland and the Great War* (2000), *The GPO and the Easter Rising* (2006), *Field Marshal Sir Henry Wilson: a political soldier* (2006), editor of *Military Correspondence of Field Marshal Sir Henry Wilson 1918–1922* (1985), and editor (with Thomas Bartlett) of *A Military History of Ireland* (1996) and *'An Irish Empire'? Aspects of Ireland and the British Empire* (1996).

Roger Moorhouse has been senior researcher and editorial assistant to Norman Davies since 1995. He is the author (with Norman Davies) of *Microcosm – Portrait of a Central European City* (2002) and of *Killing Hitler. The Third Reich and the Plots against the Führer* (2006).

Elspeth O'Riordan has taught history at King's College, London and at the Universities of St Andrews and Dundee. She is the author of *Britain and the Ruhr Crisis* (2001) and a number of articles on British foreign policy during the 1920s.

Alan Sharp is Professor of International Studies at the University of Ulster. He has published widely on British foreign policy after the First World War, with a particular focus on Lord Curzon's tenure of the Foreign Office and the career of James Headlam-Morley. He is the author of *The Versailles Settlement: Peacemaking in Paris 1919* (1991) and editor (with Glyn Stone) of *Anglo-French Relations in the Twentieth Century: Rivalry and Cooperation* (2000).

Klaus Tenfelde is Professor of Social History and Social Movements, and Director of the Institut für soziale Bewegungen at the Ruhr Universität, Bochum. He is the author of *Sozialgeschichte der Bergarbeiterschaft an der Ruhr im 19. Jahrhundert* (1977, 1981), *Proletarische Provinz. Radikalisierung und widerstand in Penzberg/Oberbayern 1900 bis 1945* (1982), *Arbeiter im Deutschen Kaiserreich* (with Gerhard Ritter) (1992), *Arbeitersekretäre.*

Karrieren in der deutschen Arbeiterbewegung vor 1914 (1993, 1996), *Mileus, politische Sozialisation und generationskonflikte im 20. Jahrhundert* (1998) and *'Krupp bleibt doch Krupp'. Ein Jahrhundertfest* (2005). He is also the editor/joint editor of some twenty further volumes.

Andrew Webster is Lecturer in Modern History at Murdoch University. He has published a number of articles on the disarmament question and is currently completing a history of international disarmament between 1899 and 1945.

THE VERSAILLES SETTLEMENT: ENFORCEMENT, COMPLIANCE, CONTESTED IDENTITIES

INTRODUCTION

The settlement at the end of the First World War has received a more sympathetic approach from historians in the last thirty years, particularly since the opening of the British and French archives in the 1960s and 1970s. These revealed more clearly the enormity of the peacemakers' task and the immense pressures upon them as they tried to restore order after over four years of industrialized warfare on an unprecedented scale. Between eight and ten million young men had been killed, many more had been seriously injured, often permanently incapacitated, and, on the Western front alone, an area equivalent to the size of Holland had been devastated. Having struggled to mobilize entire nations to meet the demands of total war, governments now had to learn, very rapidly, how to demobilize, reintegrate millions of discharged servicemen, redirect the energies of millions of women who had replaced the men called to fight, and reorientate industry to peacetime manufacture. But vast areas of Europe had no government. In an unparalleled and unique occurrence, the more or less simultaneous collapse of the Russian, Austro-Hungarian, and Ottoman empires meant that eastern and central Europe and much of the Near East, found themselves bereft of authorities that had controlled these areas for centuries. This was compounded by the territorial disruption in Germany's borderlands and the revolutionary situation within Germany itself.

The peacemakers had thus to work swiftly, partly because they needed to devote attention to their domestic responsibilities, partly because they feared that, should they leave a vacuum of power for too long, it would be filled by Bolsheviks or other undesirables. Earlier condemned as a vicious and short-sighted "peace to end all peace" merely guaranteeing that the Great War would only be the first world war, the outcomes of the Paris Peace Conference are more often now seen by scholars as a settlement that was probably the best available at the time. It was not ideal but two major international conferences in California and London in the last ten years concluded that it might have had the potential to be adapted to become the foundation of a more stable Europe and world.[1]

This volume investigates what happened next–what happened in the aftermath of Georges Clemenceau's "belle journée" and of Harold Nicolson's hangover from drinking bad, if free, champagne on 28 June 1919?[2] Many recent works have suggested that the major problem with the settlement was that it was not enforced. This volume offers some serious challenges to this new consensus. Its studies indicate that the practicalities of compliance and execution were far more problematic than has hitherto been realized. Furthermore, whilst the British subsequently sought to moderate the terms of the treaty, for the French these very same problems appeared to demand the imposition of a more rigorous and far-reaching revision of the treaty. Yet for the Germans the very same settlement posed a series of apparently insuperable challenges that the new republic could scarcely wish away. This dimension has been largely neglected in much of the anglophone literature. Thus, whilst not wishing here to underestimate the difficulties facing the peacemakers in Paris, the practicalities of execution and enforcement proved problematic in the extreme.

The governments of Europe were moving into unknown territory with little in the way of precedent to guide them. Just as the war had forced governments, businesses and individuals to adjust their concepts of the extent and possibilities of their responsibilities, so the attempt to make and enforce peace also represented a huge challenge. At the highest level political leaders faced an unfamiliar world, new structures of power, new foreign counterparts who did not necessarily respect earlier conventions of diplomatic behavior. They faced a number of difficult, often ambiguous, questions. How much could/should Germany pay to the victors? How far could the victors enforce disarmament upon the losers—and how far would (and could) the losers comply or, alternatively, resist or dissemble? How far did security depend, not just upon the disarmament of the losers, but upon a more general demilitarization? In one sense boundary changes might appear to be more straightforward—new frontiers were created and new maps appeared. There was not much chance, at least in the short-term, of ambiguity or revision on this score. Yet for the inhabitants of the Moselle (north-eastern Lorraine), which had again become German after 1871, and now, in 1918, reverted to France, or for the people living in the Polish Corridor, the change of citizenship and nationality might be exhilarating or tragic but was anything but straightforward. Identity was something too complicated to be settled simply by lines on a map or words in a treaty. The Allied occupation of the Rhineland created new problems, both on the ground and in the realm of high politics. The occupation forces and local inhabitants had to come to terms with the human and administrative repercussions whilst some, at least, must have been aware of tensions between France and its allies over the direction and ambitions of French policy in the area. Here, on the Rhine in particular, the French were seeking, not merely to enforce, but to revise the settlement. French designs for *Rhenanie* reinforced Germany's fears for the future and British suspicions about France's continental ambitions.

The European leaders faced another problem. The United States had played a major role in creating the settlement but was now withdrawing from the challenges of execution and enforcement. This reinforced, in different ways, the various doubts and reservations of the French, British and Germans. How convinced were all the powers about the practicality of the treaty terms? Did the winners trust the German government sufficiently to accept its claims that certain aspects of the treaty were impossible or undeliverable? If they did not, what were the alternatives? Was there any realistic way of imposing their terms on Germany except through the agency of a German government? If so, how could they balance the needs to maintain the domestic credibility of any democratic German administration with the requirement to deliver the unpopular treaty terms? Was this ever part of French policy in any case? The challenges ranged from the emotionally charged and unprecedented demands to deliver, to allied justice, German wartime leaders accused of new political, as opposed to operational, war crimes, to the practicalities of disarmament and reparations. German governments faced a degree of economic and social dislocation so great that its resolution would have been highly problematic even without the demands of the peace settlement.

How far did the victors trust each other? Did the settlement confirm that great powers, with their own agendas and susceptibilities, might combine to defeat a common foe but would not be able to maintain their cooperation once that menace was removed? Under these circumstances it is hardly surprising that the relative consensus achieved between the various parties at Vienna after the Revolutionary and Napoleonic Wars was not replicated after the First World War.

The papers in this volume were delivered in September 2003 at a colloquium in Glasgow devoted to the aftermath of the 1919 Paris Peace Conference. The original idea for such an investigation came from Conan Fischer of the University of Strathclyde who, together with Alan Sharp and Keith Jeffery of the University of Ulster, became the conference's organizing committee. They were generously supported by grants from the British Academy, the German History Society and their respective universities. The editors wish to express their thanks to these donors, to the contributors and participants, and to Erik Goldstein, the editor of *Diplomacy and Statecraft*, for his generous support and encouragement.

Alan Sharp
Conan Fischer

NOTES

1. See Manfred Boemeke, Gerald Feldman and Elisabeth Glaser, "Introduction" in *The Treaty of Versailles: A Reassessment after 75 Years*, Boemeke, Feldman and Glaser, eds. (Cambridge: Cambridge University Press, 1998), pp. 11–20. Zara Steiner, "The Treaty of Versailles Revisited," in Michael Dockrill and John Fisher, eds. *The Paris Peace Conference 1919: Peace without Victory?* (Basingstoke: Palgrave, 2001), pp. 13–33. Mark Mazower "Two Cheers for Versailles," *History Today* 49 (1999): Alan Sharp *The Versailles Settlement: Peace-making in Paris, 1919* (Basingstoke, Macmillan, 1991). Margaret MacMillan, *Peacemakers: The Paris Conference of 1919 and Its Attempt to End War* (London: John Murray, 2001). Antony Best, Jussi Hanhomäki, Joseph Maiolo and Kirsten Schulze, *International History of the Twentieth Century* (London, Routledge, 2004), p. 55.
2. Harold Nicolson, *Peacemaking 1919* (London, Constable, 1933), pp. 370–371.

THE ENFORCEMENT OF THE TREATY OF VERSAILLES, 1919–1923

Alan Sharp

On June 28, 1919 the peace treaty between the Allied and Associated Powers and Germany was signed in the Hall of Mirrors in the Palace of Versailles, the location itself one more episode in the humiliation and counter-humiliation of Germany by France and vice versa. After six months of intensive inter-allied negotiations the treaty was complete.[1] A British delegation member, James Headlam-Morley, anticipated that "No doubt things will become more orderly, but they will be much duller."[2] He was wrong on both counts. Drawing up the treaty represented the easy part, enforcing it would be harder. As always, the devil was in the detail—working out precisely what the wording of the clauses meant when they encountered the real world—not least because, even as they were being drafted, those clauses meant, sometimes accidentally, sometimes deliberately, different things to the different parties involved. The treaty was the product of compromises seeking to meet as many of the national interests of the main negotiators as possible. It had been drawn up under great pressure occasioned by the complex and interlinked nature of the problems it sought to address and the simultaneous need, in a world struggling to return to "normalcy," for the leaders to return to tackle pressing domestic concerns in the capitals they had abandoned for the conference. The peace conference's lack of organisational clarity also meant that maximum demands, intended for subsequent revision after dialogue with the Germans, were often incorporated unaltered when no such negotiation occurred. There were sometimes clashes between the high moral ideals set by the American president, Woodrow Wilson (and, perhaps, also the British premier, David Lloyd George) and the need to reach conclusions—"Il faut aboutir" as the formidable French prime minister, Georges Clemenceau, was wont to observe.

Where the negotiations had involved three, four, and sometimes more parties, enforcement fell mainly to two, Britain and France. Much of the treaty existed because the United States had significantly influenced the outcomes, often against the wishes of Britain or France, and sometimes both. Now they found themselves enforcing a treaty that they would not necessarily have drafted, increasingly bereft of American counsel, presence and support, and without a common interpretation of what they hoped to achieve. Lloyd George's attempt in June 1919 to modify the draft treaty terms had, with the major exception of the plebiscite in Upper Silesia, largely failed but many British decision-makers did not accept this as final. On the other hand they were aware that the French too might wish to modify the treaty—but in a different direction.[3] Further complications arose from the continuing negotiations to draft treaties with the other defeated powers, at least one of which, the rejuvenated Turkey, refused to lie down. Additionally there was the huge uncertainty represented by the former Tsarist empire of Russia, now rent by secession, foreign intervention and civil war, but increasingly in the grasp of the revolutionary force of bolshevism. It was, however, the central relationship between Britain and France, and their differing perspectives, aims and objectives coupled with their joint and individual relationships with Germany, which dominated the high politics of treaty enforcement.

This paper uses the episode of the March 1920 Kapp *Putsch* to introduce a number of issues that dominated the early years of enforcement but any such brief and schematic account must oversimplify the complexities. The "real world" was not a vision shared by the major states, nor even by individual representatives from the same country. There were disputes as to what was actually happening, disputes as to how this should be interpreted and disputes about how to deal with the disputed consequences. There were disputes between countries and between conflicting agencies within countries. From this tangle governments were supposed to create coherent policies and order.

The treaty's entry into force required the ratification of Germany and three of the main allies.[4] The Germans deposited their ratification on July 10. Arthur Balfour, Britain's foreign secretary and chief representative in Paris after the departure of Lloyd George, expected the process would be complete by mid-August,[5] but only on January 10, 1920 did the treaty enter into force. Some delay was convenient to Britain because, although technically the king could ratify the treaty, it was thought wiser to have an

Act of Parliament. This received royal assent on July 31, but now raised a further complication. The Dominions would be affronted if the British parliament was consulted but not theirs, given their growing sense of separate identities.[6] All had approved by October 3. On October 14, President Poincaré ratified the treaty for France. Like George V, he might have acted without parliamentary approval but did not do so. The treaty underwent the scrutiny of committees of the Chamber and the Senate, both accepted that Clemenceau had achieved the best attainable deal for France and the two houses approved the ratification law. Since the King of Italy had ratified the treaty on October 6, the allies were in a position to let the treaty enter into force but they did not do so.

This was not for the lack of the various bodies and agencies required to enforce the treaty. Germany had already agreed to the allied proposals for an Inter-Allied Rhineland Commission to supervise the government of the Rhineland during the occupation.[7] In July 1919 the new major allied body replacing the Council of Four, the Heads of Delegation—the representatives of the five major allied powers, Britain, France, Japan, Italy and the United States—had approved a commission to deal with the execution of the treaty with Germany and a pre-Reparations Commission to act until the treaty was in force.[8] It also agreed the composition of three separate disarmament control commissions for air, sea and land, with appropriate internal sub-divisions.[9] The French Secretary-General of the conference, Paul Dutasta, drew up a list of the actions required by the treaty, with a note of the time limits and interested countries. This was circulated on July 23.[10] A plan for the Rhine Occupation Army proposed by the French commander-in-chief of the allied armies, Marshal Ferdinand Foch, was approved on July 26.[11] Once the peace conference ended it was envisaged that an allied commission would undertake the overall supervision of the execution of the treaty and an outline of what became the Conference of Ambassadors was approved on July 28.[12] The mechanisms were ready.

The allies were not. There were concerns that, once the coercive powers available under the armistice were superseded by the treaty, it might be impossible to enforce unfulfilled armistice conditions or to force German troops to evacuate the Baltic provinces.[13] The major issues related to German failure to deliver compensation for the June scuttling of the High Seas Fleet at Scapa Flow and alleged war criminals (including important figures like Bethmann Hollweg, Hindenburg, Tirpitz and Crown Prince Rupprecht—the Kaiser having already fled to Holland which refused to surrender him).[14] Foch suggested allied occupations of Frankfurt or the Ruhr District unless the Germans agreed to meet the allied conditions. Most allied leaders in Britain and France believed Germany would concede before such drastic action was necessary but there was panic in London when Clemenceau's draft note of December 6,

1919 threatened "to place Germany in face of a rupture of armistice with all consequences which would follow therefrom" unless Germany agreed to the conditions for final ratification.[15] Lloyd George summoned George Curzon, Balfour, Andrew Bonar Law and Winston Churchill to a late evening meeting at 10 Downing Street which sent Lloyd George's private secretary, Philip Kerr, to Paris to negotiate an amended draft.[16] This was accomplished, though more on Clemenceau's terms than Lloyd George's. The Germans, as expected, backed down and, after some further tinkering, terms were agreed and the treaty entered into force on January 10, 1920.

This increased Lloyd George's determination to terminate the Paris peace conference and replace it with regular meetings of allied leaders. In early December Clemenceau accepted it would end within a fortnight of the deposit of ratifications. Thereafter "large questions of policy" would be dealt with by direct exchanges between governments and "questions of detail" would be the concern of a Conference of Ambassadors, meeting in Paris but "large questions of policy," and "questions of detail," were not defined.[17] The Paris conference thus ended on January 21, 1920, one year and three days after its opening, but Headlam-Morley's expectation of greater order was still not fulfilled.

On March 13, 1920, there was an attempted *coup* in Germany, nominally led by Wolfgang Kapp, a civil servant. Such elements of the German army that were not actively supporting Kapp's *Putsch* refused to help the government, which fled to Stuttgart and then re-established its authority by calling a general strike, paralyzing Kapp's regime. This led to the first major confrontation of treaty enforcement and it revealed a series of issues, themes and attitudes that encapsulated the essence of the problems involved and which would be a constant presence throughout the execution of the treaty. These included: the questions of what mechanisms existed to enforce the treaty; how the different agencies interacted and the nature of authority within and between them; the sanctions available to the victorious governments to enforce their will; the position and problems of the German government; the extent to which there was a single will or vision amongst the allies about the role, intentions and good faith of the Germans and their government; the relationship and suspicions existing between Britain and France and the differing aims, ambitions and approaches of the major participants.

The aftermath of the *putsch* caused more problems than the event itself. A mixture of a real and imagined communist threat in the Ruhr led both the legitimate and insurrectionary governments to request permission for extra troops to be allowed into the demilitarised zone to restore order. This revealed confusions in the allied ranks about authority and control. Although Kapp's request was ignored that of the legitimate government received contradictory answers from two allied meetings, each believing it had the overall authority. In Paris the Ambassadors' Conference heard Foch oppose the German request and suggest an allied occupation of the Ruhr. It decided to refuse the German request. In London the now peripatetic Supreme Council was simultaneously meeting to discuss the treaty with Turkey. It agreed to recommend approval of the request.[18] Curzon was anxious to maintain the authority of the Supreme Council, but in Paris the French premier, Alexandre Millerand, argued vigorously (though unsuccessfully) that the ambassadors had the power and duty to act for the allies.[19] Curzon commented acidly, "M.Millerand not only regards the Peace Conference as sitting in Paris, but as I have before remarked, he regards himself as the Peace Conference."[20]

The veteran French ambassador in London, Paul Cambon, wrote on March 29 to his brother Jules in Paris, encapsulating this confusion. "There has never been such a shambles of a conference. Here we have the supreme council which thinks it is the Peace Conference. Then there is the Council of Ministers and Ambassadors that Curzon chairs.[21] Finally we consider that the Peace Conference still remains in Paris. Its existence is entirely imaginary, it is a phantom, but we cling to it as if it were reality. In addition there is the Ambassadors' Conference, chaired by yourself or sometimes by Millerand. I'm not sure what its powers are. I just see that it undertakes the same business as we do and that the two bodies often have contradictory opinions. I don't understand any of this, and I'm not asking you to explain what's what. It's inexplicable."[22] There was thus chaos at the highest level about the overall control of peace enforcement, contributing, in this instance, to isolated action by the French, who occupied five German towns, Frankfurt, Darmstadt, Hanau, Homburg and Dieburg on April 5/6, 1920.

This confusion was ominous because the crisis revealed that the British and French governments intended to keep matters of treaty enforcement in their own hands. Lord Robert Cecil, one of the main architects of the League of Nations and a passionate believer in the new body, argued that the German troops in the forbidden area represented a threat of war that should be, according to the treaty, referred to the League. The Foreign Office admitted the strength of his case but brushed it aside—such matters were for the allied governments to settle, not the League.[23] The League might be useful for finessing the issue of self-determination when it was felt necessary to provide France with the coal of the Saar and Poland with the use of Danzig as a port without awarding either state sovereignty over the respective inhabitants. It was convenient to brush responsibility for minority protection in eastern and central Europe under the League carpet. Only when driven to desperation by their failure to reach agreement did Britain and France ask a League committee in 1922 to convert the result of the Upper Silesian plebiscite into territorial dispositions. This was an unusual and exceptional involvement of the League in treaty execution (and the British cabinet secretary, Sir Maurice Hankey's disparaging description of the committee as consisting of "Two dagoes, a pro-French Belgian and a Chink" hardly augered well). More normal was the Anglo-French rejection in 1921 of the League as a credible replacement for the Inter-Allied Military Mission Control Commission as the major enforcer of German disarmament and their continued scepticism about its potential as a future monitoring agency, despite the provisions of Article 213 of the treaty. The 1923 Corfu incident was a further example of the exclusion of the League from matters arising from treaty enforcement.[24]

Britain and France intended to keep control of treaty execution in their own hands but Lloyd George in particular distrusted traditional diplomatic methods and preferred to deal in person with his fellow allied leaders at meetings and conferences. The aftermath of the Kapp *Putsch* initiated the era of "casino diplomacy" as inter-allied and, exceptionally, international gatherings involving the Germans, were held in desirable seaside resorts, capitals and watering places. Beginning "sous the ciel bleu de San Remo"[25] the next three years saw successively gatherings of various sizes in Hythe, Boulogne, Brussels, Spa, London, Paris, London, Cannes, Genoa, London, and Paris. Conference diplomacy suited Lloyd George's style and enabled his skills of communication and persuasion to be used to great effect, at least in the context of the meeting itself. However, as Curzon told the new British government in November 1922, Lloyd George's "superior cleverness" might be a short-term asset but was frequently a long-term liability in that his conference successes could create later resentments.[26] A further potential problem was that conference diplomacy might be an effective way to round off longer-term negotiations or to force an issue to a head but it also needed to be incorporated into a continuous process of review and implementation. Frequently these high profile gatherings were not always effectively linked to the more mundane business of day-to-day diplomatic exchanges.[27] There was also the consideration that conferences, where the appropriate experts were readily available, could sometimes translate rhetoric rapidly into actual figures and forecasts, depriving diplomacy of both time and ambiguity— this was not necessarily advantageous. Conferences frequently broke up with expressions of goodwill but without discovering lasting solutions to the persistent problems of treaty execution.

The relationship between the framers of high level policy and the agencies enforcing the treaty represented a further complication. The allies had postponed the setting of a total reparations bill in Paris in 1919 because the matter was too complicated, too divisive, and too dangerous. They set up a Reparation Commission to report in 1921 "with wide lattitude as to its control and handling of the whole reparation problem"[28] but, at different times, and for differing motives, Britain and France spent much of 1920 and the early part of 1921 trying to pre-empt the functions and decisions of that commission. For the British, the commission, in the absence of the intended American chairman, was now too deeply under French control. The French insisted that they must now hold the chair, giving them an additional casting vote should the four powers usually involved in west European reparations (Britain, Belgium, France, and Italy) reach an evenly split decision. The commission, although consisting of delegates nominated by the appropriate governments, was intended to be independent of allied government control, but, when it was convenient to them, both the British and French governments, either independently or in collusion, sought to direct its deliberations. The commissioners were often resentful of such government interference. This impacted more on the French than the British because several of the succession of French delegates named to the commission were prominent politicians—Raymond Poincaré and Paul Doumer in particular. The British delegate throughout this period was Sir John Bradbury, a Treasury official without the political influence of his French colleagues. Nonetheless his "quaint diplomatic methods" were a frequent cause of Foreign Office resentment, as was his reluctance to accept guidance—"He behaves as if he were an independent state" complained Curzon.[29]

As with the workings of the Inter-Allied Military Commission of Control, charged with the disarmament of Germany and the monitoring of the treaty provisions, there was always an element of compromise between the theory of commission autonomy and the reality of political control. In 1921 it suited French premier Aristide Briand to insist upon the Reparation Commission's independence in the face of Lloyd George's pressure to bypass it, fearing that French influence in the commission would produce an impossibly inflated demand upon Germany. Lloyd George wanted the two governments to name a total for German indebtedness, because he believed he had a greater chance of influencing the French government than the commission. In fact the sums proposed by Britain at conferences in Boulogne in June 1920 and Paris in January 1921 were higher than the total named by the commission in May 1921.[30] On this occasion Lloyd George could be glad that his persistent campaign against the commission in 1920 and 1921 had failed. Agencies like the Inter-Allied Rhineland High Commission were rarely themselves matters for high level diplomacy, though they might become involved in the complexities of Anglo-French relations—the threat of withdrawal from various inter-allied bodies was considered by Britain on several occasions, including the aftermath of the Kapp episode, but never actually used.[31]

In April 1920, faced, as they interpreted it, with a German infraction of the treaty, the French, as noted previously, acted independently and occupied five German towns. It was an act of disputed legality and, as such, typified the problem of the sanctions legitimately available to the allies in the case of German non-compliance with the treaty or of deliberate acts of defiance against it. The treaty was remarkably vague about penalties and sanctions, and was especially weak when it came to measures that might, by the immediacy of their threat, encourage Germany to act with any urgency. Article 430 of the treaty allowed an extension of the occupation of the Rhineland beyond the original fifteen years if Germany did not comply with allied reparations demands and the implication of Article 429 was that such an extension could also be justified by concerns about the adequacy of guarantees against unprovoked German aggression. Neither was calculated to be of major immediate concern to a German government in the early 1920s.

Many of the actions taken by the allies in various combinations between 1920 and 1923 were of dubious legality, relying upon adaptations of clauses intended for other purposes or upon interpretations of treaty provisions disowned by their original authors. In March 1921, Article 270, which permitted the allies to make special customs arrangements for their occupied areas of Germany "to safeguard the economic interests of the population of those territories," was invoked to justify a customs barrier around the Rhineland designed to penalise the German government for not making an adequate effort to comply with the treaty. It was used again for a similar purpose during the Franco-Belgian occupation of the Ruhr beginning in January 1923.[32] That occupation was itself justified by an interpretation of Part VIII (reparations) Paragraph 18, Annex II. The paragraph stated that the allies had the right to take measures in the event of a voluntary reparations default by Germany which "may include economic and financial prohibitions and reprisals and in general such other measures." The French argued that "such other measures" could include territorial occupation, whereas the British government, and one of the original drafters, the American lawyer, John Foster Dulles, argued that the phrase clearly applied only to sanctions of an economic or financial nature.[33]

British legal objections to the 1923 Franco-Belgian occupation of the Ruhr were compromised by Lloyd George's exasperated agreement in March 1921 to an allied occupation of three German towns, Duisburg, Ruhrort and Düsseldorf. He had agreed, despite his own eloquent arguments that "from a technical point of view the Allies' case might be weak" because he perceived no other way of persuading a German government he saw as intransigent.[34] H.W. Malkin, the Foreign Office's deputy legal adviser, believed the treaty did not cover the sanctions taken and suggested "It may be that some of the means of pressure adopted are of such a nature that Germany would be entitled, if she thought fit, to treat them as involving a state of war."[35] The British Attorney General, Sir Gordon Hewart, hardly produced a ringing endorsement of their actions, suggesting that they "recite Germany's continued violations of the terms of the Treaty of Peace . . . and . . . state that these violations . . . give the Allied Governments the right to take any measure of compulsion they consider necessary or proper . . ."[36] The problem was, as Lloyd George had already conceded in 1920, occupying the Ruhr was the only effective sanction: ". . . there was no other method available for enforcing the Treaty."[37] The legality under the treaty of such an occupation was highly controversial. The allies could show a whole string of German infractions of the treaty but they had not written adequate penalties into the settlement to justify the use of force that was, ultimately, the only recourse against its breach.

This was partly because the British and Americans in Paris had feared that too specific and powerful sanctions and penalties within the treaty would be used by the French to justify future harsh actions against Germany. An enduring British suspicion of French motives and objectives complicated treaty enforcement, in particular, the belief that the French had not accepted as final the treaty's verdict that the Rhineland, albeit under occupation and with conditions and limitations, would remain German. In addition British observers believed that each French demand to occupy the Ruhr to force German compliance, or to punish a German infraction of the treaty, was really also an attempt to rectify their earlier failure within the treaty to deprive Germany of this valuable asset. Sydney Waterlow's[38] comment during the Kapp crisis was typical of many uttered by politicians and diplomats alike both before and later— "The French Government are evidently working to use the situation as a pretext for occupying the Ruhr basin and detaching the Rhineland."[39] British suspicion of "the lure of the Ruhr"[40] was a constant presence lurking on, or just below, the surface of every Franco-British encounter. There were always deep misgivings about France's possible intention to encourage separatism, undertake annexations of German territory and even to destroy the German state though British observers were divided as to whether France was driven by the desire to dominate the continent or by fear.[41]

The British faced a further dilemma—should they seek to allay French insecurity by offering a military guarantee, thus encouraging greater Anglo-French cohesion in their dealings with Germany (which meant greater French willingness to acquiesce to British proposals) or would a France, secure in the knowledge of British support, pursue policies the British considered more, not less, intransigent? The matter was the subject of prolonged debate in the early 1920s without leading to a firm

Franco-British agreement. The French found this particularly unsatisfactory, believing they had already fulfilled their side of Lloyd George's bargain in March 1919 when he offered a British guarantee to France in return for Clemenceau abandoning French claims in the Rhineland. He carefully linked his guarantee to a parallel undertaking by the United States and, when the Americans failed to deliver, the British were, in their own eyes at least, relieved of their responsibility.[42] Britain's refusal to honour its moral, if not legal, obligations reinforced French frustration with a partner that did not, in their eyes, recognise the realities of the European power balance. "The misfortune" lamented Paul Cambon "is that the English are not yet aware that Napoleon is dead."[43]

Sir Eyre Crowe, the Permanent Under-Secretary at the Foreign Office encapsulated the overall dilemma in late 1921: "From the point of view of general foreign policy, the maintenance of the Entente remains of supreme importance. Some of the Treasury and Downing Street tendencies are towards the substitution of an Entente with Germany in place of that with France. This is a chimaera under present conditions and must remain so for a long time to come. What we, and what the whole world wants, is peace. Peace must for the present rest on the execution of the peace treaties. These would hardly survive a breach between England and France at this moment."[44] Britain and France had to work together if the treaty was to be executed but the reality was that each had different visions of the post-war world and different routes to achieve those visions. The Belgian ambassador to France, Edmond de Gaiffier, himself symbolic of the part-player, part-onlooker role attributed to the lesser allies, identified two broad allied strategies. The British, Japanese and Italians wanted concessions to Germany and a revision of the treaty, whilst the French wanted its complete execution. Gaiffier thought neither practicable but these differences of viewpoint were a persistent feature of inter-allied relationships and helped to create a stalemate of mutual frustration between the two principal treaty enforcers.[45]

Once again the post-Kapp crisis illustrated a wider theme. Crowe, in April 1920, offered Curzon the alternatives of a definite breach with France—an "heroic solution" that he rejected—or that the matter should be treated as a "lover's quarrel" and that Britain should seek ". . . to build golden bridges for the retirement of the French from their present false position."[46] Curzon appreciated Crowe's advocacy of a general clearance of the air with France but added ". . . After so flagrant a case as this . . . I am not very enthusiastic about 'kissing again with tears.'"[47] Yet the relationship had to survive, whatever its frustrations, personal dislikes and thorny problems of which there were many. Lloyd George and Millerand met at San Remo and papered over the cracks, with Millerand promising no further French independent action.[48]

Kapp highlighted another constant problem: the treaty required a German government to enforce it, yet amongst the issues driving the *coup* were highly unpopular Allied demands for the disarmament and disbandment of Germany's armed forces and for the surrender of war criminals. This placed the German government under extreme pressure from the right to resist and then helped to promote the *coup*, exposing the fragility of the alliance between Weimar and the army when the revolutionary threat was from the right. The *Reichswehr* commander, Hans von Seeckt, refused to send troops to help the government, stating "*Reichswehr* does not fire on *Reichswehr*."[49] The aftermath of Kapp suggested that the republic was also threatened by communist revolutionary forces in the Ruhr and elsewhere. When the threat was from the left the *Reichswehr* did intervene vigorously, causing some British observers to blame the Ruhr problems on army brutality.[50] Could German governments withstand such pressures, retain sufficient authority to fulfil their treaty obligations and survive? Lloyd George might be provoked at times by a Stinnes or Simon but the British view tended to be somewhat patronizing, the German government was weak but doing its best and was, generally, acting in good faith. The British therefore favoured concessions to enable German governments to survive. The French believed that Germany was cheating and wanted stronger measures taken to ensure treaty execution. When the Germans said they could not execute part of the treaty the British generally accepted this; the French believed the Germans could, but would not, fulfil their obligations.

The disarmament of Germany illustrated some of these problems. In Paris all agreed to German disarmament but Foch favoured a larger conscript army, Lloyd George a smaller, long-service, volunteer force. The compromise of a long-service volunteer army of 100,000 men was not one of the more contentious issues of treaty negotiation.[51] The British doubted whether this was a sufficient force to guarantee German internal and external security and London sympathised with Germany's 1920 requests for extra time to reduce its forces to the required levels and even for larger German forces. The French were normally anxious to press execution issues to the limit but their policy could be complicated when, as in Bavaria, there might be advantage in terms of encouraging Bavarian particularism by turning a blind eye to the paramilitary forces there. Britain was unsure however whether this was to provide support for Bavarian separatism or to create an excuse for further action against German infractions of the treaty.[52] In October 1920 Curzon did unofficially warn the German ambassador, Friedrich Sthamer, "that Bavaria was building a bridge for the French to the Ruhr."[53]

By the end of 1922 most of the major disarmament issues were settled as far as they were going to be. A number of problems remained about the

police, the reconversion of munitions factories, the surrender of unautho-
rized war material and Germany also faced the very difficult task of
accounting for weapons that had either been lost or deliberately hidden in
the aftermath of defeat and of trying to locate and destroy arms held by a
wide variety of groups, many of whom were hostile to the treaty and often
also to the government. As we have discovered since in both Northern
Ireland and Iraq such matters are not easy. The final decision as to
whether Germany was disarmed was always going to be political, especially since the military experts did not agree, and, ultimately, would be
conditional.[54]

Reparations were a more difficult proposition, involving the more tangible individual self-interest of each of the allies and some awareness
that, as Sally Marks would express it seventy-five years later, "If the
Allies, and especially France, had to assume reconstruction costs on top
of domestic and foreign war debts, whereas Germany was left with only
domestic debts they would be the losers, and German economic dominance
would be tantamount to victory. Reparations would both deny Germany that
victory and spread the pain of undoing the damage done."[55] France
needed Germany to pay its reconstruction costs, but there was the added
bonus that this would also diminish Germany's ability to seek revenge.
For Britain reparations were economically and financially important, for
France they represented, in addition, security. Both were anxious to
achieve the maximum receipts possible, but for Britain this was tempered
by a greater concern than France for the survival of the German economy,
which it saw as an important element in British prosperity. The economics and technicalities of reparations probably defeated the ability of most
politicians to understand them; what they all grasped was the enormous
potential political fall-out from such a highly contentious and charged
question. Lloyd George frequently castigated French leaders for not confronting their population with the truth about probable reparations
receipts, but he was never anxious to lead by example.

From 1919–1923 the victors confronted the problem that, if the treaty
was not executed, their only real and immediate sanction was force.
Allied agencies reported German infractions and deficiencies and high
level conferences tried to interpret German actions and intentions and to
encourage Germany to fulfil its obligations. The fundamental questions
were always the same: were German failures a matter of intent or inability-
would not, or could not, Germany execute the treaty clauses? Should
force be used? If so, when, and what sort of force? Was there a credible
alternative? Inter-Allied conferences produced rousing speeches and
sometimes actions intended to be decisive—at Paris in March 1921 a
punitive customs regime was decreed to separate occupied from unoccupied Germany. These were the points at which high level diplomacy met

the real world—the study of which forms the main theme of the other papers in this collection. The British Rhineland Commissioner, Arnold Robertson, was required to institute the customs barrier along a substantial frontier without new resources or any clear directive as to the aims, objectives and mechanisms of the exercise. Disgruntled, he suggested that his only solution was to place a collecting box at the border with a notice: "England expects every German to pay his duty."[56] The problem was that some of the victors expected every German also to do his duty by the treaty and execute it in its entirety. The inadequacies of the sanctions and incentives contained in the treaty partly explained why this was an equally unrealistic expectation. The deeper problem, however, lay in the failure of the British and French to agree a common strategy and then to abide by it. They could neither agree to enforce the treaty, nor to redraft it. Their tragedy was that this contributed to the conditions that created, ultimately, what neither wanted, a renewal of hostilities on a continental and world scale.

NOTES

1. For accounts of the conference see Alan Sharp, *The Versailles Settlement: Peacemaking in Paris, 1919* (Basingstoke, 1991); Margaret MacMillan, *Peacemakers: The Paris Conference of 1919 and Its Attempt to End War* (London, 2001); Antony Lentin, *Guilt at Versailles: Lloyd George and the Pre-History of Appeasement* (London, 1985) Michael Dockrill and Douglas Goold, *Peace Without Promise; Britain and the Peace Conferences 1919–1923* (London, 1981).
2. James Headlam-Morley, *A Memoir of the Paris Peace Conference 1919*, Agnes Headlam-Morley, R. Bryant, A. Cienciala (eds.), (London, 1972), p. 180.
3. See Lentin *Guilt at Versailles*, pp. 132–54 and his later "The Worm in the Bud: 'Appeasement' at the Peace Conference" in *Lloyd George and the Lost Peace: From Versailles to Hitler, 1919–1940* (Basingstoke, 2001), pp. 67–88. Headlam-Morley suggested to Kerr, Dec. 13, 1919, that "there was a party in France led by Foch" who wanted to force a breach with Germany, to denounce the armistice and begin war again. "What is the object of this? Is it not that they think that the Treaty is in some points unduly favourable to Germany and want really to scrap the Treaty itself...?" Letter in GD 40.17.216 Lothian Papers, Scottish Record Office.
4. Article 440, Treaty of Versailles, *The Treaty of Versailles and After: Annotations of the Text of the Treaty* (New York, 1968 reprinting of 1944 US Government Printing Office edition), p. 737. (Hereafter *The Treaty*)
5. Balfour, Paris, tel. 1173, 18.7.19, HMSO, *Documents on British Foreign Policy 1919–1939: First Series* (London, 1947 onwards, multiple volumes) Vol. II, p. 39, hereafter *DBFP*.
6. Crowe told Clemenceau, 30.9.19. that "constitutionally we might not be bound to do so . . . [but] it would . . . be a practical impossibility for HMG to act before the Dominions had signified their assent." Crowe, Paris, tel. 1393, *DBFP* Vol.V, pp. 599–600.

7. "Agreement with Regard to the Military Occupation of the Territories of the Rhine," signed 28.6.19, *The Treaty* pp. 762–9.
8. IC 200, Minutes 1 and 2, 2 Jul. 1919, in *DBFP* Vol. I, pp. 1–3.
9. HD 3 Minute 11, July 9, 1919, and Appendix E, Ibid. p. 45 and pp. 52–7.
10. Balfour desp. 1412 (18639/7067/39 in FO 371/4262).
11. HD 14 Minute 4 *DBFP* Vol. I, p. 199.
12. HD 17, Minute 1, July 28, 1919, and Appendix A, Ibid. pp. 225–6 and pp. 231–2.
13. HD 70 Minute 6, Oct. 15, 1919. Ibid. pp. 961–2. This particular fear proved unjustified and the Germans evacuated the provinces in December 1919 and January 1920.
14. The allies notified the Germans of eleven headings they wanted fulfilled before the treaty came into effect. These ranged from the 42 missing locomotives (from the original demand for 5,000); 4,600 wagons (from the original 150,000); missing French and Belgian works of art; to the compensation demanded for Scapa Flow (five light cruisers and 400,000 tons of floating docks and cranes). HD 80 Appendix C, Nov. 1, 1919, Ibid. pp. 131–7. See also Willis, James F. *Prologue to Nuremberg: The Politics and Diplomacy of Punishing War Crminals of the First World War* (Westport, Conn., 1982). The earliest allied demands amounted to over 1500 men (and one woman) but these were reduced to 854 by the allied conference in Paris, Jan. 20, 1920, ICP 22, Minute 1, Ibid. pp. 927–8.
15. Crowe tel 1662, 159379/7067/39 in FO371/4265.
16. Bonar Law, Lord Privy Seal, was the Conservative leader, Churchill, then a Liberal, was Secretary of State for War. Balfour and Curzon had swapped offices in October 1919, with Curzon confirmed as Foreign Secretary and Balfour now Lord President. Kerr was also present. Cabinet 12, Appendix VI in CAB23/18.
17. Conference of London, 11–13.12.19, *DBFP* Vol. II, pp. 773–4 and 782–3.
18. Conference of Ambassadors, Mar. 18, 1920, Ibid. Vol. IX, pp. 170–179; ICP 78, Minute 1, Ibid. Vol. VIII, pp. 542–7.
19. FO tel. 353, Mar. 18, 1920, Ibid. Vol. IX, pp. 184–5; Conference of Ambassadors, Mar. 20, 1920, Ibid. pp. 193–202.
20. Curzon, minute, Apr. 6, 1920, Ibid. N1, p. 328. The German habit of addressing all notes to Millerand as president of the peace conference was a constant source of irritation to the Foreign Office, e.g., minutes on 188765/4232/18 in FO 371/3781.
21. The London conference ran from Feb. 12, 1920 to Apr. 10, 1920. Its main business was the treaty with Turkey. It split into two groups, the main allied leaders met with Lloyd George at 10 Downing Street, the foreign ministers and ambassadors met, under Curzon's chairmanship, in the Foreign Office. *DBFP* Vol. VII, p iv.
22. Paul Cambon, *Correspondance* (Paris, 1946, 3 Volumes), Vol. III, p. 383.
23. Cecil wrote to Curzon, Balfour and Lloyd George, Apr. 12, 1920, arguing that the German troop movements could be construed as contraventions of Articles 42 and 43 of the Treaty constituting a threat of war and hence the League should be summoned. Waterlow commented: ". . . Either we must sooner or later find an occasion to promote recourse to this machinery, or we must reconcile ourselves to the Covenant becoming a dead letter." 191340/4232/18 in FO371/3783.

24. Hankey T. D., see J.P. Dunbabin, "The League of Nations" Place in the International System *History*, Vol. 78 no. 254, October 1993, p .421–42 and Ruth Henig, "Britain, France and the League of Nations" in Alan Sharp and Glyn Stone (eds.), *Anglo-French Relations in the Twentieth Century: Rivalry and Cooperation* (London, 2000), pp. 139–57.
25. Poincaré's headline for his article in *Le Matin*, Apr. 19, 1920.
26. Cabinet 64 (22) Annex IV, Nov. 1, 1922 in CAB23/32).
27. Headlam-Morley noted Oct. 18, 1920: ". . . the Prime Minister did not in fact before going to a Conference consult those who were or ought to have been in a position to give him sound advice, and the decisions arrived at or the information which came out. . . . was not communicated to the Foreign Office or to the diplomatic representatives of the country. . . . Looking back over the last two years it would be difficult to point to a single problem, of real importance that has been settled; what has been done is to postpone the problems, to effect a temporary makeshift or *modus vivendi*; this no doubt is often the best thing to do, but the fact remains that our relations with France have been getting steadily worse. . . . Conferences are no more a sovereign specific for avoiding international conflict than avoiding a coal strike." FO800/149.
28. Part VIII, Paragraph 12, Annex II. *The Treaty,* p. 475.
29. Sir William Tyrrell minute, Sep. 15, 1922. C13042/99/18 in FO371/7484 and Curzon minute, Oct. 12, 1922. C14129/99/18 in FO371/7485.
30. The Boulogne agreement set a figure of 269,000,000,000 gold marks; Paris suggested 226,000,000,000 gold marks and the Reparation Commission 132,000,000,000 gold marks. Etienne Weill-Raynal, *Les Réparations Allemandes et la France* (3 vols., Paris, 1947), vol. 1 pp 547–60 and pp 593–600; Marc Trachtenberg, *Reparation in World Politics: France and European Diplomacy, 1916–1923* (New York, 1980), pp. 136–44 and pp. 201–2; Bruce Kent, *The Spoils of War: The Politics, Economics and Diplomacy of Reparations, 1918–1923* (Oxford, 1989), pp. 95–6 and pp. 123–6; A. McFadyean (Controller of Finance, British Treasury) memo. Apr. 16, 1921, CP2843 in CAB24/123.
31. FO tel. 401, Apr. 1, 1920. *DBFP* Vol. IX, p. 292. See originals on 189367/4232/18 in FO371/3781 for Curzon's addition, ". . . if the French Government persist in acting without . . . consultation of their Allies, we may have to re-examine our position and to consider whether it is worthwhile for us to continue in occupation of Rhine area."
32. Article 279, *The Treaty,* p. 559. See Curzon's revealing remark to the French Ambassador, Sainte-Aulaire, Mar. 25, 1921: "The more I looked into [this particular sanction] the more did it seem to be fraught with great difficulties and perils, not the least of which was that, in our desire to hit Germany, we might injure and even ruin the occupied territories themselves. " FO desp 887 to Paris, C6247/2740 in FO371/6020. Briand and Lloyd George had both suggested this was not an appropriate use of the Article, *DBFP*, Vol. XV, p. 8.
33. Memo, by R.W.Wigram on the legal position in the event of a German default, Dec. 18, 1922 (C17313/99/18), *DBFP*, Vol. XX, pp. 344–6; Opinion by the Solicitor-General (Thomas Inskip) on the interpretation of Paragraph 18, Annex II, Dec. 28, 1922 (C17791/99/18) Ibid. p. 358.
34. ICP 171, Mar. 2, 1921 in *DBFP*, Vol. XV, pp. 246–7 and p. 251.

35. Malkin note, Mar. 12, 1921. C5545/2704/18 in FO317/6018.
36. Hewart note, Mar. 30, 1921. C7006/2740/18 in FO371/6022.
37. ICP 137, Jul. 14, 1920, *DBFP*, Vol. VIII, p. 602.
38. An official in the Foreign Office's Central Department.
39. Minute, Mar. 16, 1920, 185720/4232/18 in FO371/3780.
40. Curzon to the Imperial Conference, June 22, 1921. E4 in CAB32/2.
41. See Alan Sharp, "Standard-bearers in a tangle: British perceptions of France after the First World War," in David Dutton (ed.), *Statecraft and Diplomacy in the Twentieth Century* (Liverpool, 1995), pp. 55–73.
42. Antony Lentin, "The Treaty That Never Was: Lloyd George and the Abortive Anglo-French Alliance of 1919," in Judith Loades (ed.), *The Life and Times of David Lloyd George* (Ipswich, 1991), pp. 115–28.
43. See Alan Sharp and Keith Jeffery, "'Après la guerre finit, Soldat anglais partit.' Anglo-French relations 1918–1925," *Diplomacy and Statecraft*, Vol. 14, No. 2, June 2003, pp. 119–38. Cambon's remark is quoted by the Comte de Sainte-Aulaire, *Confession d'un Vieux Diplomate* (Paris, 1953), p. 536.
44. Crowe minute (endorsed by Curzon) Nov. 30, 1921. *DBFP*, Vol. XVI, p. 827, n. 7.
45. In his despatch, Mar. 22, 1920, Gaiffier wrote "Accorder à l'Allemagne la revision intégrale, c'est admettre qu'on n'obtiendra rien du tout. D'autre part, déclarer avec viguer, comme le font MM. . . . Poincaré et Millerand et Foch, que la France s'en tiendra à l'exècution intégrale du traité . . . est impracticable." *Documents Diplomatiques Belges 1920–1940: La Politique de securité extérieure*, Charles De Visscher and Fernand Van Langenhove, eds. (Brussels, 1964–1966, 5 vols.), Vol. I, pp. 174–6. See Dockrill and Goold, *Peace Without Promise*: esp. p. 86, and *passim*.
46. Crowe, memo, Apr. 6, 1920, *DBFP*, Vol. IX, pp. 327–8.
47. Curzon, minute, Apr. 6, 1920, Ibid. N. 1. p. 328.
48. Derby tel. 449, 9.4.20, Ibid. pp. 361–2.
49. Quoted by Erich Eyck, *A History of the Weimar Republic* (2 volumes, New York, 1962), Vol. I, p. 150.
50. Sir Harold Stuart (Koblenz) tel. 103 Apr. 12, 1920: ". . . until the *Reichswehr* advanced, the greater part of the Ruhr was quiet." and report by Lt.Col. Ryan included in Stuart desp. 254, Apr. 17, 1920, *DBFP*, Vol. IX, p. 388 and pp. 418–27.
51. See Lorna S. Jaffe, *The Decision to Disarm Germany; British Policy towards Postwar German Disarmament, 1914–1919* (Boston, 1985).
52. Smallbones, Munich, Desp. 90, Nov. 19, 1920, and D'Abernon Desp. 1187, Nov. 23, 1920. C12249/113/18.
53. Curzon, Oct. 20, 1920, *DBFP*, Vol. X, n. 2, p. 401.
54. See Gordon Craig, *The Politics of the Prussian Army 1640–1945* (New York, 1964), pp 381–415; J. Wheeler-Bennett, *Nemesis of Power* (Basingstoke, 1967), pp. 95–153; J.H. Morgan, *Assize of Arms* Vol. I (Vol. II never published) (London, 1945); F. Bingham, "Work with the Allied Commission of Control in Germany 1919–1924," *Journal of the Royal United Services Institute*, Vol. LXIX, 1925, pp. 747–63.
55. Sally Marks, "Smoke and Mirrors: In Smoke-Filled Rooms and the Galerie des Glaces," in M.F. Boemeke, G.D. Feldman, and E.Glaser (eds.), *The Treaty of Versailles: A Reassessment after 75 Years* (Cambridge, 1998), p. 338.
56. Robertson (Koblenz) desp. 159, Apr. 18, 1921, *DBFP*, Vol. XVI, p. 544.

THE BRITISH ZONE OF OCCUPATION IN THE RHINELAND

Elspeth O'Riordan

The decisions regarding the occupation of the Rhineland after the First World War formed one part of the hugely complicated and highly political inter-allied discussions at Paris in 1919. After a brief outline of the negotiations at Paris and the formulation of the treaty clauses relating to the occupation of the Rhineland, we shall examine Treaty implementation, examining how, for the British, Rhineland occupation worked in practice between 1918 and 1923. Three specific episodes serve to illustrate the character of the occupation: events relating to the Kapp Putsch and subsequent extension of the Rhineland occupation by France (supported by Belgium) in 1920; the occupation of Frankfurt, Duisburg and Düsseldorf in response to difficulties while negotiating the London Schedule of Payments in 1921; and, finally, the impact on the British zone of the Franco-Belgian occupation of the Ruhr in 1923.

Three issues are paramount here. The first relates to the difficulties encountered in practice when attempting to implement the Treaty provisions. Secondly, the practicalities of Britain's position as an occupying power drew her further into the minefield of European politics than policy-makers would have wished, often making her vulnerable to pressure from both France and Germany as tensions between the two increased. Finally, the practicalities of policy implementation on the ground highlighted (and indeed, on occasion, exacerbated) weaknesses and inconsistencies in Britain's overall European policy at the political level. This resulted in a dynamic, symbolic policy-making relationship between the periphery and London. Through considering the specifics and detailed implementation of the Treaty of Versailles in this way, it is hoped to shed fresh light on the viability and wider record of the overall peace settlement.

THE FORMULATION OF THE RHINELAND AGREEMENT: NEGOTIATIONS AT PARIS, 1919

Even before the allied leaders convened in Paris in January 1919, the question of the Rhineland had proved contentious. At the armistice negotiations in the autumn of 1918 the lines of difference between the Allies were already revealed, for the French were eager to ensure their long-term security by changes to their eastern boundaries. Perhaps anticipating a cool reception from the British, Marshal Foch targeted the Americans. He had some success. Colonel House (Wilson's special envoy at the armistice negotiations) made crucial concessions, amounting in practice to the acceptance of some kind of allied occupation of the Rhineland. Britain, represented by Lloyd George, then had little option but to agree also.

Thus, the armistice agreement, signed on November 11, 1918, contained specific terms regarding the Rhineland: Germany must withdraw 40 kilometres beyond the right bank of the Rhine, allowing the Allies to occupy the left bank plus three bridgeheads, 30 kilometers deep on the right bank. The remaining evacuated territory would form a neutral zone.[1] The territory marked out for occupation amounted to 12,000 square miles and included sections of four German states, two thirds being in Prussia. This only represented 6.5 per cent of the Reich, but contained a disproportionate proportion of the population: eleven percent (or 7 million). It included the city of Cologne, and bordered Frankfurt, Düsseldorf and the industrial Ruhr area. The location of allied zones of occupation was dictated by tactical and political considerations regarding the position of allied armies at the end of hostilities. The British area, which included Cologne and the bridgehead opposite it, was the most densely populated of the zones.

The haggling over the Rhineland which began in November continued once the Peace Conference proper got underway at Paris. As Foch commented: "In a word, the occupation is a lever that we have in our hand and with which we can call the tune."[2] Basically, the French, driven largely by the French President, Poincaré and Foch, wanted to gain a Rhine frontier, or at least to detach the Rhineland from Germany, but this brought them into conflict with Lloyd George and Wilson. On March 14, 1919, the

British and American leaders, hoping to divert French attention away from the Rhine, offered the French Premier, Clemenceau, a tripartite defensive alliance against Germany. Clemeneau was interested, and did abandon his demand that the Rhineland be independent, but insisted that the pact itself be foolproof and be supplemented by a thirty year allied occupation of the left bank.

Two weeks of deadlock ensured, which was finally broken in early April when Wilson made concessions regarding reparations, the Saar and the Treaty of Alliance. In return, Clemenceau agreed to a compromise. He would accept the Anglo-American guarantees against future German attack, along with Allied occupation for the left bank and the strategic bridgeheads on the right bank for a period varying from at least five years in the north to fifteen years in the south. In addition, the left bank plus a 50 kilometre strip on the right bank would be permanently demilitarized. Lloyd George was absent in London when this deal was struck, essentially returning to a *fait accompli,* but, on April 22, the British Premier gave in and accepted a fifteen year occupation.[3] With the basic parameters agreed, debate now shifted to the structure and nature of the occupation.

During the armistice period, the occupation was in theory to be determined by the Luxemburg Commission, but in practice was being run by the High Command under Foch. On April 5, 1919, the British suggested replacing the Luxemburg Commission with a four member Interallied Rhineland Commission, which would have full control over political and economic matters on the left bank. To make the proposal more palatable to Paris, it was suggested that a senior French colonial official, Paul Tirard, should be chairman of the new commission and on April 14, 1919 the Supreme Economic Council accepted these proposals. The British now quickly appointed Sir Harold Stuart as their first High Commissioner.

Predictably, however, problems soon surfaced. Foch was unwilling to relinquish his Rhineland authority and although Stuart and Noyes (the US High Commissioner) were in Luxemburg on April 30, ready for work, Tirard refused to schedule even a date of arrival. There were also problems with the sub commissions of the High Commission. For example, General Payot refused to relinquish any of the Inter-Allied Military Food Committee's powers. Gradually, however, the British and Americans did make some progress. On May 10, Noyes and Stuart obtained agreement to transfer the seat of the new Commission from Luxemburg to Koblenz, situated in the US zone of occupation. By mid-May, France had bowed to the British and US pressure, and finally accepted the High Commission, allowing the entire Rhineland Agreement to form part of the ultimatum dispatched to Germany.

This final package, agreed on June 16, was a compromise at every level— from the nature and length of the occupation to the mechanics and practicalities of the High Commission. Each clause represented a matter of principle over which the Allies had haggled and battled. In these circumstances, it is certainly questionable how coordinated the agreement as a whole was, and whatever else the Commission's administrative structure was immensely complex. How would the multifarious decisions and initiatives which comprised the Rhineland Agreement come together and work in practice once the Treaty of Versailles came into operation in January 1920?

THE KAPP PUTSCH AND EVENTS OF 1920

Almost from the onset, the British found that their role as an occupying power involved them in unwelcome practical complexities. In mid-February 1920, Sir Harold Stuart reported that he suspected that the French were exploiting a deteriorating food situation in the occupied territories to their advantage. Apparently the food situation in Germany as a whole was "rapidly becoming acute," and Paul Tirard (Chairman of the Inter-Allied Rhineland High Commission) felt that the German government was neglecting food supplies to the occupied territories in favour of the rest of Germany. As a result, Tirard suggested stopping the export of food from the left to the right bank of the Rhine and prohibiting German laws in the occupied territories that gave the German government the monopoly on importing foreign food stuffs. Instead, Tirard suggested that the High Commissioners take over this function. Stuart disagreed with Tirard's judgment: "I have shown that the occupied territories, so far from being unfairly treated, have on the whole had better supplies than the rest of Germany. . ." Moreover, he strongly suspected ulterior motives on the part of the French: "I am convinced that the French High Commissioner's proposals are not primarily due to an anxiety about the food situation. They are, in my opinion, inspired by the French policy which aims at the separation of the Rhineland from the rest of Germany."[4]

The issue passes, but the incident was a portent harbinger of future events. Already the British were finding that their situation in the Rhineland left them exposed to pressure from what they identified as the more unwelcome elements of French policy. From March, this vulnerability became more acute as a result of events surrounding the Kapp Putsch. The putsch occurred on the nigh of the March 12–13, 1920. Berlin was occupied by military units which ousted Gustav Bauer's Socialist-led coalition and installed a regime led by a minor civil servant named Wolfgang Kapp. By March 17, the putsch had failed and Kapp resigned, but the incident sparked a reaction in the form of a left wing uprising in the Ruhr.

From the onset the British monitored developments in their Rhineland zone closely. On March 16, Stuart reported that while there had been no disturbances in the British zone, Soviet type workmen's councils had been started in a number of Cologne factories. More seriously, 6000 workmen were reported to have left the Cologne bridgehead to attack the Reichswehr in the neutral zone.[5] This was not an isolated incident. On March 17, the new official German government, emphasizing the seriousness of the situation, requested permission to send troops into the neutral zone.[6] For the British, this was an unwelcome development. At a meeting of the Conference of Ambassadors at Paris on March 18, the French, naturally, vehemently opposed agreeing to the German demands. Moreover, Foch, the French representative, suggested that rather than allowing German troops into the Ruhr, Allied troops should be sent in: ". . . I ask the Allied governments, after having advised them not to comply with the German request, to consider whether they should not themselves restore order to the Ruhr valley."[7]

This placed the British in a very difficult position. They did not want to see Communists gaining strength in the industrial heart of Germany, but nor did they wish to sanction the entry of German troops into the neutral zone only two months after the Treaty of Versailles had become operational—an act which the French could justifiably claim was a flagrant breach of treaty provisions. That said, the British had no intention of committing themselves to an extension of the allied occupation, but nor were they prepared to allow French troops to occupy the Ruhr. The Foreign Office tried to avoid the issue. At the Ambassador's Meeting on March 18, Derby (the British ambassador in Paris) adopted delaying tactics to avoid a final decision,[8] and again at a subsequent meeting on March 20.[9] Pressure on the British, however, was mounting. On the same day the German Chargé d'Affaires in London again asked the british Foreign Secretary, Lord Curzon, for permission to send German troops into the Ruhr.[10]

Curzon tried to find a compromise. Lloyd George suggested to the French President, Millerand, that German troops could be allowed into the Ruhr subject to two conditions: that the time limit of their occupation be fixed in advance, and that Allied officers should accompany the German troops in order to supervise operations. Curzon concluded: "His Majesty's Government are prepared to agree to the above arrangement, but cannot consent in existing circumstances to any proposal to send Allied forces into Germany."[11]

Meanwhile the situation on the spot continued to give grounds for grave concern. On March 18 Stuart had reported from Koblenz that the situation in the Ruhr was serious, with considerable fighting, and that Dortmund, Elberfeld and Bochum were now in the hands of the Communists. There was also some disruption to the British zone—a strike of 10,000 had taken place that afternoon at Wiesdorf and Schledbusch.[12] On March 24, Stuart reported that workmen in the Ruhr claimed to have

150,000 men ready to fight, and that although the situation at present was calm, "fighting might break out at any moment."[13]

Shortly thereafter, however, British information from the Ruhr began to emphasize the relative calm of the situation. On March 26, Stuart reported that "'All was quiet at Essen' and that 'There have been no excesses of any kind in the Ruhr,'"[14] and on April 1, reports from Koblenz suggested that all was quiet in the British zone and that non fighting had been reported in the Ruhr area.[15]

Despite this apparent improvement, the wider crisis now came to a head, giving grounds for suspicion that both the French and German governments were now, to some extent, seeking to instrumentalize the crisis to implement wider policy initiatives. On April 2, Grahame reported from Paris that Millerand insisted that German troops could only be authorized to enter the Ruhr if French troops simultaneously occupied 5 towns: Frankfurt, Darmstadt, Hanau, Homburg, and Dieburg.[16] The Germans, however, were no longer prepared to wait, and now claimed mitigating circumstances. On the evening of April 2, Lord Kilmarnock (the British Chargé d'Affaires in Berlin) reported that they had sent a note to the British and French governments claiming that "in view of urgent necessity German troops may enter neutral zone without waiting for consent of Allies which it is hoped to obtain subsequently."[17] On April 3, German troops entered the zone and by April 5, reports suggested that the Communist uprising was quickly being suppressed.[18] As early as April 4, the Germans emphasized that they would withdraw very soon: "German government expects that operations will be finished within seven days and that removal of small reinforcements which have entered the neutral zone in the last few days can be effected."[19]

However, British hopes that the crisis might pass were dashed when on April 5, Grahame reported a heated conversation with Millerand, who seemed bent on French action: "He . . . practically admitted to me that orders had already been given for the advance of French troops . . . I made repeated and earnest appeals to him not to take precipitate action but I fear in vain."[20] On April 6, the French occupied the 5 German towns already mentioned, thereby precipitating a serious breach with the British. Paul Cambon, the French ambassador in London, called on Bonar Law on April 6, to inform him of the French action. Cambon explained that ". . .a dangerous situation was being created in the Ruhr district, which constituted a grave violation of the treaty and a serious menace to France. In these circumstance, the French government felt that they had no choice but to take immediate and energetic measures to obtain material guarantees for the withdrawal of the German troops from the neutral zone."[21]

Bonar Law's response is significant, as it underlines how important the situation in the Rhineland was in shaping overall Anglo–French relations. He replied that:

> only yesterday he had in the most explicit terms informed M. Cambon of the strong objections entertained by His Majesty's Government to the course then proposed, and had submitted an alternative procedure. . . . It was, Mr. Bonar Law though probably the first time since the war broke out, that one of the Allies had in an important matter cited in a manner directly contrary to the expressed wish of another ally. The result, whether intended or not, was to place the British Government before a 'fait accompli'. They now found themselves in the embarrassing position of having either to declare to the world that the unity of the alliance was broken or to express approval of, an assume responsibility for, a policy which they held to be wrong and dangerous.[22]

The language used by Bonar Law emphasizes the seriousness of the breach which had occurred between the Allies only three months after the Treaty of Versailles came into operation. The term of the Rhineland Agreement were already being challenged in practice. They were proving a fertile battleground between France and Germany, inevitably drawing in Britain. Despite their efforts, the British had found it very hard to avoid being drawn into events surrounding the Kapp Putsch and subsequent Communist uprising in the Ruhr. Their response had been to try to monitor events, to avoid precipitate action, and to maintain calm in the British zone of occupation. When this policy failed to prevent German and French action, Britain was left looking on in awkward embarrassment. Being on the spot in the Rhineland only contributed to the complexity of the British position and the problems and difficulties involved when implementing the Treaty provisions amidst the tangled backdrop of the post war environment.

THE REPARATIONS CRISIS OF SPRING 1921

Ostensibly, this episode marks a direct contrast with the 1920 Kapp Putsch crisis, for this time France and Britain were united in the action taken against Germany. However, on closer examination, it is evident that, below the surface, problems with France over Rhineland and Ruhr policy remained, and that these complicated the British position. In addition, the 1921 reparations crisis illuminates the tension which existed between the formation of British policy in London and the implementation of it in practice in the British zone in the Rhineland.

By the beginning of 1921, problems with Germany over reparation payments were increasing. An allied conference was held in Paris in January 1921, which resulted in Germany being presented with a new set of proposals along with a note threatening certain sanctions should she continue to fail to meet her obligations. In early March, at the Third Conference of London, Walter Simons (the German Minister of Foreign Affairs) vehemently rejected the Paris Resolutions, suggesting instead a greatly reduced time-table of payments. Even Lloyd George, more moderate in his reparation demands at this stage than his French allies, felt that the German proposals were "frankly an offence and an exasperation"[23]

The allies agreed that unless the Germans accepted the Paris Resolutions by March 7, sanctions would be imposed. These would comprise the occupation of the Rhineland towns of Duisburg, Düsseldorf and Ruhrort, and the imposition of a customs duty in the occupied territories which amounted to a 50 per cent levy on German exports. The Germans failed to meet the conditions and so, on March 7, the imposition of sanctions was announced. These sanctions, imposed mainly at British insistence (Lloyd George pressed for the imposition of the customs levy), constituted a carefully considered compromise. Perhaps Britain genuinely desired to take a firmer line with Germany after Berlin's flagrant rejection of the Paris Resolutions. On the other hand, to regard events more cynically, the extension of the occupation would trump any hint at an economic rapprochement between France and Germany, rumors of which were circulating in the FO at this time.[24] At the same time, however, these measures would not be harsh enough either to allow France greatly increased influence over Germany or entirely to embitter the defeated country.

On the surface, British policy appeared to succeed. At the end of March, Lord D'Abernon (the British Ambassador in Berlin) commented that despite the fact that: "The military advance and occupation of Düsseldorf and Duisburg have not caused nearly the sensation of the economic measures,"[25] the real force of German bitterness was directed not towards Britain but towards France: "Feeling against France is intensely bitter. Compared with the French, the English are almost popular."[26] Thus the British had succeeded in treating Germany with relative firmness but at the same time had diverted the resulting resentment towards France: Meanwhile, Britain's show of strength towards Germany and acquiescence in the Rhineland occupations earned the country a measure a French goodwill. All in all Britain had succeeded in maintaining sufficient tension and friction between France and Germany to enable it to continue to pursue a middle path in Europe to its own advantage.

However, while at a level of high politics, London's policy concerning the March sanctions might be considered a success, the situation was very different on the ground. Ironically, it was the customs sanction, which, as mentioned, had been suggested and pushed by Lloyd George, that caused the most difficulties for British officials on the spot in the Rhineland. The new British High Commissioner, Arnold Robertson, was soon complaining; indeed even before the sanction was agreed on he telegrammed the Foreign Office emphasizing that the proposals risked precipitating economic chaos.[27] Once the sanction was underway, Robertson not only emphasized the economic problems it entailed, but also reported increasing problems with the French.

The situation did not make for good relations between the High Commissioner and the Foreign Office. On March 16, Robertson telegrammed "most urgently," complaining that: "I have received no answers to my telegrams Nos 24 to 28 inclusive. Unless I can have assurances from His Majesty's Government that necessary customs officials and reinforcements will be sent I shall have no alternative but to allow French to take over whole line."[28] This elicited a curt reply from Curzon the following day: "No British troops can be sent. We are examining possibility of sending customs officials to assist you, but it will take some time to ascertain extent to which your demands for experts can be met." He concluded: ". . . His Majesty's Government cannot admit interference by French authorities in British zone without previous agreement. You should so inform our French colleague. . ."[29]

Robertson was extremely concerned. On March 14, he had already written a very revealing letter to Waterlow at the Foreign Office:

> To tell you the honest truth, I am very anxious about these "sanctions" and do not quite see what the result of them is going to be beyond the inevitable ruin of the Rhineland. I think you will admit that the High Commission has been somewhat badly treated. We were not consulted beforehand and we are now told to draw up a Report "immediately," in fact, to frame a brand new Customs Tariff which, if it is to be done well at all, would obviously take months to prepare. None of us has the smallest idea what our Government's wish us to do, and so far I have ailed to elicit from you anything but the most meager replies to my telegrams.[30]

He did try to assist the Foreign Office, but found it almost impossible to produce a viable report on the proposed customs sanction in the time frame demanded, commenting to Curzon that: "Your Lordship will not fail to realize the difficulties confronting the High Commission in drawing up a report of this kind at a moment's notice. . . . The new frontier has been arbitrarily drawn through the middle of a thickly populated industrial area, and considerable experience will be required before a tariff can be finally settled. . . . At the present moment we have practically no data upon which to work. . . ." He continued: "I am still without guidance as to the policy of His Majesty's Government or the line they wish me to adopt. The French High Commissioner and the French Government have a definite purpose in view. . . . Their intention is to separate the Rhineland, at any rate economically, from the rest of Germany. . ."[31]

Left with little guidance from London, Robertson did his best to muddle through, operating the customs sanction as best he could. Indeed, he decided that, "The more I think of it the more convinced I am that the only way of bringing the present intolerable situation to an end is to hit the Germans as hard as we can with this customs frontier weapon. I am far from saying it is a good weapon, but I had noting to do with the choosing of it. . ."[32]

However, despite these practical problems, Robertson's efforts did pay off. On March 25, Lord D'Abernon, reported: ". . .there is remarkable apathy in respect of the military occupation. . . . They [the Germans] are more sensitive about the customs frontier on the Rhine and still more sensitive about the 50% levy on German exports."[33] The combined pressure from the sanctions probably contributed to finding a resolution to the crisis as a whole—helping to "persuade" Germany to take seriously the subsequent Allied threat of Ruhr occupation and to accept the London Schedule of Payments in May 1921.

This episode contains important lessons regarding the British and their zone of occupation in the Rhineland. Robertson's letters of complaint demonstrate the tension between central policy and practical implementation. Not only were there problems regarding lines of communication, but also regarding a lack of understanding between the Foreign Office and officials on the spot. Officials in the Rhineland certainly felt they were being treated unfairly by London. Perhaps the practicalities of sanction implementation in the Rhineland were so complex that they had to be forfeited if London was to achieve anything like a coherent overall policy. However, the implications on the ground in the Rhineland were significant, and Robertson was already highlighting the potential both for economic dislocation in the British zone and for pressure on the British position from Germany and particularly from France. All these factors were to play an even greater part two years later, when the sanctions under consideration were more serious, namely the occupation of the Ruhr.

THE OCCUPATION OF THE RUHR 1923

By late 1922 a serious breach in allied policy over reparations was imminent. When, on December 26, the Reparation Commission declared

Germany to be in default over payments, the French, with Belgian support, determined to impose sanctions and so January 11, 1923 occupied the Ruhr District. However, unlike in 1921, Britain did not support these measures leaving its overall policy in the uncomfortable state of 'benevolent neutrality'. Nowhere was the discomfort and vulnerability of this policy more exposed than on the ground—in the British zone of occupation in the Rhineland. Indeed, issues surrounding the Ruhr occupation reveal most clearly the interaction between events on the spot in the British zone of occupation, the international situation, and Britain's overall policy towards the implementation of the Treaty of Versailles.

From the onset of the occupation Britain's wider Rhineland policy was made extremely difficult. Lord Kilmarnock, who had taken over from Robertson as the British High Commissioner on the Interallied Rhineland High Commission, was left as an awkward onlooker, attending meetings but abstaining from any decisions regarding the Ruhr. However, the problems did not stop there. Once passive resistance was properly underway, the vulnerability of Britain's position became painfully clear. The German government began passing legislation to disrupt reparation deliveries, but this was in flagrant defiance of the Rhineland High Commission, which was supposed to approve all legislation in the occupied territories. In practice it left the British dependent on both French and German goodwill to prevent incidents in the British zone. Should Rhinelanders obey the German legislation and discontinue reparation deliveries, then they would be opposing the High Commission. Should the British try such offenders in the British courts, they would appear to support France, should they refuse to do so, they would seem to favour Germany. Whitehall was aware of the potential problems, but was unable to come up with any real answers, merely sending Kilmarnock rather ambiguous instructions: "If . . . you are requested to proceed against a German national in British zone for acting in accordance with the orders of his government contrary to orders of the High Commission, you should express your inability to do so but at the same time you may intimate that you will place no obstacle in the way of allied authorities enforcing their decision within the British zone provided that there can be no question of employment of either British troops or officials or of their becoming involved."[34]

The transport question arguably provides the clearest illustration of the range of problems faced by the British in their zone of occupation. This resulted primarily from the fact that the railway lines from the now occupied Ruhr area passed through the British zone on their way to France. Were the Germans to obstruct reparations deliveries through the British zone by refusing to work the railways there, then Britain would have faced very unwelcome alternatives. The British did not have sufficient technical personnel to operate the railways themselves and so, should the

French offer to send in their own staff, it would be hard for the British to refuse permission.

By early February, this very situation had arisen. The Germans refused to move the trains, and on February 6, the French requested permission to resume reparation transport across the British zone.[35] The solution which was ultimately adopted to this problem by the British illustrates key aspects of the role of the Rhineland zone of occupation in British policy. Not only does it afford ample evidence of the complexity of implementing policy in practice, but it also demonstrates the impact of the relationship between periphery and Whitehall on the policy making process as a whole.

Anxious to avoid a major policy confrontation with either France or Germany, or to have to rethink the fundamentals of British policy, the Foreign Office was left relying on officials in the Rhineland to try to cobble together some kind of compromise solution. Luckily, the resourceful Kilmarnock came up with a suggestion—allowing the French to use the Gravenbroich-Düren line. This crossed only a small northwesterly corner of the British zone which, it was argued, could easily be transferred to France. After a hastily scheduled meeting on February 15, when key French officials traveled to London, the compromise was agreed on.[36]

Agreement had been reached, but in the event it was not a particularly satisfactory one. Operational details were left to officials in the Rhineland (in essence General Godley, the Commander of the British Army of Occupation in the Rhineland, and Lord Kilmarnock) to work our with their French counterparts, but in practice problems over the railways and transportation were to rumble on throughout the Ruhr crisis. The overall vulnerability of the British position had merely been papered over, rather then radically redressed. Only the resourcefulness and patience of the men on the spot in the Rhineland, whether French or British, and the fact that in the final analysis neither the French nor the Germans pushed Britain too far prevented the crisis from coming to a head. Indeed, despite the compromise solution that had been reached, the difficulties faced by the British in the Rhineland certainly contributed, along with international pressure and domestic political criticism, to Britain abandoning a policy of benevolent neutrality and moving towards a more proactive Ruhr policy during the summer of 1923.[37]

The role of the Rhineland zone in Britain's policy towards the separatist uprisings during the autumn of 1923 contrasted markedly with the vulnerability and weakness displayed during the spring, for by then the dynamics of the Ruhr occupation had changed. In essence, the British used the leverage afforded by their zone to much more positive effect, effectively thwarting the more dangerous separatist tendencies of the French. The political chaos and economic dislocation, which followed the cessation of passive resistance on September 26, fuelled the Rhenish separatist movement, particularly in the Belgian and French zones of occupation. By October 22, smaller towns including Ems and Saarburg were in the hands of separatists, as were the public buildings in Wiesbaden, Trier, Düren and Duisburg. Reports received by the British immediately thereafter suggested that the movement was running out of steam,[38] but suddenly the situation changed. Reports filed a week later, at the end of October, spoke of its resurgence, and attributed this new lease of life to direct French involvement and encouragement.[39]

As early as October 23, a meeting was held in Sir Eyre Crowe's room at the Foreign Office to discuss the situation, with important consequences. Two approaches were agreed upon. Firstly, the British government resolved that it would only support any change in regime which was brought about in accordance with the German constitution.[40] In essence, this decision mooted the possibility of supporting the German government against the separatists, for Berlin was unlikely to agree to a completely independent Rhineland. The second stratagem was more subtle, and involved using the British zone of occupation in the Rhineland as a bulwark against separatism. It was decided that, in the interests of the maintenance of public order in the British zone, the army of occupation would suppress any acts of violence. In other words, London would refuse to allow the separatists to gain ascendancy in the British zone, without which the formation of any kind of viable independent republic would be next to impossible. In addition, Britain communicated a stern warning to its allies, both through a public speech by Prime Minister Baldwin on October 25, and through strong protests by Kilmarnock at the Rhineland Commission.

The tide turned against the separatists. The French, and particularly the Belgians, proceeded more cautiously, so that by early December the separatists had been disarmed at Duisburg, Bonn, Beuel, Königswinter, and Godesberg. The movement was clearly a spent force.

It is difficult to determine with any degree of certainty, the extent to which the movement would have waned anyway and the extent to which Britain's stance contributed to its decline. However, this episode demonstrated the increasingly uniform and coherent nature of British policy and the degree of coordination that was at last occurring between London and the Rhineland. At last the potential (and limitations) of Britain's involvement on the spot had been appreciated in London and as a result Britain's presence in the Rhineland on this occasion actually helped rather than hindered overall policy.

CONCLUSION

In March 1920, only a few months after the Treaty of Versailles came into operation, Britain found herself in a very difficult position when Communist uprisings were reported in the Ruhr and the neutral Rhineland zone. Unable to calm the escalating violence, the British were left trying to maintain order in their own zone as tensions between France and Germany escalated. When France took action against Germany by occupying 5 towns on the Rivers Rhine and Main, Britain was left looking on in awkward embarrassment.

In 1921, the situation was ostensibly less complex as France and Britain were united in the action taken against Germany. But in reality, Britain's Rhineland presence contributed to increased Anglo-French tension as France sought to interfere in the British zone. More seriously, this episode generated severe tensions within the British policy-making process, for unmistakeable problems surfaced between Whitehall and the periphery.

In 1923, Britain's international predicament was particularly serious. As in 1920 unilateral action was taken by France (and Belgium), without British consent. Once again this resulted in a range of practical problems in the British zone, particularly in the spring of 1923, when Britain's overall position was most seriously compromised. Thereafter, and by way of contrast, when the height of the Ruhr crisis had passed and passive resistance had ended, the pressure on Britain's Rhineland position eased, allowing London to formulate and pursue a more consistent and positive policy towards the ensuing separatist rising.

Each of these episodes demonstrates how hard it was, in practice, for Britain to implement the letter of Versailles—not least because of differences of interpretation between the Allies over the issue of sanctions. Britain's presence in the Rhineland represented an area of vulnerability, leaving London even more exposed to the dynamics of European politics and the increased tension between France and Germany.

Beyond this, the impact of the Rhineland zone on Britain's overall policy-making process is worthy of mention, as is the shifting pattern which occurred over the course of the three years. In 1920, relations between the centre and the periphery were characterized by a degree of tentativeness and uncertainty. In 1921, relations were at a low point and in essence one way, with the Foreign Office dictating policy. This caused severe strains between Robertson, in the Rhineland, and Curzon in the Foreign Office. In contrast, despite the worsening international situation and increased complexity of the situation in the Rhineland, the situation was much improved by 1923. The Foreign Office was now involving the periphery much more proactively in decision-making, using officials in the Rhineland to help find solutions to problems both in the spring and autumn. All in all the policy-making relationship had become much more two and symbiotic.

Examining the detail of Britain's experience in the Rhineland, has, therefore, not simply contributed towards a deeper understanding of the viability and record of the Treaty of Versailles, but also towards a fuller appreciation of the nature of Britain's foreign policy and the complex process of policy formulation during the immediate post-war period.

NOTES

1. Alan Sharp, *The Versailles Settlement: Peacemaking in Paris, 1919* (Basingstoke, 1991), p. 17.
2. K. Nelson, *Victors Divided: America and the Allies in Germany 1918–1923* (Berkeley, 1975), p. 66.
3. Sharp, *Versailles*, p. 32.
4. HMSO, *Documents on British Foreign Policy 1919–1939*, (*DBFP*), First Series, vol. IX, no. 43, p. 69. Sir H Stuart (Koblenz), unnumbered tel., Feb. 16, 1920.
5. *DBFP* vol. IX, no. 126, p. 153. Stuart, tel. 44 Mar. 16, 1920.
6. *DBFP* vol. IX, no. 137, p. 163. Kilmarnock (Berlin) tel. 136, Mar. 17, 1920.
7. *DBFP* vol. IX, no. 147, p. 170. Meeting of Conference of Ambassadors, Mar. 18, 1920.
8. Ibid.
9. *DBFP* vol IX, no. 170, p. 193. Meeting of Conference of Ambassadors, Mar. 20, 1920.
10. *DBFP* vol. IX, no. 177, p. 207. Tel. 262 to Derby (Paris), Mar. 20, 1920.
11. *DBFP* vol. IX, no. 195, p. 221. Tel. 373 to Derby, Mar. 22, 1920.
12. *DBFP* vol. IX, no. 159, p. 187. Stuart, tel. 55, Mar. 18, 1920.
13. *DBFP* vol. IX, no. 219, p. 248. Stuart, tel. 68, Mar. 24, 1920.
14. *DBFP* vol. IX, no. 226, p. 255. Stuart (unnumbered), Mar. 26, 1920.
15. *DBFP* vol. IX, no. 249, p. 283. Robertson (Koblenz), tel. 76, Apr. 1, 1920.
16. *DBFP* vol. IX, no. 265, p. 300. Sir G. Grahame (Paris), tel. 406, Apr. 2, 1920.
17. *DBFP* vol. IX, no. 268, p. 303. Kilmarnock, tel. 204, Apr. 3, 1920.
18. *DBFP* vol. IX, no. 285, p. 315. Robertson, tel. 82, Apr. 5, 1920.
19. *DBFP* vol. IX, no. 281, p. 313, Kilmarnock tel. 208, Apr. 4, 1920.
20. *DBFP* vol. IX, no. 288, p. 317, Grahame, tel. 421, Apr. 5, 1920.
21. *DBFP* vol. IX, no. 298, p. 324, tel. 419 to Derby, Apr. 6, 1920.
22. Ibid.
23. *DBFP* vol. XV, p. 325: Allied Conference Mar. 7, 1921. Speech by Lloyd George.
24. Rumors of a Franco-German rapprochement were circulating in the FO at this time. For example, on March 3, Lord Kilmarnock, the Chargé d'Affaires in Berlin, informed Curzon: "I am informed that negotiations, the prime movers in which are M.M. Stinnes, Vögler and Quaatz, three of the most prominent businessmen in Germany, are being conducted with a view to concluding a sort of trust of important French and German interests. I am likewise informed that Walther Rathenau is working in the same direction." Kilmarnock continued: "It is obvious that a Franco-German economic rapprochement is not as unthinkable as at first sight it might appear to be. It has been freely discussed, it has been openly negotiated, and it is still being advocated in both countries by persons who have the power and ability to put it into effect." [*DBFP* vol. XVI, p. 276, Kilmarnock to Curzon (letter) Mar. 3, 1921].

25. Curzon Papers, MSS Eur F 112/203, Lord D'Abernon's diary, Mar. 28, 1921.
26. Ibid.
27. *DBFP* vol. IX, no. 447, p. 474. Kilmarnock, tel. 390, Mar. 3, 1921.
28. *DBFP* vol. IX, no. 465, p. 493. Robertson (Koblenz) tel 29, Mar. 16, 1921.
29. *DBFP* vol. IX, no. 468, p. 497. Tel. 17 to Robertson Mar. 17, 1921.
30. *DBFP* vol. IX, no. 461, p. 486. Letter from Robertson (Koblenz) to Waterlow Mar. 14, 1921.
31. *DBFP* vol. IX, no. 467, p. 495. Robertson to Curzon no. 117, Mar. 16, 1921.
32. *DBFP* vol. IX, no. 475, p. 510. Letter from Robertson to Waterlow, Mar. 22, 1921.
33. Curzon Papers, MSS Eur F 112/203, Lord D'Abernon's diary, Mar. 25, 1921.
34. Public Record Office, Foreign Office (FO) 371 8705, C1167/313/18: Tel. 6 to Kilmarnock, Jan. 22, 1923.
35. FO 371 8711, C2329/313/18: Note from French Ambassador Feb. 6, 1923, and letter 482 to Crewe in reply Feb. 9, 1923.
36. FO 371 8713. C2922/313/18: Notes of meeting on Feb. 15, 1923.
37. For a fuller exposition of this argument, see Elspeth Y O'Riordan, *Britain and the Ruhr Crisis* (Basingstoke 2001), Chapter 2.
38. FO 371 8685, C18253/129/18: Ryan (Koblenz) tel. 416 Oct. 23, 1923.
39. FO 371 8685, C18430/129/18: Thurstan, Cologne, Tel. 31 Oct. 25, 1923.
40. Minute by Cdogan, 24.10.23 on FO 371 8685, C18312/129/18: Rhine Army, Cologne, to WO, 50005, Oct. 23, 1923.

"*HUT AB*," "PROMENADE WITH KAMERADE FOR SCHOKOLADE," AND THE *FLYING DUTCHMAN*: BRITISH SOLDIERS IN THE RHINELAND, 1918–1929

Keith Jeffery

Between December 1, 1918 and December 12, 1929 over 300,000 British and British Empire troops served in the British Army of Occupation in Germany. Their experience has not much troubled historians. Sir James Edmonds' volume in the British "official history of the Great War" series was published in a limited edition in 1944.[1] Although Edmonds had particularly sought out "domestic details" of the Rhine Command, including, "intercourse with inhabitants, including the ladies (professional and otherwise), restaurants and beer halls,"[2] the volume only deals with such matters in general terms. The only modern extended study of the British occupation is David Williamson's *The British in Germany*, published in 1991.[3] Williamson aimed "to show how the subaltern, private soldier, civilian officials and their dependants lived in what were at times virtually British colonies in Germany,"[4] but the book has comparatively little about personal Germano-British relations. This study explores the social history of the "British Army of the Rhine" (BAOR), especially their interactions with the German population over the three main phases of the eleven-year occupation: from the beginning of December 1918 until early 1919 covering the immediate circumstances of the Allied march into Germany and the beginning of the occupation; then to January 1920, when the possibility remained that the forces in Germany might have to be used to compel German acceptance of the Allied peace terms; and finally after 10 January 1920, when the Treaty of Versailles was ratified, the Inter-Allied Rhineland High Commission inaugurated and civil control of Occupied Germany established.

On December 1, 1918 Allied troops began to cross the German frontier. The British made a particular effort to include any men—"they were not many"—who had arrived in France in 1914, and to ensure that Dominion troops—Canadian, Newfoundland, New Zealand, Australian, and South African—were among the first to cross the frontier.[5] By December 9, British troops had reached the Rhine and by December 13, completed the occupation of an area of approximately a thousand square miles of German territory west of the Rhine, as well as the chief Rhineland city of Cologne and a "Cologne Bridgehead," extending some ten miles or so east of the city. The area contained about 1,400,000 inhabitants, of whom 600,000 lived in Cologne. To the north and west was the Belgian area of occupation, and to the south, the American and French areas.

How would Allied troops adapt to being a conquering army of occupation, and how would Germans respond? Edmonds described the Germans' attitude as "one of indifference tempered with curiosity; the officials were studiously polite." Billeting of Allied troops proved no problem—"the inhabitants, accustomed to billeting in peace time as well as in war, made few difficulties on that account."[6] Captain Charles Dudley Ward of the Welsh Guards, recorded in his diary that his billet in the outskirts of Cologne was "not at all bad but frigid politeness from the people." Their "one desire," however, "seems to be friendly. They will do anything for you & give no trouble."[7] Some Rhinelanders preferred British troops to the wartime German army. T. H. Howard spoke to an elderly female servant of a propertied German family: "'You don't find us as bad as you expected, then?' said the officer. 'All I know', she answered, 'is that the roads are safe for women now, there's no more stealing, and I don't have to sleep with a revolver under my pillow.'"[8] Percy Creek, an artilleryman billeted with an English-speaking schoolmaster in a village to the south of the bridgehead zone, recalled "how at every chance he berated the German war lords" and at first suspected "that he was trying to curry favour with the British, but when I knew him better as a kind gentle man, a scholar, who hated war, lust and greed, I realised he was sincere."[9]

Nonetheless the British high command took no chances. After consulting Marshal Foch, the overall Allied commander, the Adjutant-General established the general policy for the Army of Occupation in a memorandum issued on November 27, 1918. This preserved the basic administrative structure of German local government, and "the life of the civilian population shall so far as possible continue uninterrupted and with the minimum of interference," though under the supervision of the British military authorities. These authorities could issue regulations controlling billeting, the movement of population and the sale of alcohol. Military "Summary Courts" were set up to consider "breaches of orders issued by the British military authorities, acts to the prejudice of the British Armies, or offences against the persons or property of British or Allied subjects."[10]

On December 2, General Sir Herbert Plumer, the first commander of the British Army of Occupation issued nineteen regulations, the *Anordnungen*, which established the conditions for the initial occupation period. All civilians had to have identity cards, their movements beyond their immediate locality were severely restricted and with a curfew from 7.00 p.m. to 6.00 a.m. All methods of communication—telephone, wireless, carrier pigeon, post and telegraph—were strictly controlled and the "taking of photographs out of doors by civilians" was forbidden. The nineteenth regulation proved to be among the most irritating, for British and Germans: "All persons of the male sex will show proper respect for British officers [not, of course, the other ranks] and at the playing of the British National Anthem, in the case of civilians by raising their hats, in the case of persons in uniform by saluting."[11] This required German civilians to doff their hats to British officers, even in passing. It was, reported one journalist, "a French notion," but it was swiftly modified.[12] On January 5, 1919 an amended regulation required civilians to doff their hats only when addressing or being addressed by British officers.[13] Germans in uniform—postmen, railway servants, and policemen—had to continue to salute British officers.[14]

Some British troops applied the regulation with particular vigor:

> At least in the early days of 1919, male Germans were required to step into the roadway and uncover when passing a British officer or a party of marching troops. Failure to comply brought the sharp reminder *'Hut ab'* ('hat off'), an order which was joyfully rendered by exuberant 'other ranks' as 'hoot up, Fritz!'[15]

Such high-spirited horse-play is unsurprising when large numbers of young men are licensed to lord it over a defeated enemy. Charles Dudley Ward recorded some drink-fuelled Christmas jollities. On Christmas Day he and some fellow officers:

> went into town to see if we could get some fun. Jack said he would take us to a good place & introduced us to a low café where dancing was going on. For some unknown reason the youngsters immediately began to "rag" the place. They said it was because it annoyed them to

see Huns dancing. Anyhow we all joined in & raced round in a ring holding each others hands with the Hun dancers in the centre. As we all wear enormous pistols here they were quite alarmed & the women began to squeal. Then someone let go & Ball swung round & knocked over a table. Fearful crash of glasses. Old Vickery was there with some of his staff & they began to utter fox hunting yells. It was really funny. The civilians went out in one stream followed by us. In five minutes we had emptied the place & as Ball said once more established our superiority! We then had an excellent dinner with Rhine salmon & lager beer & got back by the last tram at nine. Everyone thought it a most successful Xmas [sic] day!![16]

This escapade followed what Ferdinand Tuohy described as "the first untoward incident of the occupation." On Christmas Eve rank and file soldiers "forcibly invaded cafés which had been set aside for warrant officers and N.C.O's, free fights, and the striking of seniors resulting." Frustration at the occupation regime's restrictions contributed to the disorder. "Victory? Pooh!," said the British Tommy, "Every second blinking place out of bounds."[17] Williamson describes it as "boisterous 'undergraduate' behaviour," undoubtedly alcohol fuelled, citing the case of "two drunken officers [who] placed chamber-pots on the heads of the statues of Kaiser Wilhelm and Kaiserin Augusta" during the evening of January 4, 1919.[18]

Dudley Ward, whose diary is vividly revealing of British officer attitudes in early-occupied Germany, enforced the "hats off" regulation in January 1919 when the Welsh Guards' regimental colours were paraded through Cologne. "A crowd of police," he noted, "ordered the civilians to take their hats off—those who didn't had them knocked off. Ball & I cut across the square & marched by the side of ours & had the greatest fun removing hats."[19] The *Anordnungen* requirement for Germans to "show proper respect" to the British was also capable of wide interpretation, as Ward further testifies:

[February 6] We still have the amusement of running in Germans for minor offences—much can be done with the charge of "behaving in an insolent manner to His Majesty's Forces"! They get imprisonment up to two months with hard labour & fine to a thousand marks. They can get more but that is the most we have done up to now, the offender being an ex-officer who tried to push his way across our parade ground![20]

British responses to perceived German insult could have more serious consequences. In May 1919 an officer believed three boys cycling past

British troops insulted them. His warning shots fatally wounded one of the cyclists. The boy's family were offered derisory compensation though the officer was cashiered "despite his plea that he had often employed similar methods in the colonies."[21]

A much resented order, issued on December 17, warned troops against fraternization with the inhabitants. "Any man," it said, "seen walking with a German woman" would be arrested.[22] A pious instruction added: "Intercourse with the inhabitants will be confined to what is essential and will be marked by courtesy and restraint."[23] This was a counsel of perfection and certainly difficult to enforce. The Americans attempted to enforce it even within the soldiers' billets, but the British Military Police only really clamped down on public behaviour. Percy Creek wrote that "the Military Police, officers and N.C.Os, who stamped on any show of fraternization in the streets, could not police every billet," and that "during the long winter evenings the Schoolmaster invited Nobby Clark and I into his parlour where his wife gave us a bowl of potatoe [*sic*] and bean soup." There were also eight females, employed in a government office in Bonn, some of whom joined Creek and the others in the evening. The Military Police later caught Creek walking with one of the girls, and he suffered the stiff penalty of fourteen days' Number One Field Punishment, roped to a gun-wheel.[24]

In February 1919 the II Corps newspaper, *The Watch on the Rhine*, published some gently satirical verses on the "no fraternizing" order:

> But stern and grim an order came
> Which caused us much surprise –
> The frauleins, from a distance love,
> But you must not fraternise.
>
> Now when a buxom fraulein says
> "Sir, have you Cho-ko-lat?"
> You have to scowl and utter "Nix"
> And other words like that.
> Of course, you still a sigh can heave,
> Or love her with your eyes;
> Don't put your arm around her waist
> 'cos then you fraternise.[25]

Fraternization with local women was difficult to stop with the British garrison 290,000-strong in January 1919.[26] "In one respect," argued Ferdinand Tuohy in his lively 1931 account of the occupation, "it was not unlike the prohibition law since in America. Enforcement of the 'no fratting' order lacked the moral sanction of officers and men alike, and so came under constant discussion—and probably, as with prohibition, led, if the truth were only known, to more consorting with *Fräulein* than would have eventuated had no ban ever existed."[27] The increasingly unenforceable rule was abolished in July 1919. T. H. Howard noted that some social tensions resulted from Rhineland girls seeking the company "of young men who possessed not only the excitement of novelty but also [he asserted] far better manners than the local youths and far more money in their pockets." Crucially, the British soldiers had "supplies of chocolate from the canteen, a delicacy for which the German girls had long been obliged to sigh in vain. So 'promenade with kamerad for schokolade?' became a recognized form of invitation which was presumably seldom refused, and Fritz and Hans found themselves left at the post."[28]

Many of these meetings were, no doubt, honorable, and there were a number of marriages between British soldiers and German women during the occupation, despite active discouragement by the military authorities. Until March 1920 marriage to a German subject was prohibited. In March 1921, the Secretary for War told parliament that "approximately 112 officers and soldiers" had married Germen women.[29] By November 1923 the number had risen to 500 and by the end of 1925, it was 648.[30] In the summer of 1919 the *Cologne Post*, the BAOR's own newspaper, warned "For five years or more the German nation has been nourished on hatred for Britain and it would be an unpleasant event for an English father if the first words his offspring spoke were 'Gott strafe England.'"[31]

There were a number of "unofficial" marriages. In September 1919 a soldier on leave told *The Times* he had seen 23 British soldiers marrying German women in Cologne Cathedral; "a German to whom he had expressed surprise told him it was quite a common thing to see British soldiers marrying German girls."[32] General Sir William Robertson, who had succeeded Plumer as General-Officer Commanding (GOC) in April 1919 responded sharply: "Report absolutely untrue. No marriages between British soldiers and Germans have taken place in Cologne Cathedral, nor have any such marriages taken place in the occupied territories as far as can be ascertained after interrogation of the German authorities."[33] The soldier reiterated his claim. "There were," he said, "several thousands of our soldiers in German billets, and throughout the day they were allowed to go where and to do what they pleased."[34]

The male–female liaisons which most exercized the authorities were those involving prostitutes, principally in Cologne itself, a "cosmopolitan city," which with the occupation "commenced to attract the worst elements of the scum of Europe."[35] One Military Police officer remarked on the large number of prostitutes in Cologne since the Armistice, so many, indeed, "that that the rumour accounting for their presence seemed almost plausible. They were supposed to have been systematically collected and left there by the Germans in 1918 on purpose to corrupt the incoming armies of occupation." But "the truth was that they gathered quite naturally wherever money was being spent without any other stimulus."[36] Prostitutes were registered in the Rhineland, and brothels operated openly, prompting criticism in Britain. In 1927 the Labor MP and temperance activist, Cecil Wilson, asked a parliamentary question about "licensed houses of prostitution" in the Allied occupation area. Commodore King, a junior War Office minister, ducked the question, replying that "there are, and have been, no licensed brothels" in the British area.[37]

In fact the British authorities condoned the operation of brothels in Cologne. In April 1920 the Dean of Lincoln complained to the Convocation of Canterbury about the British tolerance of "disorderly houses for the exploitation of women." There were, he asserted, "fifty of these houses in Cologne alone."[38] While the "worst brothels" were closed,[39] others were not. Robert Coulson found that "one of the hardest and least pleasant duties" of the Police "Special Branch" was the monitoring of prostitutes. Anyone suspected of being one was arrested and brought to police headquarters where she was examined by a doctor: "The healthy ones were released, the diseased handed over to the German police who sent them to special reformatory hospitals."[40] The incidence of venereal disease in the Rhine Army was a constant concern. In June 1920 the GOC, General Sir Thomas Morland (who succeeded Robertson in March 1920), observed that VD had increased by 350% "since the Germans took over control on signing the Peace." "We are doing all we can to combat it," he wrote, "but it is difficult in a large town of this nature where there are 30,000 women of loose character."[41] In March 1921 a Conservative MP, Captain Walter Elliot, raised the question of Rhine Army VD in parliament. The Secretary for War, Sir Laming Worthington-Evans, admitted that the incidence of VD was "not satisfactory and has been the subject of much anxious consideration ever since the area was first occupied." The incidence of the disease, however, had fallen slightly from 45.81 per 1,000 in the first quarter of 1920 to 37.80 per 1,000 a year later. Worthington-Evans assured "the House that every possible effort is unceasingly being made to reduce the amount of this disease among the troops of the British Army of the Rhine." Among the efforts was "the spread of information regarding self-disinfection as followed in the United Kingdom," where it had a marked beneficial effect.[42]

Self-disinfection and the detaining (and also deporting) of diseased women were not the only means of combating VD. The latter policy recalled the nineteenth-century campaign in Britain against the Contagious Diseases Acts and raised criticisms among feminists and others as it fell exclusively and pejoratively on women.[43] Following what Sir James Edmonds privately described as "rather ill-informed agitation at home about V.D. amongst our troops on the Rhine,"[44] in December 1922 a leading feminist, Mrs Margery Corbett Ashby, was allowed to visit Cologne to investigate. Mrs Ashby, who was Co-Honorary Secretary of the National Council of Women of Great Britain and Ireland, London Branch, found nothing very surprising. Poverty, and unemployment, among women tended to lower moral standards. Germans from other parts, she remarked, "generally consider the population of the Rhineland more pleasure-loving than in other districts." She thought the streets "seemed no worse than elsewhere, but being very narrow are crowded with very slow moving crowds, easy for new acquaintances to be formed." Her impression of the soldiers in the cafés was that they "seemed very young and nearly all seemed to have had too much drink, flushed, sleepy or excitable faces, not really drunk. A large number in twos or threes without girls." Corbett Ashby made three suggestions: that the British forces should be paid in sterling and not marks; that savings bank facilities be available in the pay rooms; and that "a corps of German Women Police should be formed," some British Women Police being sent out to work alongside them. "The German women," she argued, "could deal with the German girls, and the British women could deal with the British soldier."[45]

These recommendations were adopted,[46] but were not an unqualified success. Six British policewomen began duty in July 1923, alongside three German women. At the end of the year the GOC reported that the maintenance of the women police was "not important to welfare of Army,"[47] proposed to abandon the experiment. Corbett Ashby protested sharply in a letter to *The Times*. "Few people," she wrote, "realize the quiet and wonderful work done by them."[48] Katharine Tynan Hinkson, the Irish writer who had lived in the Rhineland for a year in 1922–23, added her support, expressing her "admiration of the spirit in which they [the women police] carried out their difficult and painful work."[49] On the other hand, the women were ridiculed in the German press, as "*Halb Mann, Halb Frau.*" Arguing that "they were costing the British taxpayers £1200" per annum, "without any noticeable result," the army withdrew them at the end of March 1925.[50] The experience of the 2nd Cameron Highlanders who arrived in Cologne in October 1923 suggests little could be done. After only a month in Germany the battalion adjutant, Captain Douglas Wimberley, wrote in his diary: "Venereal disease is a perfect curse here. We have had over ten cases already. Why the Jocks have not more sense I cannot imagine, as they have been told time and again of the dangers. We have tried everything we can to keep it down, loss of pay, punishments, precautions, etc., but it seems no use."[51] Corbett Ashby proposed a similar scheme during the Second World War, claiming the women police experiment as a success. The women police could "warn the soldiers." She said that he had been told in 1922 that this duty "was an impossible measure but," she continued, "it was carried out, was not resented and worked. On several occasions young soldiers returning home on leave, even asked the women police to look after their girls for them."[52]

The condition of the civil population also drove some women to prostitution. "Black February" 1919 was a time of great privation for the Rhinelanders. Continuing food shortages following the wartime Allied blockade brought many of the malnourished population to starvation. This, accentuated by the presence of an adequately-fed occupation army, meant, according to Ferdinand Tuohy, some sold themselves for food and consequently "transformed many a father and brother and lover into a burning Spartacist."[53] According to Robert Coulson, the hyperinflation of 1923 prompted desperate measures. An apparently decent man was charged with procuring his daughter to a soldier. "Soldiers had money and could get food from the canteen," he said. After his daughter had refused to fall in with his plans, the man "went out himself, found a soldier in a beer-house, and brought him home." Coulson's response to the case, and that of his fellow police*men*, throws interesting light on their own moral understanding: "We discussed the case in the office afterwards. We all came to the conclusion that conditions in Cologne being what they were, the girl had been wrong to refuse; the family had needed the food so urgently that to keep her personal chastity intact was a mere luxury."[54]

The composition of the Army of Occupation exacerbated discipline and behavioural problems. All the soldiers, and their families back home (not to mention the British Press), wanted demobilisation as quickly as possible. When no clear and demonstrably fair demobilisation scheme emerged, some soldiers began to "vote with their feet." Men home on leave, refused to return to France or the Army of Occupation. Early in 1919 a wave of soldiers' protests threatened the stability of the army as a whole.[55] Unrest appears to have spread to the troops in Germany, though the details are sketchy.[56] In 1943 Sir Archibald Montgomery-Massingberd, who had been Chief of Staff in the Army of Occupation in 1919, told Sir James Edmonds that there were "several very unpleasant mutinies in various units during Wully's [Sir William Robertson's] Command'. Massingberd said that Robertson had handled them "extremely well. . . . He went most carefully into each case usually on the spot to find out the cause of the outbreak. In most cases it was lack of good officers and ignorance & neglect on the part of temporary officers to look after their men & find out their small worries that led to the trouble." Robertson sorted these situations out by putting "reliable officers in command of the units to get things right." In a few other cases, however, "where it was clearly shewn that the men had no real cause for complaint & that the unrest was due to Bolshevism or pure devilment Wully came down very hard and he had little mercy."[57] Unrest, moreover, was not confined to British soldiers.

On 4 January Sir Henry Rawlinson, commander of the British Fourth Army, noted that "the Canadians" had been "rather naughty" at Cologne.[58]

Robertson's memoirs mention little beyond that there was "some discontent amongst the men,"[59] but it is clear from his private correspondence that he was concerned. Five days after taking over the command from Sir Herbert Plumer, he wrote to Winston Churchill, the Secretary of State for War, that "generally, I find rather an easy-going spirit prevailing," which he conceded was to be expected "after the tension of the last four or five years."[60] A fortnight later he noted quite a lot of low-level unrest among his troops, which he mostly put down to the unsettled condition of the post-war army, and the men's understandable impatience at the slowness of demobilization. As a contributory factor, however, he added that "it must also be remembered that the men are forbidden to 'Fraternize' with the inhabitants and therefore they are, at any rate in public, debarred from the supposed enjoyments attaching to female society."[61] In June he told the Chief of the Imperial General Staff that it was "difficult to imagine a more unorganised body or a greater lack of cohesion than I found on arrival here." A clear difficulty was the absence of any clear policy defining the actual purpose of the occupation forces and it required "constant effort to keep people up to the mark, as one and all seem to have had enough of the war, and feel that there is no very definite object towards which they should strive."[62]

Many occupation army soldiers were very young. Churchill had accelerated the release of war service soldiers in response to the demobilization crisis and filled up the Rhine Army divisions with new recruits. In March 1920, the Chief of the Imperial General Staff, Sir Henry Wilson, found battalions of the Middlesex Regiment and the Black Watch "all very young, very raw, vary untrained."[63] Such soldiers might be more liable than otherwise to cause problems. The British did not employ colonial troops in their occupation army, unlike the French who stirred deep, racially-fuelled antagonisms in Germany.[64] In a verse, "To a German complaining of the Occupation of the Rhineland after 1918," the celebrated Irish poet, medical doctor and wit, Oliver St John Gogarty compared occupied Germany with the contemporaneous situation of "occupied" Ireland:

> To have the black troops on the Rhine
> Is bad enough; but Hans
> If you were ruled by "English swine"
> You'd have the Black and Tans.[65]

The aims and role of the occupying forces were sometimes uncertain. One veteran recalled that "Army morale suffered in these early weeks in Germany through the difficulty of adjusting from the demands of active

warfare to the boring army duties of peace-time."[66] There remained
the possibility that the Army of Occupation might have to force terms
on the Germans. Major Henry Harding (of the 1/2nd County of
London Yeomanry) who had marched into Germany in December
1918 remembered that "life was interesting but really uneventful. It
chiefly consisted of training young troops and keeping the men efficient. It was not until June 1919 that we had any excitement."[67] Late
in May the Rhine Army was instructed to prepare for an advance into
Germany in order to put pressure on Germany to sign the peace treaty.
Sir William Robertson describes in his memoirs the preparations made
for this and asserts that the troops were "elated at the prospect of
going forward,"[68] an opinion flatly contradicted by Henry Harding's
recollection:

> We had orders to march on into Germany. No one knew what would
> happen. We were ready to move in our steel hats, full complement of
> ammunition and full rations, and we were to proceed at 6 p.m. The
> time came, and our orders were to delay another hour, and at 7 p.m.
> came the joyful news that Peace had at last been signed.
>
> You can imagine our feelings during those brief hours of uncertainty.
> Was the war going to commence again?[69]

The army might also have been required in March 1920 at the time of the
Kapp Putsch; and in January 1923 when the Franco-Belgian occupation
of the Ruhr occurred. How effective militarily would it have been?

The army's traditional remedy for boredom was to step up training,
encourage sport and promote "safe" recreational facilities. It created football
and field hockey fields, though "cricket pitches were limited in number."
The army authorities issued 2,380 sets of boxing gloves, 37,000 pairs of
"gym shoes," 52,700 football boots, 530 hockey sticks and 90 hockey
balls.[70] Many of the surviving accounts of the occupation emphasise lei-
sure pursuits as much as any military activities. Writing in August 1919,
Irene Laying, serving with Queen Alexandra's Imperial Nursing Service
Reserve, told her sister "We have had lots of social functions—dances,
dinners etc & we often go into Cologne, we are always greatly stared at.
All our journeys are free of charge & we travel like lords . . . our Med.
Officers have built a tennis court, so we have always that to go to."[71]
Returning to the Rhine Army in 1921, Percy Creek found that life in
Cologne was now "jam for the British soldier, the strict fraternising rules
had been eased. . . . The German mark was on the ground and an English
shilling would enable one to have a meal at one of the better restaurants."
Creek spent "several very pleasant evenings at the Café Germania. We

had a seat in the balcony and after a meal we listened to a violinist playing the beautiful songs of Schubert, Strauss and Brahms."[72]

The opera appears in many accounts of Cologne life. Early in the occupation seats at every performance were reserved in the Cologne opera house for British troops. These were "allocated, in turn, to the various units stationed within easy reach of Cologne."[73] One officer recorded in March 1919 he not only saw "a fine performance of the 'Flying Dutchman,'" but also "enjoyed the comfort of a well-appointed hotel," which cost him nothing as the Germans "had to pay for it themselves."[74] He was lucky to have seen a Wagner opera. In April 1919, Colonel Edward Beddington took over as Plumer's Intelligence chief in Cologne. This position made him not only "head of the Secret Service," but, curiously, also responsible for approving the opera programme. Once a week, he recalled in his memoirs, the director of the opera would come and submit his programme: "All I did was to cut out too much Wagner if such, as it often was, was included and make him substitute something lighter."[75]

For the British, German hyperinflation brought astonishing local wealth. The extremely advantageous

> rate of exchange enabled all ranks to make full use of what was to most of them a unique opportunity of hearing famous operas performed by first-class singers. . . . A striking example of the effect of exchange rates was that on one typical occasion a British officer drove to the Opera House in a taxi, viewed the performance from one of the best seats, partook of the substantial meal [served at the interval] and a half-bottle of wine, drove back to his hotel and found that his evening had cost him a total of elevenpence [i.e., less than five decimal pence].[76]

Not all treated the performances with respect. Douglas Wimberley recalled in 1924 deliberately behaving badly at the opera to insult the Germans on the stage and in the audience. There were "about five of us," he wrote, "sitting in one of the boxes and all putting our legs, in their light tartan trews, up on the front of the theatre box, and pretending to go to sleep, instead of listening to some over-fat German blonde singing lustily in some Wagner opera."[77] By contrast, Sir Alexander Godley, GOC Rhine Command from March 1922 to June 1924, wrote that "I went to Cologne wondering if I should ever be able to sit out a Wagner opera," but "came away a Wagner 'fan.'"[78] His memoirs suggest recreation to have been more significant for Godley than military or political affairs. There were "delightful expeditions" to the surrounding countryside, where "the wooded and mountainous country . . . was ideal for picnics"; his period of command coincided with the decennial performance of the Oberammergau Passion play; the racing "was great fun"; there was excellent shooting to be had; the "golf-links were only a mile from my back gate"; and "our annual horse show was a great event."[79]

Katharine Tynan observed that "the Opera is perhaps the only place in Cologne except the public conveyances where Germans and English sit side by side,"[80] evidence of the social self-sufficiency of the Rhine Army. There was pressure for fraternisation, but many soldiers tried to avoid Germans. As one ranker told Ferdinand Tuohy, "What's the use of a place where you can't understand a word of what's going on? Only tarts to guttenacht and wieviel to? And 'aving to be'ave an' look like mucking dolls all the time. Give me a good old Saturday night in Blighty!"[81] The occupying army and civilian population became increasingly separate as the occupation became established, especially after Sir William Robertson permitted British army wives to join their spouses in Germany in mid-1919.

Robert Coulson arrived just after Christmas 1922. "Life in Cologne was much the same as in any other garrison abroad. I need not have been concerned with the problem of whether to avoid Germans or not; there was no question of any personal contact with them. The garrison, at least the officers and their wives—especially the wives—kept entirely to themselves."[82] Ferdinand Tuohy argued that following the arrival of the wives, the BAOR began "to assume that self-contained, almost segregated air which was to characterize it for the remainder of its life." He also asserted that the British women "kept up the hatreds of the War more,"[83] a point echoed by Katharine Tynan, who asserted that "British wives," especially those "whose minds are not cultivated," are "apt to be the repositories of a crude patriotism." She reported "a terrible meeting" with the wife of an NCO in a crowded tram. "Wot I says is, w'y didn't we do wot the French wanted us to do—beat'em right back to Berlin? Let 'em 'ave it proper. These yere 'Uns they're not 'alf-beaten yet." Tynan's embarrassment was compounded by her assumption that most of the Germans on the tram could understand English.[84]

Despite all this there was surprisingly little serious or violent overt antagonism between British and German. In 1919 a German ex-serviceman, Sergeant Swaboda, murdered a New Zealander. He evaded prosecution for six years by staying out of the Occupied Area. On his return he was convicted and sentenced to death. The GOC commuted this to life imprisonment. He was released after the occupation ceased in 1929.[85] In February 1923 a British soldier shot dead a German civilian "during a brawl in a Cologne café." He went unpunished.[86] Two other cases of murder came before the Summary Court while Sir John Du Cane was GOC (1924–7), but neither appears to have been political.[87] In October 1924, a Scottish soldier, Private George Halliday of the Cameron Highlanders, "in company with another soldier" met a woman (Du Cane says she was a prostitute) in a café at 10.30 p.m. An hour later the other soldier left the two together, and at about midnight "screams were heard by several German witnesses who saw Louisa Fuchs stabbed repeatedly with a bayonet by a Scots soldier whom they could not identify." Halliday returned to barracks, but his bayonet was later found to have "traces of fresh human blood on the blade and hilt." He was found guilty and sentenced to death. Du Cane, having ascertained "that according to German law unpremeditated murder is not punishable by death," had the man's sentence commuted to fifteen years' penal servitude.[88] In December 1924, a Private Wright of the West Yorkshire Regiment, shot dead Lance-Corporal Whitham of the Cameron Highlanders (an ill-starred regiment, it seems), and so badly wounded "a German girl name Marie Stasiak, who was with him," that she later died. It was suggested in *The Times* "that jealousy was the motive of the crime." At his court-martial Wright's defense was "pathological drunken-ness." He was sentenced to death, but also had his sentence commuted, this time to life. Du Cane believed it "very undesirable to have a soldier shot by a firing party in the circumstances."[89]

Both these "crimes of passion" might have occurred as easily in a British garrison town. A more ambiguous case occurred in 1928 when a German policeman, "*Landjäger* Haas," died after an exchange with some British soldiers of the Manchester Regiment. The Britons had been walking in the countryside and were approached by Haas who "spoke to them in German, presumably intimating that they were trespassing." The men did not understand, and an argument ensued, during which Haas was knocked to the ground. He "was suffering from an internal complaint and his fall was the cause of its aggravation with the result that he died." The soldier concerned was acquitted of murder "on the ground that the blow was not the direct cause of death." The affair stimulated critical comment in the German press, especially in the Berlin satirical journal, *Kladderadatsch*.[90]

Sir John Du Cane stated that while he was GOC "there was no case of a murderous assault by a German on a British soldier."[91] *The Times* did report a number of German attacks in 1924 suggesting that the potential for violent, if non-lethal, confrontations remained. Some Germans assaulted Captain Shaw of the Royal Army Medical Corps. He was returning from a cricket match when he "found the road blocked by several carts" which would not move. He was not in uniform, and, after failing to ascertain the name of the most obstructive German, seized the name-plate from his cart. The German "struck him with his whip" and others joined the assault, even though Shaw "repeatedly shouted in English that he was a British officer." He was rescued "by two other Germans." Three men were prosecuted. All "denied knowing that the driver of the motor-car was a British officer." One of the Germans, Wilhelm Muhr was sentenced to five years' imprisonment.[92]

Captain Codyre, of the Duke of Cornwall's Light Infantry (DCLI), was returning to his camp at about midnight on July 31, when a dog in the accused's garden "began barking furiously." Codyre "threw some small stones at the dog twice," but the dog escaped and bit Codyre. A man "accompanying the dog," struck Codyre on the head "with a long instrument." Codyre "shouted that he was a British officer and got away." At his trial, the accused, Herr Goethling, "said that there had been frequent thefts of fruit from his garden at night, and that when stones were thrown at his dog by a person who subsequently ran away he thought that it must be a thief, and pursued him with a pitchfork. It was," he added, "too dark to see that it was a British officer whom he had pursued in error." Goethling, as the prosecutor accepted, had not planned to attack Codyre, who must have appeared to him as a drunk or thief. The president of the court, however, in an ineffably supererogatory remark, "expressed the opinion that it was the duty of the inhabitants to make sure, by every means in their power, that they did not attack British soldiers."[93]

Germans did burgle British quarters. A officer of the DCLI awoke to find a German "holding his own service revolver to his head, while three other men ransacked the room." As they left he "snatched an automatic pistol from beneath his pillow," shot one man dead "and severely wounded another." A band of robbers was arrested and much stolen property—"chiefly British"—recovered.[94] In another case a German received twelve years from a military court for the burglary of British officers' quarters in Cologne. A second man received four years "for striking a British policewoman," and the appropriately-named Heinrich Half, "a one-legged man," got six years' imprisonment "for a violent assault on a military policeman."[95]

What are we to make of these cases? It is difficult to make any hard and fast judgment. Only in 1924 did *The Times* report such significant cases of violence, yet the BAOR was steadily reducing in number. Perhaps the burglaries reflect a normalisation of the relationship as much as anything else. As German national self-confidence recovered, so "ordinary decent crime" towards the British, as much as towards anyone else, began to re-establish itself.[96]

For the most part, Germans and British treated each other with forbearance, if not also tolerance. British military ceremonies including on Armistice Day, were well attended by Germans and witnessed in respectful silence. Some sporadic hissing was reported when the British left Cologne to move to Wiesbaden for the last three years of the occupation, but that scarcely rates as a major political demonstration. Neither does the occasion, raised before the Summary Court in Wiesbaden, when a German "was charged with throwing a potato at a passing British officer at the wheel of his car."[97] Perhaps a comment from a young officer to Ferdinand

Tuohy best sums up the Germano-British relationship as demonstrated through the whole occupation experience: "The Bôche? Oh, he's been all right on the whole. Minds his own business and doesn't give any lip."[98] *Mutatis mutandis*, the same might generally be said of the BAOR.

NOTES

1. Sir James Edmonds, *The Occupation of the Rhineland, 1918–1929* (London, 1944; facsimile edn 1987). For the history of the volume, see the introduction to the 1987 reprint by G. M. Bayliss.
2. Edmonds to Lieut.-Colonel F. M. A. Morris, Sept. 26, 1942 (United Kingdom National Archives (henceforward TNA), CAB 45/81, file (i) general correspondence).
3. David G. Williamson, *The British in Germany, 1918–1930: The Reluctant Occupiers* (Oxford and New York, 1991). See also J. Garston, "Armies of occupation: II The British in Germany 1918–1929," *History Today*, 11 (1961), pp. 479–89. And also the research of Richard Robinson, who alerted me to many important aspects of the subject (Richard Robinson, "Britain and the occupation of the Rhineland, 1918–1929" (MA thesis, University of Ulster, 1990)).
4. Ibid., p. 4. David Williamson, "Cologne and the British," History Today, 27 (1977), pp. 695–702, is more focused on social aspects but is both short and unreferenced. British Army of the Rhine records were destroyed during the London blitz (see Note, Sept. 24, 1943, TNA, CAB 45/81, file (i) general correspondence).
5. Edmonds, *Occupation of the Rhineland*, p. 86.
6. Ibid., p. 89.
7. Diary of C. H. Dudley Ward, Dec. 22, 1919 (Dudley Ward papers, Imperial War Museum (IWM)).
8. T. H. Howard, "Tales of E. O. T. A.: I–The British Army of the Rhine," *Army Quarterly*, vol. 47 (1943–44), p. 93.
9. "One Man's Story," p. 58 (Percy Creek papers, IWM 87/31/1).
10. Edmonds, *Occupation of the Rhineland*, pp. 62–6.
11. Ibid., pp. 76–9.
12. Ferdinand Touhy, *Occupied 1918–1930: A Postscript to the Western Front* (London, 1931), p. 42.
13. Edmonds, *Occupation of the Rhineland*, p. 136.
14. Major E. E. Gawthorn, "The British Army of the Rhine; a retrospect," *Journal of the Royal United Service Institution*, 74/496 (1929), p. 762.
15. Howard, "Tales of E.O.T.A.," p. 94.
16. Dudley Ward diary, Dec. 25, 1918.
17. Tuohy, *Occupied*, p. 44.
18. Williamson, *British in Germany*, p. 57.
19. Dudley Ward diary, Jan. 6, 1919.
20. Ibid., Feb. 6, 1919.
21. Williamson, *British in Germany*, p. 56.
22. Edmonds, *Occupation of the Rhineland*, p. 83.

23. Touhy, *Occupied*, p. 110.
24. Creek, "One Man's Story," pp. 59–60. Field Punishment No. 1 was abolished in 1923.
25. *The Watch on the Rhine*, no. 10, Feb. 1, 1919 (IWM, Papers of Capt. W. G. Cook, 77/183/1).
26. Edmonds, *Occupation of the Rhineland*, p. 147. 1919 saw a very rapid decline in troop numbers. Figures for British troops in Germany on 1 Jan. are as follows: 1920: 40,594; 1921: 12,421; 1922: 4,630; 1923: 8,730; 1924: 8,873; 1925; 8,118. (ibid., p. 181). In 1921–22 troop numbers fluctuated. Some supervised a League of Nations plebiscite in Silesia, and others were recalled to Britain because of industrial unrest.
27. Tuohy, *Occupied*, p. 106.
28. Howard, "Tales of E.O.T.A.," p. 94.
29. Hansard, Mar. 1, 1921, 138 H.C. Deb. 5s, col. 1591.
30. Edmonds, *Occupation of the Rhineland*, p. 120; Secretary for War in House of Commons, *Hansard*, July 29, 1926, 198 H.C. Deb. 5s, col. 2320.
31. *Colongne Post*, July 25, 1919 (quoted in Williamson, *The British in Germany*, p. 58).
32. *The Times*, Sep. 17, 1919.
33. Ibid., Sep. 23, 1919.
34. Ibid., Sep. 24, 1919.
35. Gawthorn, "British Army of the Rhine," p. 760.
36. "Apex" (Robert Gustavus Coulson), *The Uneasy Triangle: Four Years of the Occupation* (London, 1931), p. 33.
37. *Hansard*, Dec. 13, 1927, 211 H.C. Deb. 5s, col. 2111.
38. "Vice in the Army," *The Times*, Apr. 30, 1920.
39. Edmonds, *Occupation of the Rhineland*, p. 120.
40. "Apex," *The Uneasy Triangle*, pp. 33–6.
41. Morland to Sir Henry Wilson, Jun. 25, 1920 (IWM Wilson papers, HHW 2/57/6).
42. Hansard, Mar. 15, 1921, 139 H.C. Deb. 5s, col. 1262.
43. See Lesley A. Hall, "Venereal diseases and society in Britain, from the Contagious Diseases Acts to the National Health Service," in Roger Davidson and Lesley A. Hall (eds.), *Sex, Sin and Suffering: Venereal Disease and European Society since 1870* (London, 2001), pp. 120–36.
44. General notes on the Occupation of the Rhineland (TNA CAB 45/81, file (ii)).
45. Mrs Corbett Ashby, Visit to Cologne, Dec. 7th–11th, 1922: Report and Recommendations (IWM, Papers of Capt. Arthur Brian Ashby, p. 63).
46. See copies of letters by Mrs Corbett Ashby, Nov. 25, and Dec. 3, 1942 (ibid.).
47. General notes on the Occupation of the Rhineland (TNA CAB 45/81, file (ii)).
48. *The Times*, Dec. 24, 1923.
49. Ibid., Jan. 2, 1924. Katharine Tynan wrote a sadly anodyne account of her time in Germany: *Life in the Occupied Area* (London, n.d. [1925]).
50. Edmonds, *Occupation of the Rhineland*, p. 209; General notes on the Occupation of the Rhineland (TNA CAB 45/81, file (ii)).
51. Diary entry for Nov. 4, 1923, quoted in Major-General Douglas Wimberley, "Scottish Soldier," (ts autobiography), p. 200 (IWM Wimberley papers, pp./MCR/182).
52. Copy of letter to *The Times*, Nov. 25, 1942 (IWM, Papers of Capt. Arthur Brian Ashby, p. 63).

53. Tuohy, *Occupied*, p. 48.
54. "Apex," *Uneasy Triangle*, pp. 49–50.
55. See Keith Jeffery, "The post-war army," in Ian F. W. Beckett and Keith Simpson (eds.), *A Nation in Arms: A Social Study of the British Army in the First World War* (Manchester, 1985; London, corrected edn, 1990), pp. 212–15 and Keith Jeffery, *The British Army and the Crisis of Empire, 1918–1922* (Manchester, 1984), chs 2 and 3.
56. None of the studies on post-war military unrest mention the BAOR: Andrew Rothstein, *The Soldiers' Strikes of 1919* (London, 1980); Gloden Dallas and Douglas Gill, *The Unknown Army: Mutinies in the British Army in World War I* (London, 1985); and Dave Lamb, *Mutinies: 1917–1920* (Oxford & London, n.d.).
57. Montgomery-Massingberd to Edmonds, Jan. 23, 1943 (TNA CAB 45/81(i)).
58. What precisely this refers to is not clear. In his study of post-war unrest in the Canadian Expeditionary Force Desmond Morton says nothing about Canadian soldiers in Cologne (Desmond Morton, "Kicking and complaining": demobilization riots in the Canadian Expeditionary Force, 1918–19," *Canadian Historical Review,* 61(3) (1980), pp. 334–60).
59. Sir William Robertson, *From Private to Field-Marshal* (London, 1921), p. 364.
60. Robertson to Churchill, Apr. 27, 1919 (Liddell Hart Centre for Military Archives (LHCMA), Robertson papers, 6/4/4).
61. Robertson to Secretary, War Office, May 11, 1919 (ibid., 6/4/6).
62. Robertson to Sir Henry Wilson, Jun. 6, 1919 (IWM Wilson papers, HHW 2/1A/19b).
63. Wilson diary, Mar. 12, 1920 (IWM Wilson papers).
64. Edmonds says bluntly that the use of "coloured troops" was "a mistake" (*The Occupation of the Rhineland*, p. 203). See also Keith Nelson, "The 'Black Horror on the Rhine': Race as a Factor in Post-World War One Diplomacy" *Journal of Modern History* 42 (1970), pp. 606–27.
65. A. Norman Jeffares, *The Poems and Plays of Oliver St John Gogarty* (Gerrard's Cross, 2001), p. 422. The "Black and Tans" were in effect a military gendarmerie reinforcing the civil police during the 1919–21 Irish war of independence, whose ill-disciplined activities did much to undermine the legitimacy of British rule in Ireland.
66. "Some reminiscences in 1977/80 on the First Great War Years 1916/19" (IWM A. J. Jamieson papers, 88/52/1).
67. "First World War memoirs" (1929) (IWM Papers of Maj. Henry Norman Harding, 77/154/1).
68. Robertson, *From Private to Field-Marshal*, p. 365.
68. "First World War memoirs" (1929). Harding's manuscript diary backs up this recollection: June 23, 1919 "Packed up ready to move. Rumours all day. At 7.7 the Brig. came & told us the Huns had decided to sign. Great jubilation in the camp. Rained heavily" (IWM Papers of Maj. Henry Norman Harding, 77/154/1).
70. Edmonds, *Occupation of the Rhineland*, p. 118.
71. Irene Laying to Nellie Laying, Aug. 21, 1919 (IWM, Papers of Mrs Irene Edgar).
72. Creek, "One Man's Story," p. 66.

73. Diary entry, Feb. 26, 1919 (IWM, First World War papers of Lieut. C. Carter, pp./MCR/141).
74. Ibid., Mar. 5, 1919.
75. Edward Beddington, "My Life" (ts memoirs), p. 178 (LHCMA, Beddington papers).
76. Howard, "Tales of E.O.T.A.," p. 97.
77. Wimberley, "Scottish Soldier," p. 212 (IWM Wimberley papers, pp./MCR/182).
78. Sir Alexander Godley, *Life of An Irish Soldier* (London, 1939), p. 290.
79. Ibid., pp. 281–2, 190–1. A note in the "Official History" files rather confirms the priority given to recreation. "I feel bound to say that," wrote F. B. Bourdillon of the Foreign Office, "if the provision of polo grounds was one of the charges imposed on Germany as part of the costs of the army of occupation, I should be disinclined to advertise the fact!" (Bourdillon to Sir James Edmonds, Sep. 15, 1943, TNA CAB 45/81, file (ix) Comments, Foreign Office).
80. Tynan, *Life in the Occupied Area*, p. 258.
81. Tuohy, *Occupied*, p. 287.
82. "Apex," *The Uneasy Triangle*, p. 7.
83. Tuohy, *Occupied*, pp. 220–1.
84. Tynan, *Life in the Occupied Area*, pp. 206–7.
85. Tuohy, *Occupied*, p. 147; General Sir John Du Cane (GOC, BAOR, 1924–7) says it was an Australian soldier (Du Cane to Sir James Edmonds, Aug. 28, 1944 (TNA, CAB 45/81, file (i): general correspondence)).
86. Or, at least, it was not reported in the papers (information from *The Times*, Feb. 10, 1923).
87. Du Cane to Edmonds, Aug. 28, 1944 (TNA, CAB 45/81). There are some records in the UK National Archives in the Home Office series HO144 concerning these crimes, but these are all under a one hundred–year closure.
88. *The Times*, Nov. 17, and Dec. 1, 1924; Du Cane to Edmonds, Aug. 28, 1944 (TNA, CAB 45/81).
89. *The Times*, 24, Dec. 27, 1924 and Mar. 4, 1925; Du Cane to Edmonds, Aug. 28, 1944 (TNA, CAB 45/81). Du Cane's opinion does raise the question of what circumstances would have to obtain for him to approve an execution.
90. Report on Rhineland Occupation from Apr. 30, 1927 to Dec. 12, 1929, by Lieut.-Gen. Sir William Thwaites, Mar. 26, 1930 (TNA CAB 45/81, file (ii)).
91. Du Cane to Edmonds, Aug. 28, 1944 (TNA, CAB 45/81).
92. *The Times*, Aug. 7, 1924.
93. Ibid., Aug. 15, 1924. Goethling was found guilty, but *The Times* did not report what sentence he received.
94. Ibid., Oct. 22, 1924.
95. Ibid., Dec. 8, 1924.
96. "Ordinary decent crime" is a term used in contemporary Northern Ireland to distinguish activities such as burglary from politically-motivated crime.
97. Touhy, *Occupied*, p. 249.
98. Ibid.

FRENCH POLICY IN THE RHINELAND 1919–1924

Stanislas Jeannesson

There is no doubt that France, at least until the London Conference of 1924 which inaugurated a new period in international relations with the implementation of the Dawes Plan and the evacuation of the Ruhr, had an active policy in the territories she had occupied on the left bank of the Rhine in accordance with the Treaty of Versailles and the Rhineland Agreement.

Numerous aspects of this policy have already been the subject of detailed studies, in particular the works and articles of Walter MacDougall, Marc Trachtenberg, Jacques Bariéty, Georges-Henri Soutou, which are now considered as classics.[1] This paper makes no claim at all to summarize those well-known theses at the risk of distorting them. Instead what it attempts to do is use the relevant issues raised by the author's research about the occupation of the Ruhr[2] in order to understand France's policy in the Rhineland: its main functions; its overall consistency; its place in the global policy of France, and its final failure.

The ambitions of France are demonstrated by the extent of her presence in the Rhineland. Indeed, her area of occupation covered the southern part of the left bank, around the bridgehead of Mainz, that is to say 75% of the occupied territories, whereas the British, American and Belgian occupation only represented respectively 6%, 9%, and 10% of the whole. This predominance was further reinforced in January 1923, when the region controlled by the United States around Koblenz passed under

French command. The French would also be in the Rhineland longer than their allies because the Treaty of Versailles had planned a gradual evacuation from the north to the south every five years, to be completed in 1935 with the Mainz zone. The number of military personnel grew in proportion: on February 1, 1920, it amounted to 94.000 French soldiers under the command of General Degoutte who was, in addition, responsible for the joint command of the occupation forces, a total of 130.000 men.[3]

What was entirely new was that the Rhineland Agreement subordinated military command to a civilian administration, the Inter-Allied Rhineland High Commission (*Haute Commission Interalliée des Territoires Rhénans*), with its headquarters in Koblenz. It was the supreme representative of the four occupying powers. This organisation had tremendous power, especially from a legal standpoint. It could, if necessary, enact decrees which had the force of law, to ensure safety, the maintenance and needs of the military forces (article 1). It could also, at any time, declare martial law over the whole territory or part of it, and thus return control to the occupation forces (article 13). For all questions concerning the occupied territories, the Rhineland Commission reached decisions by majority voting. If the votes were tied, the French representative, president by law, had the casting vote. In practice, after the departure of the American delegate, the British High Commissioner often found himself isolated from his French and Belgian colleagues. On the other hand, each High Commissioner had exclusive responsibility for all affairs concerning his own area, enabling him to develop an individual policy. He was assisted by a general delegate and the heads of various legal, economic or financial departments, created for the purpose. In each of the 72 Districts (*Kreise*) the High Commissioners were represented by delegates who acted as go-betweens with the local authorities. Thus, contrary to what Lloyd George had expected by placing military authority under the control of a civilian organism, the exceptional powers of the High Commission, as well as its decision-making practices, made it a perfect instrument to further possible French ambitions.[4]

In all this the personality and the ideas of the French High Commissioner Paul Tirard played a crucial role. Trained in Morocco by Lyautey, he had become General Secretary of the protectorate in 1913. When he arrived in Koblenz, Tirard felt invested with a mission which was not only technical and administrative but also political, and, in the broad sense of the word, civilizing[5]. He saw himself as an instrument to establish France, her values and spirit in the Rhineland. After a century of Prussian domination and after the *Kulturkampf*, the history of France was re-engaging with the history of the Rhineland. He believed that France had to renew the policy of men like Richelieu and Vergennes, the generals of the Revolution and the Imperial prefects to create preferential political economic and cultural ties in the region and imprint itself on the distinctive identity of the Rhineland. "What should be our interpretation of the measures of the treaty toward the Rhineland?," he wondered in 1922. "Our history, our traditions, the acts of our governments, those of Richelieu as well as those of the revolutionary armies clearly established it. It had to be a French policy, a liberal and benevolent one, caring about ensuring peace on our borders. In short, it had to be a generous one."[6]

These phrases were vague but hid concrete issues and a precise programme. French Rhineland policy was fundamentally based on the idea shared by many—that the Treaty of Versailles was not sufficient to ensure France's safety. It is known that, during the Peace Conference, the French delegation had claimed the creation of neutral demilitarized buffer-states along the Rhine. Yet, facing British and American hostility, Clemenceau had, however reluctantly, accepted the Rhineland compromise, that is a military occupation of the left bank of the Rhine limited to a maximum of fifteen years and the demilitarization of the region. The *Reich* remained sovereign and theoretically kept its political prerogative. In return for French concessions, Wilson and Lloyd George offered to guarantee France immediate military assistance in case of unprovoked German attack. That is why, when learning that the American Senate would not ratify the Treaty of Versailles and that consequently this guarantee was no longer in place, many, not only in political and military circles but also in journalism and the media, felt betrayed. They believed it logical and legitimate for France to return to her initial conception, to endeavour to ensure her security in the Rhineland by herself and to try to remedy the dangerous weaknesses of the Treaty of Versailles.

These ideas were championed in Paris by a "lobby of the Rhineland" which claimed the detachment of the occupied territories and the independence of the Rhineland or, at least, its autonomy within the *Reich*. The most extreme positions were adopted by the Committee of the Left Bank of the Rhine which called for the return of General Mangin. Their ideas and language were too radical to have a real influence on the government. But there was also a group of personalities, writers and journalists, particularly at the School of Political Sciences and at the University of Strasbourg, who were close to Tirard or politicians like Alexandre Millerand and Raymond Poincaré. They included his close friend Jacques Bardoux, René Pinon, Georges Blondel, Raymond Recouly, Louis Barthou, Louis Marin, Léon Daudet, and Maurice Barrès.[7] However, the importance of this lobby must not be exaggerated. Their activism and sensational declarations very often put the Quai d'Orsay in an awkward position and damaged the more subtle policy worked out in the field. Tirard complained bitterly about it.[8]

For Tirard, who shared many of General Degoutte's ideas, French policy in the Rhineland should operate on three levels according to the circumstances. In the first instance, and in a general way, it had to develop within the bounds of the Treaty of Versailles and the Weimar constitution with regard to Germany's home policy. At this stage, therefore, the policy was to withdraw the Rhinelanders little by little from Germany's grasp, to bring them more under French influence, and thus to encourage the creation of an autonomous Rhineland. At the same time French policy had to take care not to offend the legal and constitutional wishes of the population. "The prime goal of our action in the occupied territories," he wrote as early as October 1919, "appears to me to be as follows: encouraging the efforts of the Rhineland population, without any interference into the home policy of the *Reich*, towards a regionalism freed from Prussian or Bavarian domination and generally to give this population the opportunity to make their pacific will heard, within the different councils of the Empire."[9]

The stress was essentially put on propaganda especially in the cultural and social fields[10] with the creation and circulation of the French press, the organisation of exhibitions and conferences or artistic tours to make French culture known in the Rhineland. French classes, charities and soup kitchens also had a role and, in addition, discreet support, financial or otherwise, was offered to federalist and separatist parties whilst being careful not to compromise them.

Religious policy provided a privileged field of action, given the resentment of Prussian Protestant domination among the people of the Rhineland who were, by an overwhelming majority, Catholic. The resumption of diplomatic relations between Paris and the Vatican was quite a good opportunity to influence the Holy See in favor of French interests. The results were not always convincing because Rome wished also to maintain good relations with the German government. Nonetheless France did obtain the appointment of a bishop to act as head chaplain for the army in the Rhineland and to liaise with the local clergy and, of course unofficially, to keep watch over the appointment of the Rhineland bishops.[11]

In terms of economic policy, Tirard claimed many times, albeit unsuccessfully, that commercial preference should be granted to products from the Rhineland exported to France. He was faced with the opposition both of French industrialists, who hoped to protect the home market, and the French government, which initially refused to exempt the occupied territories from the obligations imposed throughout Germany. Its aim at this point remained the implementation of the Treaty of Versailles. Federalist tendencies were not to be encouraged in whichever region, by making it believe that this would permit it to avoid any of the treaty measures. French policy was limited to encouraging the establishment of shops and French companies on the left bank. This policy enjoyed mild success.

The second level of French policy would be appropriate if the unity of the *Reich* seemed threatened by secession or if failures in the execution of the treaty led the Allies to impose economic and customs sanctions on the Rhineland. In such circumstances Tirard believed that France must take the earliest opportunity to use fully the exceptional powers of the High Commission and to apply a policy of surety and security, hastening the creation of an autonomous entity. From 1919 to 1922, he sent notes to the Quai d'Orsay which outlined the measures to be taken in case of a favourable German situation:[12]

1. A total control of the legislation to be applied in the occupied territories through ordinances enacted by the High Commission.
2. Setting up of tariff barriers with a reorientation of the Rhineland trade towards the west.
3. Removal of Prussian and Bavarian civil servants from the administration and the police.
4. Reworking the monetary system and creating a possible currency for the Rhineland.
5. Election of a responsible local assembly with a direct collaboration with the occupation authorities.

These measures were designed to encourage the setting up of an autonomous Rhenish State, maintained inside the *Reich* and closely controlled by the Rhineland Commission. This would have amounted to a protectorate under French tutelage, an arrangement which the emergence of an independent state would not have allowed.

The third level envisaged a wider German scenario. The Rhineland issue should not be isolated from the global treatment of the German question. As Degoutte wrote in April 1923, three months after the beginning of the occupation of the Ruhr, "It looks difficult to study the specific question of the Rhineland autonomy independently of the more general question of Germany's reorganization."[13] The whole country, driven by the example of the Rhineland, should move towards federalism and reject the unitary Weimar constitution. The autonomy of the Rhineland territories, where "Prussian hegemony" was at its strongest, should be only a first step leading to the return of a pre-Bismarckian Germany, "one of principalities and duchies," too much concerned with inner rivalry to become a danger for neighbouring countries. "Our interest," continued Degoutte, "is that the new states constitute homogeneous blocks as different as possible from each other, teeming with oppositions of all kinds—religious, political or economic; a Catholic, monarchic and rural Bavaria alongside a Protestant, socialist, working-class Saxony alongside a middle-class, moderate Swabia with mixed religions."[14]

This raises an obvious and important question. How could this weakened, divided, and disunited Germany cope with the obligations imposed by the treaty? How could it pay the 132 billion gold-marks in reparations? Two conceptions of occupation confronted each other. Did occupation aim at safeguarding the fulfilment of Germany's obligations, particularly the financial clauses and reparations, or was its purpose the security of the French and Belgian borders? Was it necessary to make it a priority to obtain regular payments which obviously required a reinforcement of taxation from the German state as well as the economic revival of the country? If so, the presence of troops on the left bank might be considered as a simple mean of pressure. Or was security a priority, leading to the encouragement of a divided Germany, which implied an active policy in the Rhineland to create favourable conditions for the development of federalism? Choosing security implied, in the long run, a rupture with the American and British allies who were in favour of strengthening a unitary Germany and who shared a concern about possible French predominance on the continent. Choosing in favour of reparations implied staying within the limits of the treaty and inclining towards an overall conception of European affairs.

That said the French leaders in the Rhineland had made up their minds between the two choices. As Degoutte wrote on March 6, 1920, "It seems that between the mortal danger of a unitary Germany and the promising prospects of a federalist one, the concern for maintaining the future of France and peace in the world, does not allow any indecision."[15] The Rhineland was where France had to reap the fruits of victory and take advantage of her position towards Germany and her allies. What did Paris think? After Clemenceau's departure, foreign policy in France was dominated by three personalities, each of whom was both prime minister (President of the Cabinet) and Minister of Foreign Affairs: Alexandre Millerand, from January to September 1920; Aristide Briand, from January 1921 to January 1922; and Raymond Poincaré, from 1922 until May 1924—three personalities, with three different conceptions of policy in the Rhineland and Germany.[16]

Millerand did not stay long in power at this level, but continued to take a close interest in German affairs, and the question of reparations in particular, after his election to the Presidency of the Republic on September 23, 1920. He defined the room for manoeuvre in the Rhineland with great, even excessive, subtlety. Right from the start, he conceived his policy in the Rhineland as an element in a wider strategy leading to the reorganization of Weimar Germany. The directives he sent to Tirard in Koblenz and to Dard in Munich can be summed up in three points. First, autonomist movements (not separatist movements which were the dreams of a misguided minority) and the federalist tendencies of the *Land* governments were to be encouraged. The creation of a diplomatic legation in the Bavarian capital in July 1920 could be explained this way. Millerand wrote to Dard:

> Already feelings of local autonomy are re-emerging in the former confederate states and even in those parts of Prussia which were most recently subjugated by it; there are indications of that local autonomy which made Germany the most divided nation in Europe. Maintaining this division has been a tradition in our policy during the past centuries. The unity of Germany has now become a threat for our security and can only be counterbalanced by a military alliance with Russia which is not easy to reinstate now. Therefore, our vital interest commits us to favour particularism, which will help establish a counterweight to the influence of unitary and militarist Prussia, within the framework of federalism.[17]

Secondly French representatives were to avoid anything that might be interpreted as an act of propaganda or as interference in German home affairs so as not to discredit autonomist movements and give their opponents an opportunity to stir up Francophobe and patriotic views against them. It was only necessary to grant those movements "a sympathy all the more efficient because it will be very discreet."[18] Tirard approved of this; his entire policy, he asserted, consisted in "keeping contacts with such elements in the Rhineland and supporting them discreetly without compromising them."[19] Thirdly they should remain within the framework of the Treaty of Versailles. Above all, France aimed at strict respect for the treaty clauses and it was out of the question to encourage the sense of federalism by promising to exempt such or such region from the obligations of the treaty. This problem soon arose in reactionary monarchist Bavaria, which sought to maintain the *Einwohnerwehren*, an armed militia whose disbanding was being planned. Contrary to Dard's advice, the Quai d'Orsay refused any preferential treatment.[20] In addition it was not immediately understood that supporting federalism often helped to develop monarchist and ultra-nationalist tendencies which advocated much more hostile views than those of Berlin. The Quai d'Orsay waited until Hitler's *Putsch* in November 1923 to break off any contact with the Nazis. Supporting Hitler was not the best means to make France secure.

With Briand, the context changed. Germany neither disarmed nor paid as it should have done. The French government thus moved towards sanctions, a policy that would help to create one of the scenarios envisaged by Tirard who viewed their imposition with favour. For the first time, France had the opportunity to apply the Rhineland policy for which Tirard had long hoped. On March 3, 1921 the Allies agreed sanctions including the occupation of Düsseldorf, Duisburg and Ruhrort, whilst tariffs were to be collected on the eastern border of the occupied territories, implying the setting up of a customs cordon between the Rhineland and the rest of Germany. This sanction was enforced on April 20, despite Great Britain's objections and Germany's concern and protests. Yet it was not accompanied by further measures suggested by Tirard, such as the opening of the western border of the occupied territories which would have openly given it a political meaning. It was lifted a few months later, in September, after Germany had accepted the amount of reparations set on May 3 and made the choice of *Erfüllungspolitik* (a policy of fulfilling the treaty).

It seems that for Briand the setting up of a customs barrier on the Rhine was only meant to exert pressure on Germany, by playing upon the very fear of a Rhineland policy. From that point of view it was quite successful. Beyond that, the only effect of the sanction was to disrupt the region's economy and to stir up the anger of the people in the Rhineland against France. Throughout the year, Briand asked Tirard not to interfere in the German home affairs. As he wrote to him: "During the talks you may have with Rhenish personalities, it seems to me preferable that you show pure disinterestedness."[21] These recommendations suggest that the main purpose of French diplomacy was not an active policy aimed at detaching the Rhineland.

There is finally the famous episode of the Ruhr occupation, which was to provide advocates of a Rhineland policy with a new opportunity to attain their goals. There is not space here to review factors such as the resistance of the population or the disastrous situation of German finances, instead examining those which reveal a deliberate French policy to separate the Rhineland from the rest of the country and treat it as an autonomous entity.[22] They included a massive eviction of Prussian civil servants compelled to leave the occupied territories with their families at a day's notice and involving about 150,000 Germans. A Franco-Belgian railway company in charge of exploiting the rail network was created, which was to be handed over to a managing company funded by Rhenish, French and Belgian capital. A real economic boundary to the east of the occupied territories aimed to deprive Germany of most the Ruhr and the Rhineland resources as early as February 1923. There were also attempts at creating a local currency (discussions between French, Rhenish, and Belgian bankers had made enough progress to give birth, on 1 December, to a detailed project defining in thirty-six articles the statutes of a future jointly funded bank of issue[23]). There were negotiations between various political leaders from Hessen, the Palatinate and the Rhineland favouring a degree of autonomy for their region (though these were coming more or less to an end). The contacts between Tirard and Adenauer are well-known even if they were the most advanced.[24]

I will content myself with a few more remarks. One must bear in mind that this policy did not suddenly emerge from the acts of German resistance or from the circumstances of the autumn of 1923. It had been seriously envisaged from the outset and even constitutes one of the major objectives of the occupation of the Ruhr. Indeed, it had been decided in August 1922, after the failure of the London conference, firstly for purely economic reasons so as to force Germany to resume her payments and in the meantime to gather on the spot the coal she did not deliver. It was the theory of gage productif (the productive seizure of German state assets) that Poincaré openly defended to justify the operation. However, a few months later, under the influence of Tirard, Degoutte, Foch and others, more political objectives concerning specifically the Rhineland became superimposed on the project planned during the summer. The council (Cabinet) held at the Elysée on November 27, 1922 was decisive in that respect. Tirard put forward the hypothesis of an inevitable campaign of German resistance and reiterated the main points of his programme: eviction of civil servants, re-establishment of a tariff cordon on the Rhine, creation of a Rhenish currency. Poincaré concluded the meeting with the words: "In March or April, we shall witness the disintegration of Germany."[25] The ensuing change of direction was favoured by the Minister of Finance, Charles de Lasteyrie, whose office was quite doubtful about any purely economic benefits from the exploitation of the pledge. The occupation would be costly and would only yield in return a heap of devalued marks. As he wrote to Poincaré: "From a financial point of view, the occupation of the Ruhr can in no way be justified. Its sole interest is political,"[26] The French troops did not enter the Ruhr on January 11, 1923 merely to fetch coal.[27]

In March 1923, in the thick of the *Ruhrkampf*, Poincaré addressed a questionnaire to most French ministries, seeking their views on a detailed study from Paul Tirard about the future organization of a possible Rhineland state.[28] The consensus favoured an autonomous Rhineland state within the *Reich* but closely controlled and occupied for a long period by the French High Commission. Its boundaries should include not only the left bank of the Rhine and the three bridgeheads but also a part of the Ruhr in order to increase its economic independence. Moreover, the evacuation of the Ruhr should occur according to the German payments, the last soldiers leaving the territory when the last mark was paid. It thus overstepped the limits of the Treaty of Versailles which, in fact, established no link between the military occupation and the payment of reparations. The date for the evacuation of the Rhineland had been arbitrarily set by the Peace Conference for 1935 and Poincaré, then President of the Republic and without real power, had bitterly reproached Clemenceau for agreeing to this date. Now Tirard did not hesitate to speak of an occupation "sustained for several generations."[29] Contrary to the image we have of a

Poincaré anxious about the meticulous execution of the slightest article of the treaty, the year 1923 rather shows him determined to profit from the right of the strongest, here to improve the treaty to the benefit of France's security. What is of course surprising is that these grand projects ignored the most elementary realities of the international situation, let alone the very existence of Great Britain.

It seems that four elements can account for the sudden ruin of the Rhineland policy. In the first place, Poincaré's decision to support the separatist *Putsch* in Aachen on October 1, 1923, contradicted the whole policy conducted for years in the region. Probably ill-informed, he over-estimated the influence of the persons involved in the *Putsch*. Even if he quickly realized his mistake, the harm had been done. From then on, Rhenish politicians became much more cautious before undertaking any negotiations with Tirard.

Secondly there was the strong hostility of Great Britain to the French plans and particularly to the creation of a local currency. On January 2, 1924, the Bank of England responded negatively to the proposals of Paribas regarding the creation of a new issuing body.[30] In addition, Belgium's disapproval of French support for the separatists encouraged it to distance itself from Paris and move closer to London.

Thirdly, under the guidance of Chancellor Wilhelm Marx, a Rhenish Centre Party politician who came to power December 4, 1923, Germany managed to restore her political unity by taking in hand her financial situation with the help of Great Britain. Marx's forceful speeches and policies helped the thwart French policies.

Finally the financial difficulties France experienced from January 1924 inverted the balance of power between it and Germany. France could no longer afford to undertake a large-scale policy in the Rhineland. Besides, not everybody at the Quai d'Orsay blindly subscribed to Poincaré's risky choices. Such was the case with Jacques Seydoux, *sous-directeur des relations commerciales*, in charge of coordinating the occupation of the Ruhr from Paris. His growing influence drove Poincaré, from January 1924 onwards, to shelve his plans for the Rhineland and instead focus on settling of the question of reparations. It left the way open for the Dawes Plan, which contained a practical solution to the German payments problem, but implied that the evacuation of the Ruhr and the restoration of German sovereignty over the whole territory formed part of this solution.

The need to obtain the best possible deal with regard to the two questions which prevailed in France's foreign policy after the war, the issues of reparations and security, contained contradictions which Poincaré could not overcome despite his strong will. Torn between several options, deluding itself about recovered power and its capacity to impose conception by coercion, persuading itself that the First World War was first an affair between it and Germany, France was left unable accurately to judge the new international order and to appreciate the reality of the new international settlement. The failure of France's Rhineland policy not only marked the limits of power, it also revealed how difficult it was to escape from the rules of the traditional European balance.

NOTES

1. Walter McDougall, *France's Rhineland Diplomacy 1914–1924* (Princeton, 1978); Marc Trachtenberg, *Reparation in World Politics. France and European economic Diplomacy 1916–1923* (New York, 1980); Jacques Bariéty, *Les Relations franco-allemandes après la Première Guerre mondiale* (Paris, 1977); Georges-Henri Soutou, "La France et les marches de l'Est," *Revue Historique*, 528 (1978), pp. 341–88.
2. Stanislas Jeanneson, *Poincaré, la France et la Ruhr 1922–1924* (Strasbourg, 1998).
3. François-André Paoli, *L'Armée française de 1919 à 1939* (Paris, 1968).
4. Jacques Bariéty, *Les Relations franco-allemandes*, pp. 51–61.
5. Paul Tirard, *La France sur le Rhin* (Paris, 1930); Pierre Jardin, "La politique rhénane de Paul Tirard," *Revue d'Allemagne*, 2 (1989), pp. 208–16.
6. *La Rhénanie* (Paris, 1922), (foreword by Tirard): "Quelle devait être notre interprétation des dispositions du traité à l'égard de la Rhénanie. Notre histoire, nos traditions, les actes de nos gouvernements, ceux de Richelieu comme ceux des armées révolutionnaires la dictaient en lettre claires: ce devait être une politique française, libérale, bienveillante, soucieuse d'assurer la paix sur nos frontières. Ce devait être une politique généreuse."
7. For example: Georges Blondel, *La Rhénanie, son passé, son avenir* (Paris, 1921); Maurice Barres, *Le Génie du Rhin* (Paris, 1921); Raymond Recouly, *La barrière du Rhin* (Paris, 1923).
8. Documents Diplomatiques Français (DDF), 1920 vol. 1 (Paris, 1997), pp. 56–7.
9. Archives nationales (AN), AJ9, 3774, Oct. 29, 1919. "L'objectif initial de notre action dans les territoires occupés me paraît être le suivant: favoriser sans immixtion dans la politique intérieure du *Reich*, les efforts de la population rhénane vers un régionalisme affranchi de la tutelle prussienne ou bavaroise, et en général, assurer à ces populations la possibilité pour elles de faire entendre leurs voix et leur volonté pacifique au sein des conseils d'Empire."
10. Paul Tirard, *L'art français en Rhénanie pendant l'occupation* (Strasbourg, 1930).
11. Jean-Marie Mayeur, "La politique religieuse du gouvernement français et l'affaire rhénane (1920–1923)," *Problèmes de la Rhénanie 1919–1930* (Metz, 1975).
12. AN, AJ9, 3774 and 3776.
13. Service Historique de l'Armée de Terre (SHAT), 2N, 237, Apr. 2, 1923. "Il paraît difficile d'étudier la question particulière de l'autonomie rhénane sans se préoccuper de la question plus générale de la réorganisation de l'Allemagne."
14. Ibid., "Notre intérêt est que les nouveaux Etats constituent des blocs homogènes aussi différents l'un de l'autre que possible et entre qui les oppositions de toutes sortes, religieuses, politiques, économiques, abondent. Ainsi, une Bavière catholique, monarchiste et paysanne auprès d'une Saxe protestante, socialiste et ouvrière, d'une Souabe mixte au point de vue religieux, bourgeoise et modérée."

15. SHAT, 7N, 2655. "Il semble qu'entre le danger mortel d'une Allemagne unitaire et les perspectives pleines de promesses d'une Allemagne fédéraliste, le souci d'assurer l'avenir de la France et la paix du monde ne nous permettent pas d'hésiter. Pour quelque temps encore, la solution fédéraliste est possible. Hâtons-nous d'en profiter."

16. Marjorie Farrar, *Principled Pragmatist. The political Career of Alexandre Millerand* (New York, 1991); François Roth, *Raymond Poincaré* (Paris, 2000); John Keiger, *Raymond Poincaré* (Cambridge, 1997).

17. DDF, 1920 tome 2, Peter Lang, 1999, pp. 219–222 : general directives addressed to Dard by Millerand when he took office in Munich on July 2, 1920. "Déjà renaissent dans les anciens Etats confédérés et dans les parties même de la Prusse les plus récemment assujetties par elle, les sentiments d'autonomie locale qui firent jadis de l'Allemagne la nation la plus divisée de l'Europe. Entretenir cette division était dans les siècles passés une tradition de notre politique; nous assurions ainsi notre prépondérance sur le continent. L'unité de l'Allemagne, devenue menaçante pour notre sécurité, n'a pu être contrebalancée que par l'alliance militaire de la Russie, qu'il n'est pas aisé de remplacer aujourd'hui. Notre intérêt primordial nous engage donc à favoriser les tendances particularistes qui, dans le cadre du fédéralisme, contribueront à créer un contrepoids à l'influence de la Prusse unitaire et militariste."

18. "Une sympathie d'autant plus efficace qu'elle sera plus discrète."

19. DDF, 1920 tome 1, pp. 235–237, Feb. 21, 1920. "Tenir le contact avec les éléments rhénans et les soutenir discrètement sans les compromettre."

20. DDF, 1920 vol. 3, pp. 358–60 and 468–71.

21. Ministère des Affaires étrangères (MAE), Rive gauche du Rhin, 26, 154–155, July 29, 1921. "Dans les entretiens que vous pouvez avoir avec les personnalités rhénanes, il me semblerait préférable que votre attitude fût celle d'un absolu désintéressement."

22. Stanislas Jeanneson, *Poincaré, la France et la Ruhr*; Conan Fischer, *The Ruhr Crisis 1923–1924* (Oxford, 2003).

23. AN, AJ9, 6383.

24. Karl-Dietrich Erdmann, *Adenauer in der Rheinlandpolitik nach dem ersten Weltkrieg* (Stuttgart, 1966); Henning Kohler, *Adenauer und die rheinische Republik* (Opladen, 1986).

25. MAE, Papiers Millerand, carton 26. "En mars ou avril, on aura la désorganisation de l'Allemagne."

26. MAE, Relations commerciales, 69, 225–228, Aug. 24, 1922. "Au point de vue financier, l'occupation de la Ruhr ne peut en aucune façon se justifier. Elle n'a d'intérêt qu'au point de vue politique."

27. Stanislas Jeanneson, "Pourquoi la France a-t-elle occupé la Ruhr?," *Vingtième Siècle*, 51 (1996), pp. 56–7.

28. SHAT, 2N, 237; AN, AJ9, 3779; Pierre Jardin, "Le Conseil Supérieur de la Défense Nationale et les projets d'organisation d'un Etat rhénan (mars 1923)," *Francia*, (1992), 3, pp. 81–96.

29. "Maintenue pendant plusieurs générations," AN, AJ9, 3779, 24, Mar. 24, 1923.

30. AN, AJ9, 6383.

THE REPARATIONS DEBATE

Gerald D. Feldman

This is not intended to be a research-based paper. I have not done research on reparations for some time, but preparing for this conference has given me a welcome opportunity to ponder some of the latest literature and think anew about problems that engaged me when I worked on the German inflation of the early 1920s, but also on the depression of the early 1930s in Central Europe. Also, some of the organizers of the gathering in Glasgow attended the conference on Versailles hosted by the Center for German and European Studies at Berkeley in May 1994 and also sponsored by the German Historical Institute in Washington, D.C. and viewed this symposium as something of a successor to the earlier one. The 1994 conference volume appeared as an edited volume, *The Treaty of Versailles. A Reassessment after 75 Years* in 1998, and I think it contributed substantially to providing new perspectives on Versailles and demonstrated the richness of the subject.[1] In any case, I find it gratifying that some of those involved believe, as I do, that the 1994 conference was a point of departure, that yet newer perspective are possible and that there remains more to be done. Versailles, despite the dismissive attitude of some historians on the cutting edge of the great cultural abyss, remains fundamental to our understanding of twentieth century history and deserves repeated revisiting.

The reparations debate, as we have come to know and love, has been of course concentrated on the question of German capacity and willingness to pay. No one has accused the Germans of honestly and forthrightly attempting to fulfill their obligations under the Treaty, and there is a genuine consensus that the policy of fulfillment had, as its purpose, the demonstration that fulfillment was not possible. There has, however, been a debate as to whether it was economically and politically possible for the Germans to pay the reparations bill and the degree to which they deliberately pursued policies of inflation and deflation in order to undermine the reparations settlement. At the 1994 Berkeley conference, Sally Marks and Steven Schuker insisted that the Germans deliberately and consciously pursued a policy of inflation and hyperinflation to escape paying a reparations bill that had already been significantly reduced by the division of the 132 billion gold mark indebtedness into A, B, and C Bonds.[2] My own position in the debate was, and remains, that Marks and Schuker inhabit a creditor's utopia where nations are constantly paying their bills and doing so on time. Yet in the real world, especially the real world of Weimar Germany, social and political circumstances did not permit such a policy. Indeed the right-wing forces, who were the only ones capable of employing the dictatorial tactics necessary to implement the socioeconomic measures necessary for fulfillment, were in fact the strongest opponents of paying reparations.[3]

An interesting twist was provided in the discussion by Niall Ferguson, who argued that the German balance of payments made fulfillment impossible but that the Germans were mistaken in thinking that inflation and dumping practices would bring the Allies to terms by producing even higher unemployment than already existed among the victors. Ferguson argued that the Germans should have taken advantage of the relative stabilization of 1920 to stabilize permanently and that this would have deprived the Allies of the German market and the advantages they were getting from the overheated German economy and its reconstruction.[4] It is worth noting that Ferguson's view complements the claim of Carl-Ludwig Holtfrerich that the German inflation helped to dampen and bring a speedy end to the economic crisis of 1920–1921 because there was at least one major industrial nation, namely Germany, with a high demand for goods and services.[5] In Ferguson's view, if the Germans had reduced this demand by a stabilization policy, then the Allies would have lost the German market and come to realize that reparations and German recovery were incompatible but also that reparations and recovery from the depression were incompatible. My own position is that German stabilization in 1920–1921 is not a credible counterfactual because there was such a strong inflation consensus in Germany in 1920–1921. The real chance came in the fall of 1922 when the inflation consensus was being replaced by a stabilization consensus, thereby providing at least a slight chance to avoid the Ruhr catastrophe or possibly make it less protracted. This opportunity was not taken, and we know what happened.[6]

While there was some mention in the 1994 discussions of the role of reparations after the stabilization and a parallel was drawn between the instrumentalization of inflation and, during the world economic crisis, of deflation in the struggle against reparations, the role reparations played in the post-1924 period was not discussed at all. It has not, in fact, received much attention until fairly recently. There are at least two good reasons, however, for taking a closer look at the post-inflation history of reparations. First, it has taken on a new significance thanks to recent scholarly work. Second, the arrangements made during the post-1924 phase had a curious and significant though quite neglected afterlife following the Second World War with the result that the entire reparations debate can be viewed from a somewhat different perspective from the usual one.

Certainly the most important recent scholarly contribution placing reparations center stage is the work of the German economic historian, Albrecht Ritschl, *The German Business Cycle, 1924–1934: Domestic Activity, Foreign Debt, and Reparations from the Dawes Plan to the Debt Default.*[7] The book is more accessible to "normal historians" than it appears when one just leafs through it, since Ritschl has been careful to present his central historical arguments in non-econometric form. Thus, readers not versed in econometrics can understand the argument even if they must take the models and the econometrics behind them on faith or simply ignore them.

Ritschl defines three reparations regimes in the post-inflation period. The first of these, from 1924 to 1928 is characterized by a recycling of reparations payments through American credits, the famous Dawes loans. Under the Dawes Plan, Germany was obligated to make reparations payments of one billion gold *Reichsmark* in the first year, rising to 2.5 billion over a period of four years. The money was to be taken from the reorganized *Reichsbahn,* customs taxes, and excises, but transfer protection was provided should Germany be unable to pay the reparations, and the *Reichsbank* was reorganized with foreign representatives on its Supervisory Board. The transfers and carrying out of the plan were placed under the supervision of an Agent-General, Parker Gilbert. An initial loan of 800,000,000 *Reichsmark* was made to Germany and was followed by a host of commercial loans that fueled the Germany recovery. It enabled Germany, after a very brief period of austerity, to enjoy an artificial boom characterized by increased public spending, social expenditures, and high wages, or at least wages higher than what was justified by investment and productivity according to Knut Borchardt and Harold James.[8] The fundamental problem, however, was that the Dawes Plan had established an implicit competition between the private international, above all American, credits used to finance the German economy and the reparations debts that was resolved by using the former to pay the latter. So long as those reparations debts were financed by foreign credits, the private debts received priority. The Dawes Plan evaded the issue of settling a final reparations sum, and this was an obvious source of uncertainty.

By 1928–1929, however, the foreign credits were diminishing substantially, and the Young Plan, which was to be the second reparations regime, was intended to create a situation in which, on the one hand, the controls on the German economy under the Dawes Plan and the occupation of the Rhineland were ended and, on the other hand, the total reparations bill was reduced to 114 billion *Reichsmark* to be paid over 59 years. The Germans were obligated to make direct reparations transfers from their budget and a transportation tax according to a fixed annuity schedule, a third of which was to be paid unconditionally and the remainder of which was postponable in the event of transfer difficulties. The annuity was to rise from 748 million *Reichsmark* in 1929–30 to a sum somewhat under 2 billion *Reichsmark* per year in 1930–31 and then somewhat over 2 billion in the late 1930s until the final payment was made in 1988. The Bank for International Settlements was set up in Basel to manage the payments and provide for Central Bank cooperation. The second reparations regime, therefore, was the Young Plan regime in which reparations payments had priority and, unhappily, came at a time when the economy was in a slump and doubly burdened the German balance of payments since the Germans had to cover both the obligatory reparations payments and the servicing of their foreign private debt. They also lacked the type of fiscal arrangement available to the British so that a genuine crisis developed each month when they had to pay the civil service and make transfers to the federal states. It was this triple bind, according to Ritshl—joined by Theo Balderston and Ulrich Bachmann, who have also worked on the fiscal crisis[9]—that imposed an austerity policy on Germany and made it impossible to fight the depression with borrowing and public expenditure and required the austerity policy pursued by Brüning instead. Just as the Dawes regime created the basis of what Knut Borchardt defined as the "crisis before the crisis" so the Young Plan regime deprived Brüning of freedom of maneuver, the other important thesis of Borchardt concerning the fatal situation of the Weimar Republic.

Ritschl, however, gives the discussion of Brüning's policies an interesting interpretative turn by stressing the dilemma of Germany as a sovereign debtor. States that do not pay their debts cannot be taken to court and thus present a special problem for creditors, a situation of which we have become very conscious since 1945, particularly with respect to

Third World countries. Indeed, in its fiscal organization and financial condition between 1929 and 1933, Germany may in fact be compared to a Third World country. Ritschl, of course, is not the first person to note the constraints on German domestic borrowing and expenditure and the domestic battle over, for example, urban borrowing during the 1924–1928 period. William McNeil's book on *American Money and the Weimar Republic* of 1986 discussed these issues,[10] but the specific role of reparations and the problems created by pushing reparations to the forefront under the Young Plan have, as far as I know, not received attention as a problem in sovereign debt. Needless to say, refusal to honor the conditions of the Young Plan could have led to sanctions against Germany, but as Ritschl points out, there is a limit to the costs in welfare that a sovereign debtor can tolerate through such sanctions. This limit is reached at the point where the costs of fulfillment and maintaining one's status as an acceptable credit risk, be these costs in actual economic welfare, be they in political destabilization, are deemed to exceed those entailed by "dropping out," that is, retreating from the international economic order altogether and pursuing a policy of debt repudiation and autarchy.

This was, of course, the option favored by the extreme right and left, and it was an option of which Brüning was well aware and which, according to Ritschl, he viewed as an undesirable but real alternative to his own policy of trying to reintegrate Germany into the world economy by fulfilling Germany's obligations but working toward an international settlement involving the revision of the Young Plan and basically the liquidation of reparations. If commercial debts could once again be given primacy, then Germany would hopefully be in a position to borrow and pursue a more expansive financial policy at home. This goal was not always consistently followed, however, because of Brüning's need to pacify the right. A prime illustration was the ill-timed and ill-fated Austro-German customs union scheme that was launched in March 1931 and probably had more to do with the strategy of the German foreign minister Curtius and the Foreign Office than the Brüning programme. It was nonetheless a gesture to the right-wing programme, and the reaction to it by the Allies only reinforced Brüning's recognition that the end of reparations would have to be worked toward by this continued deflationary policy and be realized when the political constellation was favorable in the United States and in Europe.

In Ritschl's view, the traditional charge against Brüning that he deliberately made the depression deeper in order to end reparations is the reverse of what actually moved Brüning, namely, that deflation became ever more necessary precisely because he could not end reparations in 1931. This argument seems to be born out by the evidence from the Cabinet protocols. As Brüning put the matter to his cabinet on May 7, 1931:

> Two things are necessary: Domestically, it is necessary that with the issuance of the emergency decree the impression is created among the people that the revision is already on its way; abroad, however, one must create the impression that we are striving to fulfill the plan. The entire complex must be kept in motion until the beginning of 1932. Until then Germany must not allow there to be decisive negotiations.[11]

Brüning feared that if things moved too quickly, it would have the reverse effect of what was desired and that sedation at home and abroad was necessary. The banking crisis and the Hoover Moratorium changed the situation, but even then the domestic political situation in France remained a source of concern and the Germans were uncertain as to how far they could go. The standstill agreements with Germany's commercial creditors, however, did give a priority to commercial debts despite French objections, and by October the Germans were prepared to talk about the need for a "final solution" to the reparations question. This was not, it should be emphasized, some purely German reaction to the situation, but rather the reflection of growing consensus that reparations had to end. Thus, in August 1931, a member of James Warburg's staff reported back from Berlin: "I don't believe anybody over here thinks that after six months foreign debts can be paid, nor could anybody guess when, if ever, the foreign current indebtedness of Germany can be repaid. The thing that makes it seem so hopeless to me is that the recovery of Germany seems . . . to be fundamentally based on a cancellation of reparations and it seems to be universally believed, both in Germany and elsewhere, that it is just a question of time before reparations will be cancelled."[12] Probably the major obstacle to this was the unwillingness of the United States to cancel the Anglo-French debts.

In mid-May 1932, just prior to the Lausanne Conference, that situation was no better, and the primary problem was preventing the conference from being a total failure. The French were formally maintaining their position that the unconditional portion of the Young Plan payments had to continue, while privately becoming increasingly willing to accept some compromise in the form of a lump payment of three billion *Reichsmark* or a lien on railroad profits in return for agreeing to end reparations. As the well-connected Warburg reported, the banker Carl Melchior from the Warburg Bank who had been there back in Versailles and was now a member of the Wiggins Committee, and international committee set up to deal with the world economic problems, was invited along with Schwerin von Krosigk, a ministerial director in the Finance Ministry and later

Finance Minister under Hitler, to meet with French officials in Geneva to "see if they can find a solution for the Lausanne Conference along the lines of some single, final effort to be made by Germany in consideration of being freed once and for all of reparations payments." As Warburg reported,

> Melchior's position, with which I entirely agree, is that he is quite willing to undertake this mission if desired, but that he consider it futile for two reasons: first, Brüning having stated categorically that no further payments would be made, it is inconsistent for Germany now to make any overtures before the Lausanne Conference, particularly in view of the Nazi flare-up which would undoubtedly occur if he now backed down; second, if the mission is merely to reiterate Brüning's statement that Germany will not pay another penny, it would seem better either not to embark upon the mission at all, or else to go to Paris to make this statement as politely as possible rather than have the French come to Geneva to be kicked in the face. I have no idea how the matter will develop but it is significant because it shows that, in spite of Brüning's drastic utterances to the contrary, he realizes that the Lausanne Conference is foredoomed to failure unless Germany makes some concession. Last night I met the Belgian Ambassador...and he expressed exactly the same view, namely, that Germany must make some nominal concession in order to accomplish the desired result.[13]

Brüning was not, at this point, prepared to make such concessions but, in his last cabinet discussion on reparations on May 27 before his resignation on May 30, Brüning argued that they had to demand an end to reparations, but that "this demand will to be sure hardly be possible to realize immediately, at least not at this conference. The other side will not be prepared to recognize that Germany in the future will not be in a position to attain surpluses with which to pay reparations."[14] Indeed, Brüning was prepared to argue that the 1.5 billion interest burden on the existing private foreign debt was a consequence of having to pay reparations and was getting ever more burdensome because of the continuing deflation. Brüning hoped, however, to avoid Germany being blamed for a failure at Lausanne by stressing the second goal of the conference, which was to find solutions to the world economic crisis. In general, Brüning's behavior before his departure from office and, indeed his desire to continue the policy of emergency decrees, which Hindenburg now refused him, would appear to confirm the Ritschl argument that he did not pursue deflation to end reparations but rather because he needed to end reparations in order to change the situation internally while maintaining Germany's participation in the international economic order, or what was left of it.[15] The tragedy, of course, was that reparations were eliminated at Lausanne after Brüning had left office, while Brüning's reliance on emergency decrees had paved the way for a right-wing rule that would eventually lead to the third phase of reparations history, namely, the blocking of transfers and the autarchy policy pursued by Schacht after the Nazi takeover. Ritschl suggest that Brüning, if he had stayed in office, might have used success after Lausanne to pursue an expansive economic policy at home while seeking German reintegration into the world economy.

There are a number of aspects to Ritschl's study, which I find particularly refreshing. He insists that Brüning's deflationary policy was not motivated by cyclical considerations, that is, a belief that a pro-cyclical policy was the most appropriate course to pursue as a matter of economic principal, but rather that it was a political policy required by the goal of retaining Germany's place in the international economic order. In this connection, Ritschl in no way argues that the Germans were economic victims of reparations but rather that they were victims of their constant efforts to evade reparations and putting off taking measures to pay until they had no other choice but to agree to the young Plan which came just at the time that Germany entered the Great Depression. Similarly, while he cannot find any possibility of Germany pursuing a successful policy of fulfillment, he does not think this is because Germany was incapable of paying reparations: "Had Germany possessed a political culture after the First World War that might have made the fulfillment of reparations obligations thinkable without inflation, political murder, street battles and, in the end, dictatorship and a war of revenge, then the German reparations after the First World War would probably be little more than a footnote in history, a curiosity of financial history like perhaps Britain's horrendous state debt after the Napoleonic Wars."[16]

While there is a bit of exaggeration in suggesting that reparations would have been a footnote in history, Ritschl's entire work is based on counterfactual propositions that seek to discover ways in which a satisfactory solution might have been found, and he finds none. The most convincing argument in the book in any case pertains to the competition between reparations payments and commercial debts and the problems of the sovereign debtor. Ritschl does not pay sufficient attention to the role of the Allies, by skirting not only around the American practice of intervening and then withdrawing from international economic issues, but also the failure of the French to find a suitable policy, this a product in large part of its domestic political conflicts, and Britain's increasing preoccupation with the Far East, its own nationalistic tendencies, and its growing tendency to appease Germany and drag a dependent France along what was to become a very dangerous road. For an exploration of these aspects of the problem, one must turn to the recent study of Lausanne by Philipp Heyde.[17]

In any case, what the recent historiography does suggest is that there is much work to be done toward the creation of a new and more comprehensive and international treatment of the reparations question since there are a great many unanswered questions. However, the perspective of such studies can no longer be the old debate's about the transfer problem and capacity to pay. I would like in conclusion to argue briefly that some attention should be paid to the implications of what happened after the Second World War. The creation of the Federal Republic of Germany, which considered itself and was regarded as the legal successor to the Weimar Republic and the National Socialist regime, involved among other things its progressive reestablishment as a sovereign state that was obligated to repay old debts and could undertake sovereign debts. I am referring, of course, to the fact that the Dawes loans and the Young Plan loans as well as the lesser known Krueger and the Lee-Higginson-Credit had by no means passed into oblivion after the war and were ultimately subject to repayments negotiated at the international London Debt Agreement meetings in 1951–1952 and ratified in1953.

While the subject of some investigation by Christoph Buchheim, the entire arrangement has largely been neglected in the literature with the exception of a book and other writings by Hermann Josef Abs, who was the chief German negotiator and who always preferred to write his own history. In 1991 Abs produced a study, *Decisions*, that framed the London Debt Agreement and his own role very much in the context of the alleged mistakes of the past.[18] It should be noted, however, that this was very much in the spirit of German opinion back in the 1950s. Although the situation in 1951 was obviously very different from that of the interwar period, Germany having been the beneficiary of the Marshall Plan and of the western interest in her recovery generated by the Cold War, it is remarkable how aggressive the Germans were in stating their position and the extent to which the Germans were able to use the history of the interwar period to press for what they considered an acceptable settlement. In March 1952, for example, the *Spiegel* reported: "Many experts in West Germany fear that in the wood-paneled chambers of Lancaster House a historical period will be repeated. Also, after the First World War the representatives of the creditors and those entitled to reparations pressed for 'the greatest possible German payments.'" *Spiegel* quoted Hjalmar Schacht on the Dawes Plan, when he argued that Germany did not have enough of an export surplus to pay for food and raw materials, let alone to pay for reparations and *Spiegel* went on to claim "that the situation today is hardly better. But in London the delegations from 30 countries have in the next weeks the chance to avoid the gross mistakes of the reparations policy after World War I, through which whose overburdening of the Germany economy significantly contributed to the world economic crisis of 1931." Hermann Abs believed that a fair settlement for both sides was to be achieved "though moderation on the creditor side and courage on the debtor side."[19]

Exactly what kind of courage was meant is, of course, somewhat ambiguous. Did he mean the courage to accept appropriate burdens, or did he mean the courage to say "No," a type of courage in which the Germans had become well practiced? Whatever the case, just as in 1932 there was a consensus between Germany and the Anglo-American powers that the competition between reparations and commercial debts had to end by getting rid of reparations, so in 1951 there was a consensus—unsuccessfully contested only by the Netherlands and Norway—that a competition between reparations and commercial debts had to be excluded from the start. Claims, for example, for the payment of forced labourers in German plants during the war as demanded by the Dutch would simply have to be put off until Germany was unified, as would interest payments on the interwar loans. As it turned out, they were not put off to eternity thanks to the unification of Germany, and Germany has been paying off the interest as well as struggling successfully to settle with claimants to restitution and reparation at a price well below those damages for which it was responsible. Abs rated the significance of the London Debt Agreement to be the equivalent of that of the Marshall Plan, and argued that it was the linchpin in Germany's effort to become credit-worthy again. He went on to note that it never achieved the kind of role in the public consciousness that reparations did, and concluded that its successful and unnoticed implementation was in fact a measure of its success. Another measure of its success can be found if one uses one's search engine to find the London Debt Agreement on websites, where it appears endlessly in connection with the debt restructuring of underdeveloped countries as a kind of model of how deciding to do the politically possible and necessary can create credit-worthiness and sustain the world economic and capitalist system.

From this perspective, the reparations debate during the interwar period and the historical debate that followed seem beside the point because the politics of the interwar period appear as nothing but a formula for inevitable disaster. Whether debtor's utopia for sovereign debtors is any more desirable than the creditor's utopia advocated by the few remaining stalwarts who do so is another question. Whatever the case, reparations was a matter of politics, and the Germans, by combining the London Debt Agreement with an agreement with Israel and this with equalization to burdens legislation to satisfy domestic demands certainly demonstrated that Bonn was not Weimar.

NOTES

1. Manfred F. Boemeke, Gerald D. Feldman, and Elisabeth Glaser (eds.), *The Treaty of Versailles. A Reassessment after 75 Years* (Cambridge and New York, 1998).
2. Stephen A. Schuker, "The Rhineland Question: West European Security at the Paris Peace Conference of 1919," and Sally Marks, "Smoke and Mirrors: In Smoke-Filled Rooms and the Galerie de Glaces," in ibid., pp. 275–312 and pp. 337–70.
3. Gerald D. Feldman, "A Comment," ibid., pp. 441–47.
4. Niall Ferguson, "The Balance of Payments Question: Versailles and After," ibid., pp. 401–40.
5. Carl-Ludwig Holtfrerich, *The German Inflation 1914–1923* (Berlin and New York, 1986), pp. 211–20.
6. Gerald D. Feldman, *The Great Disorder. Politics, Economics, and Society in the German Inflation, 1914–1924* (New York and Oxford, 1993, 1997), pp. 418–46.
7. Albrecht Ritschl, *Deutschlands Krise und Konjunktur: Binnenkonjunktur, Auslandsverschuldung und Reparationsproblem zwischen Dawes-Plan und Transfersperre 1924–1934* (Berlin, 2002).
8. Knut Borchardt, "Zwangslagen und Handlungsspielräume in der grossen Wirtschaftskrise der frühen dreißiger Jahre: Zur Revision des uberlieferten Geschichtsbildes," *Jahrbuch der Bayerischen Akademie der Wissenschaften* (1979), pp. 85–132; Harold James, *The German Slump. Politics and Economics 1924–1936* (Oxford, 1986), ch. 6.
9. Theo Balderston, *The Origins and Course of the German Economic Crisis, 1924–1933* (Berlin, 1993) and Ulrich Bachmann, *Reichskasse und öffentlicher Kredit in der Weimarer Republik 1924–1932* (Frankfurt a.M., 1996).
10. William C. McNeil, *American Money and the Weimar Republic* (New York, 1986).
11. *Akten der Reichskanzlei. Weimarer Republik. De Kabinette Brüning I u II. 30 März 1930 bis Oktober, 10 1931 Oktober, 10 1931 bis Juni, 1 1932* (Boppard am Rhein, 1982), vol. 2, Cabinet meeting May 7, 1931, pp. 1058–59.
12. Letter to James N. Rosenberg, Aug, 23 1931, James Warburg Papers, Box 2, John F. Kennedy Library, Boston, Massachusetts.
13. James Warburg to Lucien Nachmann May 19, 1932, ibid., Box 4.
14. Cabinet Meeting, May 27, 1932, *Akten der Reichskanzlei. Weimarer Republik. Die Kabinette Brüning I u II. März 30, 1930 bis Oktober, 10 1931. 10. Oktober 1931 bis 1. Juni 1932* (Boppard am Rhein, 1982), vol. 3, pp. 2575–77.
15. Ritschl, *Krise und Konjunktur,* p. 176.
16. Ibid., pp. 242–3.
17. Philipp Heyde, *Das Ende der Reparationen: Deutschland, Frankreich und der Youngplan 1929–1932* (Paderborn, 1998), and "Frankreich und das Ende der Reparationen. Das Scheitern der französischen Stabilisierungskonzepte in der Weltwirtschaftskrise 1930–1932" *Vierteljahrshefte für Zeitgeschichte,* 48/1 (2000), pp. 37–74.
18. Christopher Buchheim, "Das Londoner Schuldenabkommen," in: Ludolf Herbst (ed.), *Westdeutschland 1945–1955. Unterwerfung, Kontrolle, Integration*

(Munich, 1986), pp. 219–29. Hermann Josef Abs, "Das Londoner Schulden-abkommen" in: *Zeitfragen der Geld-und Wirtschaftspolitik* Internetausgabe 36 (2002), pp. 1–23; Hermann J. Abs, *Entscheidungen 1949–1953. Die Entste-hung des Londoner Schuldenabkommens* (Mainz and Munich, 1991).

19. See "Aus verblichenen Reichen," *Der Spiegel* 10/1952, (Mar. 5, 1952), pp. 7–9, and "Jeden Tag ein paar Millionen," ibid. 33/1952 (Aug. 13, 1952), pp. 6–7.

THE HUMAN PRICE OF REPARATIONS

Conan Fischer

I

Even while drafting the Versailles settlement, the Allies anticipated problems with German reparations. Quite apart from French fears (or hopes) of German bad faith,[1] the text of the treaty itself conceded that the planned interim levy of 20 billion gold marks would not be credited in full to the reparations account. The partial military occupation of Germany had first call on the monies, and thereafter the cost of "such supplies of food and raw materials as maybe judged by the Governments of the Principal Allied and Associated Powers to be essential to enable Germany to meet her obligations for reparations."[2] Germany, after all, had faced near starvation during the winters of 1916 and 1917 and the situation remained precarious following the end of hostilities. A malnourished and radicalized workforce was unlikely to produce the consignments of coal, coke, chemicals and other products set out in the Treaty. Furthermore, the settlement demanded compensation in kind to France and Belgium within three months for the 370,900 head of livestock requisitioned during the course of the war;[3] an understandable requirement, but one liable to undermine still further Germany's exhausted agricultural sector.

The Allies did subsequently permit Berlin to utilise the reparations account to secure food supplies, for example at the 1920 Spa Conference on coal deliveries.[4] However, the concessions were modest and successive German governments struggled to feed the country whilst simultaneously paying reparations, whether in part or in full, whether willingly or unwillingly. The taxation for reparations purposes of a dwindling base of liquid assets, declining profits, and falling real wages was equally problematic, prompting Gerald Feldman to ask: "Could German leaders mediate a distributional conflict whose major function, no matter who won, appeared to be serving the well-being of Germany's enemies?"[5] The great hunger of the post-war years had complex origins, some of which are traceable back to German wartime agricultural and rationing policy, but in the bitter years of defeat this was easily forgotten. Not surprisingly, the human price of reparations came to demand in turn a very high political price of the Weimar Republic.

II

In times of acute dislocation, rational economic decision making often goes by the board. With money losing its value and food remaining in acutely short supply, German farmers succumbed to the temptation of hoarding. This was essentially a symptom rather than the cause of the deeper crisis, but the authorities had cities to feed and the military was deployed into the countryside to root out the provisions that farmers had withheld from market.[6] For all this, however, food remained in desperately short supply and, if anything, matters deteriorated from year to year. The German bread grain harvest had yielded over 14.6 million tons in 1913 (on post-1919 territory), but only some 9.9 million tons in 1921, and just 7.3 million tons in 1922. Grain imports had also declined sharply, and whilst this was offset by a drastic curtailment of exports, it could not prevent overall bread grain consumption in Germany standing 42 per cent lower in 1922 than it had in 1913. Dairy cattle were yielding 1,500 litres of milk annually, as against 2,200 litres before the war, and per capita consumption of milk had fallen by 64 percent.[7] Consumption of edible fats was down 43 per cent per head,[8] whilst livestock markets saw progressively fewer animals presented for slaughter. In the case of Essen half as many beasts were offered in 1922 as before the war.[9] These animals themselves were often in very poor condition.

Official records reveal that the food crisis came to dominate entire Cabinet meetings. It intervened repeatedly during the discussion of reparations or budgetary affairs, lending much policy making an altogether reactive character. Agricultural issues that might have seemed relatively trivial or even farcical in ordinary times assumed the dimension of full-blown national crises, as in the autumn of 1921 when the Rhenish potato crop failed. This should have been a local affair, for the key Pomeranian harvest had been successful and had produced a healthy surplus. In other words there was no national potato shortage, but panic buying in Pomerania by western municipalities and businesses led to soaring prices, which threatened to put this relatively humble staple beyond the pocket of many ordinary consumers.[10] Transport deficiencies added to the sense of burgeoning crisis, for the peace settlement required of Germany the surrender of many canal barges,[11] while the German Railways were chronically short of freight wagons. Some had been surrendered to the Allies as reparations,[12] whilst of the remainder a proportion were committed to delivering consignments of reparations in kind,[13] leaving the increasingly valuable potato harvest temporarily stranded in Pomerania.[14]

On 22 November senior politicians and officials met to resolve the issue, which, of course, formed part of the wider and seemingly intractable food crisis. The Prussian Minister President, Otto Braun, warned that the Communists might easily exploit the situation to their advantage.[15] The city of Berlin had added to the panic by offering Pomeranian growers double the going rate for their potatoes; "racketeering prices" as one senior minister complained.[16] By this time the transport crisis had been partially addressed, but the increasingly wild mood that gripped the potato trade demanded further action. Although an earlier proposal to regulate the potato trade had been rejected in Cabinet, special government permits were now to be issued to selected dealers, without which potato trading was declared illegal. The assembled ministers and civil servants took the opportunity also to impose pricing controls on retailers of edible fats, the availability of which compared unfavourably with the war years.[17]

Such episodes were all too typical of the immediate post-war era. Despite the challenges faced after Versailles in the realm of high politics, Germany's most senior politicians and civil servants agonised repeatedly and at length over the securing of grain imports, bread supplies, potatoes, fish, or milk.[18] Over 100 decrees and subsidiary ordinances had been issued by late 1921 to combat racketeering and other malpractices, but, as the trade unions acidly observed in November, this torrent of legislation was incoherent to the point where it "left nothing more to desire in terms of its opacity."[19] They urged the government to simplify the statute book, protesting that a "second sell-out of Germany had begun" and warning that public confidence was hanging by a thread.[20]

This hardly came as news to the authorities. In September, confronted with schools full of half-starved children, the National Ministry of Education warned that "the prevailing situation [in Berlin] has triggered widespread unrest within the urban population"[21] and requested 500 million marks from the public purse to feed the country's urban schoolchildren.[22] According to medical officers' reports, at least half these children were malnourished, provoking Education Ministry officials to conclude in emotion-laden language that:

> Biological research has demonstrated that long-term malnourishment during the period of pre-adult growth results in irreversible loss of height and weight. Disruption of the orderly development of a high proportion of children will result inevitably in a degeneration of the race. The Englishman Baden-Powell's words - 'We shall have to wait until 1940 to see who really won the war' - thereby assume a particular significance. Given the context in which the words were uttered, this can only mean that it will first become apparent in 1940 how far the enemy blockade degraded Germany's children.[23]

Milk was regarded as an indispensable part of children's diets and on 29 November it was finally agreed to release 400 million marks to address the exceptional milk shortages being suffered by many communities. The national government could barely see its way to raising the necessary funds and requested supplementary funding from the federal states and municipalities, but accepted that some local authorities had nothing to give.[24] In any case there was a more fundamental obstacle. Germany's emaciated dairy herds were quite simply failing to yield the necessary milk; the extra money chasing dwindling supplies merely threatened to send the price of milk soaring. Local government was, therefore, advised to use the cash to raise and then regulate milk production:

> The most effective way of improving milk supplies, where these are scarce, is by buying up animal feed, particularly foreign feed, to be distributed to dairymen at a subsidised rate. The communes would deliver [the feed] and ensure that the increased milk production benefited these communes through the use of communal dairies.[25]

Days earlier the Cabinet had agreed to underwrite a Quaker-run food aid program for malnourished children,[26] but the public purse failed to address the wider problem effectively and matters continued to deteriorate. In August 1922 the authorities noted further falls in milk production, expressed concern over potato and sugar supplies, and observed that a chronic coal shortage was keeping the country's fishing fleets in port.[27] Periodic restrictions were imposed on the importing of "luxury" goods, such as "coffee, tea, spirits, tropical fruit, and chocolate,"[28] and on the use domestically of sugar by distilleries and barley by breweries.[29] Efforts were also made periodically to control prices and in November 1921 unofficial, roving anti-racketeering commissions were granted retrospective approval and their membership extended to include trade union representatives.[30] However, the ominous and accelerating rate of inflation condemned all these efforts to Canute-like failure.

In official eyes it was hard to ignore the apparent link between a chronic scarcity of foreign exchange, which could have been used to import food, and the massive outflows of hard currency occasioned by the payment of reparations and other Allied imposts.[31] A civil service report to the Cabinet in November 1921 which stated that: "One must understand that three different obligations always bear on us concurrently—1) the provision of food supplies, 2) reparations obligations, 3) clearing payment obligations,"[32] was lent graphic substance during the spring and early summer of 1922. Under the terms of the 1921 London Agreement, Germany was scheduled to pay 50 million marks monthly in reparations, but also a further 37 million marks (not credited to the reparations account as such) to cover clearing costs, that is Germanys international obligations over and above reparations.[33] In April 1922 the government needed to spend this latter sum twice; to cover clearing costs, but also to fund food imports. As Secretary of State Hirsch explained to the Cabinet:

> If we accede to the Foreign Currency Sub-Committee's decision to release 40m gold marks to the National Grain Bureau, then the country's further obligations towards the clearing process, including those on May, 15, cannot be met. The issue of whether the 40m gold marks should be released [to the Grain Bureau] is, therefore identical to the question of whether we wish or do not wish to make the [clearing] payment on May, 15.[34]

The government considered placing the question of food supplies on the agenda of the 1922 Genoa Conference, but Finance Minister Andreas Hermes remarked gloomily that with famine even more severe in Eastern Europe, it was unlikely that the Allies would give Germany a sympathetic hearing.[35] That said, alternatives were not readily to hand and the government reasoned that the use as a last resort of Germany's gold reserves to secure food imports would prove merely to be a one-off solution to a seemingly intractable, longer term crisis.[36] This option was rejected and Hermes was forced to concede that the only escape from the deepening crisis lay in resort to the printing press.[37]

Parallel to these financial deliberations ran a debate over how much extra work might be squeezed out of the country's half-starved workforce to address the demands of the reparations schedule.[38] Businessmen were heard to complain that the German revolutionary settlement of 1918–1920, which included a statutory guarantee of the eight hour day, was demanding too high a price of the economy and compromising the country's ability to pay reparations.[39] Government ministers noted that Ruhr coal had become so expensive that Germany's transport infrastructure was using more and more British-mined coal, which did nothing for the balance of payments account.[40] However, the eight hour day formed the keystone of a far-reaching accord between organised labour, industry and government that might be taken to define the very substance and ethos of the post-war revolutionary settlement. The National Labour Ministry tried to square the circle by arguing that higher output, the payment of reparations, and the integrity of the German Revolution were interconnected, continuing:

> Since Germany would 'free itself all the faster, the faster it paid off the compensation and reparations accounts through work', the . . . Ministry supported the intensified exploitation of every opportunity for rationalisation "in the immediate interest even of the working class." Taylorism could serve as 'an instrument of national liberation' under the democratic control of the new state.[41]

This, however, was more easily said than done, particularly in the coal mining sector, which was required to deliver some 15 per cent of its output as reparations.[42] Wage rises looked impressive when expressed in furiously depreciating paper marks, but by late 1922 the real income of a face worker in the Ruhr's coal mines was less than a third of his British counterpart's. Before the war their respective real incomes had been broadly equal.[43] The mining companies were scarcely in a position to pay more, with output per man shift collapsing, war time emergency taxes (such as the *Kohlensteuer*) remaining on the statute book, and profitability compromised to the point where some companies were forced to pass their dividend payments.[44] The mining unions agreed to extra half shifts in the industry to meet the reparations schedule, but at an appalling cost to the miners' personal health.[45] Even before this, the average daily calorie intake of a typical Ruhr mining family was condemning it to creeping starvation.[46]

III

It was in this atmosphere, during the summer of 1922, that Germany announced a moratorium on cash payments to the reparations account. Chancellor Wirth declared defiantly on 30 August that: "The entire nation understands the slogan 'bread first, then reparations,'"[47] but to Paris it appeared that the German authorities had engineered the whole payments crisis in order to destroy the reparations regime. The issue, of whether Germany "could not" or "would not" pay reparations has been widely aired in the academic literature, although more recently compliance has come again to be regarded as problematic, if not untenable in the immediate post-war years.[48] Of immediate significance to us, however, is the manner in which the burgeoning reparations crisis impacted on the German people and the wider health of the German polity.

The victor powers themselves failed to agree on the matter. The French authorities remained convinced that Berlin had engineered the whole crisis in order to destroy the reparations regime. Poincaré in particular regarded the payment of reparations as a touchstone of Germany's inherent good faith; their non-payment as confirmation of his long-standing and deepening scepticism on the issue. The British authorities were less fixated on reparations, worrying equally about the recovery of war debt,[49] not least from France. Sections of the British press, such as *The Economist*, openly doubted the viability and deeper wisdom of the reparations regime in any case; doubts nourished by the writings of John Maynard Keynes among others.[50] Efforts to resolve these Franco-British differences in August 1922 failed, prompting Paris to elaborate plans for unilateral action against Germany.[51] The seizure of the Ruhr District had been contemplated for some time as a suitable "sanctions territory," for it constituted a valuable source of reparations in kind and promised to provide a steady stream of tax and customs revenues to the French exchequer, through the substitution of the German fiscal regime by a French-run equivalent.[52] Beyond this, the Ruhr's heavy industry constituted the core of Germany's military-industrial complex, and the industrialists themselves were perceived by Paris to be a particularly influential, revanchist force in German political life.[53] After a series of further, increasingly half-hearted attempts at mediation, France and her Belgian ally invaded the Ruhr District on January 11, 1923.

IV

Poincaré insisted that the invasion's purpose was merely to extract reparations,[54] and whilst recent research has shown that these protestations were disingenuous to say the least,[55] a connection between the invasion and the reparations question was clear to all concerned. The extraordinary misery consequently visited on the people of the Ruhr, and also of the occupied Rhineland, can, therefore, be regarded as the ultimate human price of the reparations regime.

Many key French decision makers, including the chief of military operations, General Jean-Marie Degoutte, did not anticipate trouble. German

compliance, he assumed, would deliver France the double bonus of reparations and economic control of the greatest concentration of coal mining
and heavy industry on the European continent.[56] Instead the invading
Allies were confronted by a determined campaign of obstruction, dubbed
passive resistance, which was largely conducted not by generals and coal
mining magnates, but by the new German Republic's staunchest supporters—
unionized workers and blue-collar civil servants. The reasons for this
extraordinary turn of events have been discussed elsewhere,[57] but its
impact was devastating. Rather than bringing a truculent government to
heel through a decisive show of force, the French authorities were sucked
inexorably into an unplanned, thankless, and sometimes brutal campaign
against the entire population of the occupied territories.

Soon enough food, or more precisely the absence of food, became a
weapon in France's armoury. Collaboration, it was made clear, would
secure food supplies to the Ruhr, resistance would result in famine.[58] The
German Cabinet remained acutely aware of the wider political ramifica-
tions of the food crisis, and on January 17, 1923 concluded that material
shortages combined with the delicate question of public morale demanded
the regulation of the restaurant trade. Only one meat dish was to be
offered on any menu, the use of butter in restaurants was banned, consumption of eggs was restricted and the use of milk in hot chocolate
drinks completely forbidden. Immediate closure awaited any transgressor
of these new regulations.[59] However, efforts such as these were cosmetic
in the final analysis. Matters deteriorated and the food blockade itself was
intensified after a particularly serious terrorist outrage against Belgian
elements of the occupying army on June, 30.[60] Shops came to open but
briefly each day, if at all, and long queues of malnourished housewives
queued for whatever might be on offer in scenes reminiscent of the worst
days of the war. Potatoes fetched 3,000 marks a ton on July, 20, but
10,000 marks on 25th.[61] In early August the authorities in Bochum
warned Berlin that food supplies across the Ruhr verged on total collapse,[62] and shortly thereafter riots swept the region. Reports from
Gelsenkirchen described harrowing scenes as blood literally flowed in the
streets; other towns and cities suffered a similar fate.[63]

The Ruhr's children were already chronically malnourished and thus
highly vulnerable in terms of their health even before the invasion.
"Dietary conditions resembling those of the final war years" as one report
put it, had left them underweight and prey to chronic diseases such as
tuberculosis and rickets.[64] Words sometimes seemed almost to fail the
officials whose job it was to relay these increasingly grim tidings to their
political superiors, with one remarking bleakly that observers "had ceased
to expect to see children who looked normal."[65] Photographic evidence of
stick-limbed, pot-bellied infants, such as currently grace famine relief

posters, provided grim confirmation, were any needed.[66] Thus of the 50,000 children aged 2 to 10 years in Dortmund, 10 per cent were acutely disabled by rickets, which was to discount entirely the many more suffering from less acute forms of the illness.[67]

The health of the Ruhr's children continued to deteriorate as the 1923 food blockade took its toll. By the summer the death rate for unweaned babies had increased by 15-33 per cent since the New Year,[68] while children of school age also fared very poorly. In Hamborn, for example, where an estimated 75 per cent of children were noticeably malnourished, some schools saw attendance collapse to just 15 per cent of their roll. In Essen the proportion of school children in attendance was estimated at 55 per cent. Not surprisingly, viral infections ran riot across the region, leaving only a third of children in the Rees District free of infection.[69] Psychiatric problems also became increasingly common, with chronic bed wetting one indication among many.[70]

Even during the earlier phase of the occupation local officials expressed fears that the combined impact of starvation and wretched environmental conditions would cause many children to die,[71] prompting the evacuation of as many such children as possible to unoccupied Germany.[72] There were earlier precedents to draw on, for during and immediately after the war a Rural Visits Scheme had seen children from the Ruhr and other urban areas spend summers on farms, to build them up for the rigours of the coming winter. Revived in 1923, the Scheme witnessed cooperation between state agencies, the churches, Red Cross and larger employers, as needy children were identified, prepared for evacuation and then placed on farms that normally volunteered to care for them free of charge.[73] Officials estimated on 31 March that some 200,000 children would have to be evacuated in this way, although the number eventually reached 300,000.[74] Germany's farmers had responded generously, offering 500,000 free places for *Ruhrkinder* in their own homes.[75]

However, the very process of evacuation now revealed how shockingly degraded everyday living conditions had become in the Ruhr. Regulations stipulated that evacuees had to possess a basic minimum of essential clothing,[76] but growing numbers of children were evidently wandering around in rags, without footwear and without a change of clothing. The authorities in Buer warned that "the placement of a large number of children in the countryside is bedevilled by the lack of necessary clothing," while in Recklinghausen 90 per cent of potential evacuees faced exclusion from the programme for identical reasons.[77] Cruellest of all, as officials in Witten observed, was that children from the poorest families, who most needed to be evacuated, were those quite unable to afford a bare minimum of clothing.[78]

Nonetheless, administrative districts, or even large industrial combines, were twinned with rural districts in unoccupied Germany.[79] Trainloads of children began their long and uncertain journey out of the Ruhr, but it was literally a voyage into the unknown with visits by parents—if the French permitted them to leave the Ruhr at all—only possible if their children became seriously ill.[80] Many parents found the whole business heart-wrenching, some remembering unhappy experiences during the similar wartime evacuations.[81] With the Allied authorities always liable to interrupt telegraph traffic, adequate notice of evacuations, or sometimes of their cancellation, could not always be given. This left weak and hungry children liable to face journeys of a day or more with little food or water, or left farmers to make lengthy and time-consuming journeys to their nearest station to collect their *Ruhrkind*, only to discover that the train had not arrived at all.[82]

Once the children did arrive, they tumbled out onto remote, rural station platforms ragged, starving, and deeply disturbed. Sending them back was out of the question, but nor could they remain in such a shocking state. The parents could not help them, the local authorities in the Ruhr no more so, leaving the burdens of occupation and passive resistance to be borne by the unlikeliest of people in the most unlikely ways. As a report from the eastern District of Guben explained:

> The Rural District of Guben received about 1,300 children from the District of Recklinghausen. . . . Almost all the children arrived virtually in rags. Only about 5 to 10 per cent were provided with good clothing, almost none had a change of underwear. Educational materials had to be found for their schooling, for the children had not been provided with these either. Hospital fees have so far amounted to 4 million marks and it should be noted that the doctors are providing their services free of charge. Shoe repairs are also consuming considerable sums of money. . . . The billeting of 1,250 children in the District is . . . very demanding. In individual cases the foster parents have provided clothing, underclothes and shoes and in the process spent well over 1 million marks on a child.[83]

For all that, the evacuation program achieved its primary objective. On their return to the Ruhr in the autumn, health checks revealed that the great majority of evacuees had been restored to good health.[84] It was, therefore, all the more depressing for doctors, parents and, no doubt, the children when starvation once again took hold during the autumn. Officials noted despondently that the evacuees had returned "at the worst possible moment."[85] Unemployment hit 90 per cent in many Ruhr towns as the national government, in an effort to balance its budget and stabilise the currency, suspended the torrent of employment subsidies that had permitted a semblance of economic normality to endure in the occupied territories. Simultaneously it cut back savagely on welfare benefits. Medical and welfare officers could only console themselves that most children would survive at least, to be evacuated again during 1924.[86]

V

Throughout these traumatic months, distraught parents were convinced that the invaders and the wider reparations regime were to blame. On January, 23, for example, works council delegates from mines in the Wanne district, typically family men, lambasted the local French garrison commander over intensifying food shortages, declaring that:

> Since the war they had worked under utterly wretched conditions. Despite the fact that thousands of workers had had no meat on the table for a month at a time, that there wasn't even margarine for their bread, the miners' unions had accepted overtime agreements so as to maximise reparations deliveries to France. . . . The German working class had starved, frozen, and toiled to meet the obligations to France as far as possible. In particular the miners knew that the German people had done its duty.[87]

Similarly, long-suffering miners at the von der Heydt mine were infuriated when French troops requested use of their pit baths, and couched their refusal in terms that, again, made direct reference to the reparations question:

> Working-class families are suffering great poverty and deprivation because of the occupation; problems that were already present in sufficient measure beforehand. We have had our bellyful of incursions into our jurisdiction, the constraints on our freedom of assembly, the piratical attacks on peaceful citizens, the treacherous shooting of miners. We demand freedom, work, and bread, but you have brought hunger, deprivation, misery, and decay. We didn't invite you, nor do we want you here. We have demonstrated through years of overtime that we support our government's fulfilment policy. You have substituted violence for justice, sanctions for fulfilment; our defensive struggle has flared up in response to this.[88]

Permission to use the baths was denied, and, with discretion the better part of valour, the French military decided not to press the point.

VI

The human price of the post-1918 reparations crisis was borne in disproportionate measure by the more vulnerable sections of German society, although even many accustomed to a more comfortable existence were devastated by the trauma of hyperinflation. With the benefit of a good dose of hindsight Germany's political and economic leaders might have dealt better with the complex challenges of the post-Versailles era, but, as we have seen, beyond the major political challenges of defeat and revolution, the remorseless food shortages repeatedly demanded attention from politicians and civil servants alike. The German government was scarcely a free agent when it came to paying or not paying reparations, and the cold-blooded practicalities of meeting the Allied schedules were compromised enormously by degradation of Germany's "human capital" through war and thereafter by an imperfect peace.

Looking beyond these immediate issues, the longer term political and ethical impact of this flood tide of human misery was altogether more sinister, for the famine and associated reparations regime arguably nourished a new political discourse. The Nazis had played no part in the Ruhr business at all, but the wider experiences of the post-war years lent core elements of their ideology far greater appeal than might otherwise have been the case. Self-sufficiency in food production, hostility to international financial institutions and mechanisms, and to the Jews who allegedly dominated these mechanisms, for example, were notions whose resonance in the minds of typical voters may have owed less to atavistic bigotry or some abstract fondness for a pre-industrial idyll, and more to the human catastrophe that scourged Germany for a generation after 1914. In such extraordinary times the grotesque creed of Nazism could assume the guise of a timely solution to contemporary problems; a political movement both proportionate and reasonable. Unwittingly, the human tragedy within post-war Germany, itself the incidental by-product of a complex global peace settlement, helped set in train an altogether more devastating human catastrophe.

NOTES

1. Conan Fischer, *The Ruhr Crisis, 1923–1924* (Oxford, 2003), p. 12.
2. HMSO, *The Treaty of Peace between the Allied and Associated Powers and Germany . . . Signed at Versailles, June 28th 1919* (London, 1928), p. 247, Article 251. See also p. 207, Article 235.
3. HMSO, *Treaty of Peace*, p. 233, Annex VI, 6.
4. Gerd Meyer, "Die Reparationspolitik: Ihre außen- und innenpolitischen Rückwirkungen," in Karl Dietrich Bracher, Manfred Funke, Hans-Adolf Jacobsen (eds.), *Die Weimarer Republik 1918–1933. Politik, Wirtschaft, Gesellschaft* (Bonn, 1998), p. 331.
5. Gerald D Feldman, *The Great Disorder: Politics, Economics and Society in the German Inflation, 1914–1924* (New York, 1997), p. 428.
6. e.g., Richard Bessel, *Germany after the First World War* (Oxford, 1995), pp. 214–16.

7. E. Jüngst, "Zur Abwehr," *Glückauf. Berg- und Hüttenmännische Zeitschrift*, 59/9 (1923), pp. 220–1.
8. Jüngst, "Zur Abwehr," p. 221.
9. Nordrhein-Westfälisches Hauptstaatsarchiv Düsseldorf (HStAD), Regierung Düsseldorf (R Dü) 16445(59–60), Bericht vom Landrat Essen am 18/8.
10. *Akten der Reichskanzlei. Weimarer Republik. Die Kabinette Wirth I und II, 10. Mai bis Oktober 26, 1921. Oktober 26, 1921 bis November 22, 1922.* ed. Karl Dietrich Erdmann and Ingrid Schulze-Bidlingsmaier (Boppard am Rhein, 1973) (henceforward *RK Wirth I/II*), Nr 153, Nov, 22 1921, p. 426.
11. HMSO, *Treaty of Peace*, p. 176, Article 339.
12. Notably those deemed to be in situ in territories surrendered by Germany to the Allies. Thus, HMSO, *Treaty of Peace*, p. 39, Article 56, p. 125, Article 256, p. 55, Article 92.
13. Fischer, *Ruhr Crisis*, 151–2.
14. *RK Wirth II*, Nr 153, Nov. 22, 1921, p. 426.
15. *RK Wirth II*, Nr 153, Nov. 22, 1921, p. 427.
16. Ibid.
17. *RK Wirth II*, Nr 153, Nov. 22, 1921, p. 426.
18. Thus: *RK Wirth I*, Nr 3, May, 17 1921, p. 4; Nr 22, June, 6 1921, p. 47; *RK Wirth II*, Nr 142, Nov. 14, 1921, p. 395; Nr 154, Nov. 24, 1921, pp. 428–30; Nr 291, June, 13 1922, p. 873; Nr 355, Aug. 25, 1922, p. 1053. The preceding is a small selection of such cases during the 18 months of the Wirth Chancellorship.
19. *RK Wirth II*, Nr 156, Nov. 26, 1921, p. 435 n. 1.
20. Ibid.
21. *RK Wirth I*, Nr 103, Sept. 28, 1921, p. 294 n. 2.
22. *RK Wirth I*, Nr 103, Sept. 28, 1921, p. 294 n. 1.
23. Ibid. cf. Jüngst, "Zur Abwehr," p. 221.
24. *RK Wirth II*, Nr 158, Nov. 29, 1921, p. 445.
25. Ibid. cf. *RK Wirth II*, Nr 154, Nov. 24, 1921, p. 433 n. 11.
26. *RK Wirth II*, Nr 154, Nov. 24, 1921, p. 433.
27. *RK Wirth II*, Nr 355, Aug. 25, 1922, pp. 1053–6. cf. Nr 358, Aug. 28, 1922, p. 1065.
28. *RK Wirth I*, Nr 3, May 17, 1921, p. 4.
29. *RK Wirth II*, Nr 358, Aug 28, 1922, p. 1064.
30. *RK Wirth II*, Nr 158, Nov. 29, 1921, p. 444.
31. Thus: *RK Wirth I*, Nr 3, May 17, 1921, p. 4.
32. *RK Wirth II*, Nr 154, Nov. 24, 1921, p. 430.
33. *RK Wirth II*, Nr 291, Jun. 13, 1922, p. 873.
34. *RK Wirth II*, Nr 247, Apr. 17, 1922, p. 708.
35. *RK Wirth II*, Nr 247, Apr. 17, 1922, pp. 707–8. See also *RK Wirth II*, Nr 241a, Apr. 5, 1922, pp. 674–7.
36. *RK Wirth II*, Nr 361, Aug. 30, 1922, p. 1071–3.
37. *RK Wirth II*, Nr 361, Aug. 30, 1922, p. 1071.
38. *RK Wirth II*, Nr 145, Nov. 15, 1921, pp. 403–7. See also *RK Wirth II*, Nr 393, 30 Oct. 1922, p. 1144.
39. Feldman, *Disorder*, 486–9. cf. Carl Bergmann, *The History of Reparations* (Boston & New York, 1927), pp. 148–54; Peter Krüger, *Die Außenpolitik der Republik von Weimar* (Darmstadt, 1985), p. 194.

40. *RK Wirth II*, Nr 145, Nov. 15, 1921, p. 406–7.

41. Quoted in: Gunther Mai, "'Wenn der Mensch Hunger hat hört alles auf.' Wirtschaftliche und soziale Ausgangsbedingungen der Weimarer Republik (1919–1924)" in Werner Abelshauser (ed.), *Die Weimarer Republik als Wohlfahrtsstaat. . . .*(Vierteljahresschrift für Sozial- und Wirtschaftsgeschichte, suppl. 81, 1986), p. 60 n. 105.

42. Alfred Baedeker, *Jahrbuch für den Oberbergamtsbezirk Dortmund 1922/25* (Essen, 1925), p. 560, table XV.

43. Jüngst, "Zur Abwehr," p. 220.

44. Jüngst, "Zur Abwehr," pp. 219–20.

45. Werner Plumpe, *Betriebliche Mitbestimmung in der Weimarer Republik. Fallstudien zum Ruhrbergbau und zur Chemischen Industrie* (Munich, 1999) pp. 136–7; Karin Hartewig, "Anarchie auf dem Warenmarkt." Die Lebenshaltung von Bergarbeiterfamilien im Ruhrgebiet zwischen Kriegswirtschaft und Inflation (1914–1923)," in Klaus Tenfelde (ed.), *Arbeiter im 20. Jahrhundert* (Stuttgart, 1991), pp. 268–71; Berndt Weisbrod, "Arbeitgeberpolitik und Arbeitsbedingungen im Ruhrbergbau. Vom 'Herr im Haus' zur Mitbestimmung," in Gerald Feldman and Klaus Tenfelde (eds.), *Arbeiter, Unternehmer und Staat im Bergbau. Industrielle Beziehungen im internationalen Vergleich* (Munich, 1989), pp. 136–7.

46. Hartewig, "Anarchie," pp. 268–70.

47. *RK Wirth II*, Nr 362, p. 1072.

48. For a full discussion see Gerald Feldman, "The Reparations Debate" in this volume. Cf. Niall Ferguson, "The Balance of Payments Question: Versailles and After," in Manfred F Boemeke, Gerald D Feldman, and Elisabeth Glaser (eds.), *The Treaty of Versailles: A Reassessment after 75 Years* (Cambridge, 1998), pp. 401–40.

49. Among the many contributions to this discussion see: Denise Artaud, "Die Hintergründe der Ruhrbesetzung 1923. Das Problem der interallierten Schulden," *Vierteljahreshefte für Zeitgeschichte*, 27(2), 1979, pp. 246–7; Arthur Turner, "Keynes, the Treasury and French War Debts in the 1920s," *European History Quarterly*, 27/4, 1997, p. 514.

50. Dietmar Petzina, "Is Germany Prosperous? Die Reparationsfrage in der Diskussion angelsächsischer Experten zwischen 1918 und 1925," in Christoph Buchheim, Michael Hutter and Harold James (eds.), *Zerrissene Zwischenkriegszeit. Wirtschaftshistorische Beiträge. Knut Borchardt zum 65. Geburtstag* (Baden-Baden, 1994), pp. 241–62.

51. Stanislas Jeannesson, *Poincaré, la France et la Ruhr (1922–1924). Histoire d'une occupation* (Strasbourg, 1998), pp. 92–5.

52. For example: Adrien Dariac cited in Hans Spethmann, *Zwölf Jahre Ruhrbergbau . . ., iii. Der Ruhrkampf 1923 bis 1925 in seinen Leitlinien* (Berlin, 1929), pp. 31–2.

53. Thus: Nordrhein-Westfälisches Staatsarchiv Münster (StAM), Zentrale Nord. Nachrichtenstelle (ZN) Nr 55; Librarie du Progrès, *Die Zerstörungen in Nordfrankreich und der Wiederaufbau* (Paris, [1923?]), pp. 22–3; *Akten zur deutschen Auswärtigen Politik 1918–1945. Serie A: 1918–1925. Band VII, 1. Januar bis Mai 31, 1923*, ed. Hans-Georg Fleck, Peter Grupp and Roland Thimme, eds. (Göttingen, 1989), Arnold Rechberg an Hugo Stinnes. Abschrift. Berlin, Feb. 19, 1923, p. 211. See also: p. 213 n. 8.

54. Spethmann, *Ruhrbergbau iii*, appendix 5, pp. 314–5.

55. For example: Fischer, *Ruhr Crisis*; Jeannesson, *Poincaré*; Georges-Henri Soutou, "Vom Rhein zur Ruhr: Absichten und Planungen der französischen Regierung," in Gerd Krumeich and Joachim Schröder (eds.), *Der Schatten dees Weltkrieges. Die Ruhrbesetzung 1923* (Essen, 2004), pp. 63–83.

56. Hermann J Rupieper, *The Cuno Government and Reparations 1922–23: Politics and Economics* (The Hague, 1979), pp. 82–3; Barbara Müller, *Passiver Widerstand im Ruhrkampf. Eine Fallstudie zur gewaltlosen zwischenstaatlichen Konfliktaustragung und ihren Erfolgsbedingungen* (Münster, 1996), p. 114. However, Marshal Foch was among the French military leaders who were less sanguine.

57. Fischer, *Ruhr Crisis*, ch 3.

58. Fischer, *Ruhr Crisis*, pp. 108–17.

59. *Akten der Reichskanzlei. Weimarer Republik. Das Kabinett Cuno. November 22, 1922 bis August 12, 1923*, ed. Karl Dp.ietrich Erdmann, Wolfgang Mommsen, and Karl-Heinz Harbeck (Boppard am Rhein, 1968), Nr 47, Jan. 17, 1923, p. 155.

60. The Hochp.feld Bridge bombing. See Michael Ruck, *Die Freien Gewerkschaften im Ruhrkampf 1923* (Frankfurt am Main, 1986), p. 406.

61. Deutsches Bergbau-Museum Bochum, Bergbau-Archiv (BBA), Bestand 32: Hibernia Bergwerksgesellschaft, Herne (32)/4365, "Erschreckende Wirkungen der Verkehrssperre. Die Lebensmittelversorgung hört auf," *Kölnische Zeitung*, 516, July 23, 1923.

62. BBA 32/4365, "Englische Kohlen im Ruhrgebiet," *Kölnische Zeitung*, 540, Aug. 6, 1923.

63. HStAD R Dü 16345 (13–18), Aug. 19, 1923, III. Ernährungslage.

64. StAM Provinzialstelle für Landaufenthalt (PfL) Nr 3, Der Preußische Minister für Volkswohlfahrt. Betrifft: Aufnahme von Kindern der städtischen und Industriebevölkerung in ländlichen Familien, Berlin, Jan. 18, 1923; cf. Hartewig, "Anarchie," p. 271.

65. StAM ZN Nr 53, "Das Kinderelend im Industriegebiet. Der Einfluß der Rachitis und der Tuberkulose auf die Kinder im besetzten Gebiet." Undated.

66. Ibid.

67. Ibid.

68. HStAD R Dü 16584 (2–4), July 7, 1923.

69. Ibid.

70. StAM PfL Nr 3, Merkblatt für die Entsendung von Kindern zum Landaufenthalt. Undated.

71. Thus: StAM PfL Nr 24, Kreisausschuß des Landkreises Hörde. J.Nr.VII 446/23. Hörde, Feb. 2, 1923.

72. StAM PfL Nr 3, Zentralstelle für Kinderhilfe im Ruhr- Rheingebiet. Abt. Aufnahme. Berlin. Mar. 31, 1923.

73. Fischer, *Ruhr Crisis*, pp. 119–21.

74. Fischer, *Ruhr Crisis*, p. 133.

75. StAM PfL Nr 19, Konzept. Provinzialstelle für Unterbringung der Kinder. Nr 70. Münster, Feb. 23, 1923.

76. See note 70.

77. StAM PfL Nr 24, Der Magistrat. Jugendamt. Abt. VIIc. Betrifft: Landaufenthalt von Stadtkindern. Buer, Feb. 24, 1923; Stadt. Wohlfahrtsamt. Allg. Fürsorgeamt. J.Nr.IIa. Recklinghausen, Feb. 20, 1923.
78. StAM PfL Nr 24, Der Magistrat. Gesundheitsfürsorge. Tagebuch-Nr. IXb. Betrifft: Unterbringung von Kindern des besetzten Gebietes. Witten, Feb. 9, 1923.
79. See note 70.
80. StAM PfL Nr 3, Der preußische Minister für Volkswohlfahrt. Richtlinien für die Unterbringung von Kindern der städtischen und Industriebevölkerung auf dem Lande. Berlin, Jan. 18, 1923.
81. StAM PfL Nr 17, Caritas-Verband für das Bistum Paderborn. An die Provinzialstelle für Landaufenthalt von Stadtkindern in Münster i. W. Paderborn, Feb. 19, 1923.
82. Fischer, *Ruhr Crisis*, pp. 125–6.
83. StAM PfL Nr 24, Kreiswohlfahrtsamt. Betrifft: Bekleidung der Ruhrkinder. Guben, July 13, 1923.
84. Fischer, *Ruhr Crisis*, p. 133.
85. StAM PfL Nr 32, Amt Eickel. Gesundheitsamt. Tgb.Nr.I 8179. Betr. Messungen und Wägungen von Landkindern. Eickel, Mar. 18, 1923.
85. Thus: StAM PfL Nr 32, Der Amtmann. Nr P. Betrifft: Landaufenthalt 1923. Wanne, Apr. 6, 1924.
87. BBA 32/4371, Abschrift. Protokoll über die Besprechung der Arbeitervertreter der hiesigen 6 Schachtanlagen mit dem Kommandeur der Besatzungstruppe, Oberst Homgie, vom Infant. Regiment 147 [Jan. 23, 1923].
88. BBA 32/4364, Entschließung, quoted in "So reden Bergarbeiter," *Gelsenkirchener Allgemeine Zeitung*, Feb. 26, 1923.

REPARATIONS IN THE LONG RUN: STUDYING THE LESSONS OF HISTORY

Patricia Clavin

The long-running controversy over whether Germany could afford to pay reparations appears finally to be coming to an end. In his recent summary of the scholarly debate Conan Fischer quotes Gerry Feldman's typically pithy assessment that "the only people who really believed that the Germans could fulfil their reparations obligations . . . are some historians" and it is a fast declining number of historians at that.[1] The intention of this paper is to demonstrate that when it comes to what might be termed "historic" assessments of the German capacity to pay reparations, there were others who believed Germany could have met the demands made of it. During the Second World War, officials in the United States and Great Britain undertook an extensive study of the history of the reparations imposed on Germany in the wake of the First World War, with the intention of ensuring that their imposition after the Second World War would be more successful for all the parties involved. The work foreshadowed the much more rigorously evidenced scholarship of historians of German reparations in the subsequent half-century and, as well as providing us with the opportunity to revisit the historiography of German reparations, takes as its central pre-occupation the issues of enforcement and compliance that concern us in this volume. Both groups, government officials and historians, engaged in a sustained debate about how far the failure of the German reparation settlement was the result of German non-compliance or Allied weakness. Here important differences emerged between the two groups, a difference that reminds of the us of the ways in which present-minded concerns shape the interpretation of the evidence before policy-makers.

The decision to impose reparations against Germany once again was taken at the inter-allied conference held in Moscow in late 1943.[2] Among the self-styled United Nations, it was the Soviet Union which was the most determined to secure reparations, not just from Germany but also from her allies "to compensate for all the damage they had done during the war."[3] The Netherlands and Britain, too, staked an early interest in the subject, although they sought to speak for all interested parties, arguing that reparations should be made simultaneously to all claimant countries in agreed proportions of the total amount to be levied. Having suffered the most, it was predictable that the Russians took the view that compensation should be paid first to those countries that had suffered the greatest damage in proportion to their national wealth. This paper, however, will pay particular attention to the evolution of American policy on reparations in relation to that of other interested powers, and to the role of history in that policy, for a number of inter-related reasons.

Firstly, British policy on the topic sought largely to follow American policy in the hope that co-operation on reparations would help to secure a favourable American response to more contentious issues in Anglo-American relations, such as the future treatment of the Sterling Area. This is not to deny that, in private, there were notable and interesting differences between the two powers regarding the lessons to be drawn from the history of reparations imposed by the Versailles Settlement. The British were much less pre-occupied with learning such lessons, the only nod in such a direction being that any settlement should "appear just now and ten years hence," and that the term "reparation" itself was "charged with emotional content and suffer[s] from association with past failure." The British certainly assumed that the German territory on which payments were to be imposed would be unified, that payments should be made over as short a period as practicable, and that an "elastic formula" be used to determine German capacity to pay. (These last two points were subsequently adopted in American policy documents.) The British, on the whole, were much more focused on the internal condition of Germany, again adopting a much more present-minded approach, and were more favourable than the State Department and OSS to the notion of deliveries in kind (here there was a greater match with the US Treasury Department). They were also much less optimistic than the Americans regarding the ability of the Allies to control German economic output to secure reparations payments and much more suspicious of the USSR. As Keynes put it in a meeting with high-ranking US officials in September 1943: "Would anyone want German industry run by Soviet Commissars?"[4]

The second reason why the perspective of the United States is of particular interest lies in their conscious effort to study the question of reparation payments in a less self-interested fashion than other governments. As the administration recognized in 1944, the admissible claims it "would be able to present for reparation will in all probability be small in comparison with the claims of devastated nations."[5] The Americans' primary focus was expressed as "the bearing which reparations will exercise on the achievement of long-term peace aims."[6] This was a matter of considerable concern for the United States given what they regarded as both the "wide divergence of thinking" on reparations, and the troubling history of reparations after the First World War.[7] As we know, by 1948 the deterioration of East—West relations meant that those powers which were allied to and led by the United States abandoned further claims for reparation, a process facilitated by the Marshall Plan, in order to create a strong West Germany as a bulwark to Soviet expansion. By then many of the assumptions, strategy and tactics of American diplomacy, too, had changed significantly from those that had shaped American foreign policy planning during the Second World War. However, for some six years after the outbreak of war, it was widely anticipated that reparations would be levied against a defeated Germany. Accordingly the lessons of the Versailles Settlement were the subject of vigorous study by the United States government.

This American pre-occupation with the lessons of history is the third and final factor underpinning this paper's particular concern with American reparation policy during the Second World War. President Franklin D. Roosevelt often spoke of calling history to the bar as a bruised witness, to offer truthful testimony to help understand the economic and political crises of the interwar period, so as to develop more successful policies for the future.[8] The determination to learn and apply the lessons of history was a strong force in shaping the concepts and strategy of foreign policy during this period, and thus avoid what was seen as a disastrous chain-reaction after 1919: the failure of the diplomatic and economic order triggered by the Great Depression, the widespread collapse of liberal democracy around the world, and a bloody second world war waged within a generation of the first. Catastrophic though these developments were, they created an incentive and a window of opportunity for policy-makers to re-evaluate their existing policies towards Europe and to develop alternatives to them. Events after 1940 also helped to eliminate some policy choices that were no longer viable, notably isolationism, as well as providing a strong incentive to heed voices that sought to chart new paths in foreign policy.

Yet this emphasis on lesson learning is surprisingly absent from the historiography. Structural change, interest group politics or ideology form the dominant modes through which scholars have sought to account for the evolution of American foreign economic policy during the Second World War.[9] The American abandonment of the notion of collecting extensive reparations from Germany, in favor of waging a Cold War against the Soviet Union, is usually accounted for through the demise of the frequently misrepresented Morgenthau Plan for the treatment of Germany. The study of how the lessons of post-First World War reparations were developed, articulated, and their consequences for foreign policy reveal a new aspect of American policy towards post-war Europe.

Almost all the documentation regarding plans for the peace drafted by the range of competing agencies charged with developing America's post-war policies were infused by historical accounts of Germany during and after the First World War, the history of Germany's experience of reparations, and the challenges posed by interwar indebtedness as a whole. Among the range of official agencies involved in formulation US policy towards Europe were the Foreign Economic Administration (FEA), various State Department committees, the Research and Analysis Branch of the Office of Strategic Services (OSS), the US Treasury, a host of advisors linked with the White House, and the Board of the Federal Reserve in New York. Historians have strongly criticized the varied historical picture of Germany drawn by these sometimes-competing sets of American policymakers, arguing that this explains why US policy towards Germany at the end of the war remained incoherent. This emphasis on the failure of US policy toward Germany is misplaced however. The focus of all the agencies engaged in post-war planning was not so much how to manage Germany, but how to manage Germany in a significantly different international order from that created after the First World War.[10] It is within this broader context of how to reconstruct a new world order for political and economic relations that many of the reasons for American double-think in its policy towards Germany become clear.

When it came to the history of reparations, the lessons of history drawn by American advisors found their clearest expression in a lengthy document drawn up by the Executive Committee on Economic foreign Policy of the FEA entitled "The Reparation Problem: the Experience after World War One" which was charged with developing a "Viable Plan for Post-War Germany."[11] The report's opening statement was a significant indication that these students of history were not impervious to the perils of such an approach to policy-making: "The experience of the past, while not necessarily the basis for the formulation for the future, may serve to indicate avoidable errors." Any history professor marking a student essay on the practise of history would applaud their caution. Nor is it easy to dispute these amateur historians' two opening observations that: "Isolated measures and ingenious devices are not sufficient in solving the complicated problems of German reparation and that the main error of statesmanship after 1918 was that the war had been an unfortunate interlude rather than the cause of a shift in long run tendencies necessitating basic changes in national policies."[12]

The Committee waded through a great deal of evidence, but whittled its conclusions down to principally four political and seven economic lessons. The first political lesson was that the Allies' attempt to place German payment on a moral basis through the imposition of "war guilt," rather than the barefaced imposition of reparations as an indemnity payable by the loser, the established practise after earlier conflicts, constituted a grave error. "It gave a ready handle," the Committee argued, "to German propaganda and confused Allied opinion, helping to intensify the conflict between the former allies at a number of critical periods."[13] Echoing more recent work by professional historians, the American administration recognised during the Second World War that Wilson's Fourteen Points played an important role in opening the door to reparations. However, it also believed that Wilson himself concluded that the German peace terms imposed on Russia at Brest-Litovsk significantly compromised their validity, and that the inclusion of war widows' pensions and separation allowances (a British negotiating demand) in the Versailles settlement played a crucial role in fuelling German resentment.[14]

Divisions between the Allies regarding the volume and nature of reparations to be imposed, their subsequent attempts to put the payments onto a more stable basis during and after major crises, notably those of the Ruhr Occupation and the Great Depression, featured in a number of lessons drawn by American planners. They argued that a consistent commitment from the United States would have gone a long way towards resolving problems regarding the implementation of any settlement devised.[15] Interestingly, in recent decades international historians have shifted the national focus from the United States to the study of French policy, although the starting point of their work remans the eloquent and barbed critique of French policy articulated by John Maynard Keynes. Key studies include the works of Schuker, Trachtenberg and Jeanesson.[16] In 1944, there were further echoes of more recent research (Costigliola, Leffler, Kent and Clavin), when the impact of the problematic relationship between reparations and inter-Allied war debts on diplomatic and economic relations in the interwar period was condemned.[17]

American planners for post-war Europe stressed that the key reason Versailles failed was "the lack of consistency in policy and enforcement of the settlement." In the words of one State Department official in 1944: "Constant uncertainty in liberal quarters and a deliberate policy of sabotage among the revisionists, [meant that] Germany failed to make those internal economic adjustments which were necessary in a sincere effort to make reparation payments."[18] It was the lack of Allied will to enforce the settlement that made German compliance essential to the success of the 1920s reparations agreements. In the eyes of planners of the second postwar settlement, too much stress had been placed on safe-guarding German sovereignty: "Although military occupation occurred, it was assumed that economic controls would infringe too much on German rights." In 1944, all the planners agreed that: "In retrospect it is difficult to understand the failure after 1918 to control German economic life."[19] By the time these American lessons of history were drafted, the Second World War had made management of the economy an obvious fact of life. So much so, in fact, that no-one thought to look for instances of when control by an occupying power had failed to produce the desired results, such as the occupation of the Ruhr in 1923 (aspects of which are detailed elsewhere in this volume). Thus American planners condemned what they described as the 'insufficient effort' exerted by the Allies after 1918 to back up the liberal government in Germany, notably in what they regarded as the "first critical post-war months."[20]

Unsurprisingly, almost all of the political lessons drawn by the Americans at this stage in the war stressed the shortcomings of Allied, not German, policies when it came to ensuring a successful reparations settlement. This emphasis on enforcement rather than compliance speaks volumes for both the contex in which these lessons were drawn and the audience these authors sought to address. The same emphasis on Allied responsibilities and the international context of the reparations settlement can also be seen in the economic lessons of history determined by American post-war planners. The Allies of the First World War were castigated for their tardiness in developing a plan for collecting and distributing reparations. France was presented as a victim of this inter-Allied failure, for the delay permitted "the development of huge unpayable debts in France . . . [that] led to a growing emphasis on reparation as an aid to solving national fiscal problems." The deliveries in kind were judged to be of "relatively little assistance in the actual rebuilding." The view, of course, stood in sharp contrast to Henry Morgenthau Jnr's plan which envisioned a fundamental restructuring of the German economy based on extensive deliveries in kind. Britain, too, thought deliveries in kind would be important in facilitating early restructuring.[21] Similarly, the tendency of France and other recipient countries, who wanted to use reparations to resolve budget problems and to avoid increasing taxation, was presented as a failure on the part of all those present at the Paris Peace Conference, for only "prompt unified action by the creditor countries could have adapted reparation in a practical manner to reconstruction."[22]

When it came to the thorny question of whether Germany could afford to pay, the majority of American advisors believed that, on balance, it could. But, leaving aside Germany's apparent lack of political will to do so, they argued that the rudimentary understanding of monetary policy and fundamental weaknesses in the functioning of the international economy as a whole, in essence condemned any effort made to failure. The 1944 report on the lessons of the Paris Peace settlement broadly challenged "the widespread acceptance of the view that the total bill for reparation was too high." It examined Germany's ability to pay based on an assessment of the productive capacity of the German economy and its relationship with estimates for international trade during the period. In 1944 the general view was given that German productive capactiy (although what was understood by "productive capacity" is rather ambiguous) had outstripped that of Great Britain and almost equalled that of the United States after 1924, enabling Germany to meet its reparation obligations.[23]

Despite recognizing some of the serious weaknesses in the German economy, these wartime students, in contrast to present day scholars of German reparations, were strongly influenced by the performance of the German war economy in the Second World War. The Americans were especially impressed by Germany's ability to devote 60 per cent of its production to preparations for the war and to extract what they calculated to be around $12.8 billion of "tribute" from nine occupied countries by the end of September 1943.[24] Indeed, the efficiency of the German war economy thanks to what were described as "thoroughgoing totalitarian controls" (a characterisation since challenged by historians of Nazi Germany at war), was an essential element in American reparation calculations; different scenarios were developed depending on whether German capital equipment was subject to "heavy" or "moderate" devastation.[25] Ironically, however, the members of the Reparation Subcommittee, having castigated the Allies for their failure to promptly determine a feasible reparations sum in 1919, went on to experience similar diffulties themselves.

When it came to assessing the economic shortcomings of the reparations settlement, however, American planners in 1944 did not judge the central failings to be errors in fixing the appropriate sum or in determining Germany's capacity to pay—the main topics that have pre-occupied professional historians since. The former correctly identified many of the weaknesses in the German banking and fiscal systems and the unsettling role played by Dawes Plan loans, but put many of these problems down to a "lack of control by the Allies."[26] This stress on enforcement rather than compliance[27] also contrasts with most post-1960 historians of German reparations, who have emphasized, in varying measure, Germany's ability and/or will to comply with the reparation settlements of the 1920s.

Present-minded preoccupations, notably the clear determination to break with the past when it came to the poor performance of the international economy in the inter-war years, were the strongest influence on the composition of American lessons from the Versailles Peace Treaty. While scathing of what they condemned as the "rudimentary notions as to monetary relations held during and after the First World War," American policymakers sought to underline the ways in which the present was better than the past when it came to the management of economic relations: "It is sometimes forgotten that there were no national income series available, that there were no measures of production, that trade statistics were fragmentary, and that there was little understanding of the relation between budgetary practices, currency conditions, and the value of money on the exchanges."[28] In their words, "the history of the past twenty-five years indicates the need for a comprehensive and coherent plan carefully coordinated with both economic and political programs."[29]

This was one of two occasions on which the present was recognised as not only different to, but better than the past, and in both instances the lessons were articulated in such a way as to underline Americans' need to exert control over the circumstances in which a reparations settlement might be imposed. The second occasion related to policy-planners' criticisms of American lending to Germany in the 1920s. It was viewed as unproductive and working counter to the effective collection of reparations given the instability short-term loans helped to trigger by the end of decade. By 1944, American officials believed that it was "difficult in retrospect to see why this situation was allowed to develop as it did, but once it got out of hand it doomed to failure attempts to collect substantial reparation."[30] What is particularly remarkable about American self-criticism regarding its foreign policy in the 1920s, is not just that it resembles the views of many historians writing since 1945, but that it actually began to reflect the critique made of its foreign policy throughout the interwar period by a range of European statemen and intellectuals.

American lessons of history were not born in the USA. They were influenced by state to state dialogue between American and non-American politicians and government officials, but also by a wide variety of non-American experts in foreign policy, in economics, in finance and in history who shared and exchanged their ideas, skills and values across national boundaries during the interwar and war period. Here, study of the contribution of agencies originating outside the United States colours the better established and more substantial appreciation of the role played by key Americans and interest group constellations in US foreign policy.

The work of the Economic and Financial Organization of the League of Nations, arguably made an important contribution both before and during the Second World War, in generating an epistemic community or knowledge-based network of experts who shared a similar view as to the history of reparations in the interwar period. This helped the American government frame key issues, propose policy and provide a narrative to explain it to the general public.[31] A range of publications and individuals deserve to be mentioned, but most noteworthy were the efforts of Alexander Loveday, the Director of the Economic, Financial and Transit Department of the League of Nations who also served as the Director of the League's Princeton Mission during the war, and a series of League publications that explored the history of the interwar economy.[32] League-sponsored studies surface again and again in documents relating to American plans for the reparations settlement, as well as planning efforts more generally.

A group of what might be described as Keynesian critics of the reparation settlement, who, over time, had allowed their views of the post-war settlement to become infused with a particular understanding of the malfunctioning of the international economy as a whole, were a distinct, though integrated, group which intersected with the League.[33] As we have seen, Keynes' published view of the settlement in 1919 was by no means adopted wholesale by US post-war planners, but it was widely recognized in the United States that this perspective of the Versailles Treaty had, in the words of one American official, "a far reaching influence both in Germany and outside" with which it had to engage.[34] But it was Keynesian economics, far more than *The Economic Consequences of the Peace*, which shaped American reparation politics in the Second World War.

The League was connected to a further group of non-American foreign policy experts, many of whom had attended the Peace Conference. These were well networked through institutions like the Royal Institute of International Affairs (founded in 1920) and transnational educational schemes that sponsored the exchange of visiting professors, speaking tours and summer schools.[35] Most striking within the critique of Versailles embedded in the views and assumptions of this transnational community, and reflected in policy documents prepared by the American administration, was the strong link drawn between the malfunctioning of the international economy, the failure of American foreign economic policy, and the inability of Germany to meet the reparation demands imposed upon it. The successful enforcement of reparations demands after the end of the Second World War, it argued, was dependent upon stable international monetary relations, a reduction in the levels of international protectionism, and the absence of any complicating war debts. In the 1930s the Untied States had largely rejected this interpretation of the failure of Versailles; by the mid-1940s it formed a cornerstone of US policy towards reparations.

But this emphasis on the international system, and the need for Allied co-operation to impose a successful settlement—in other words the focus on enforcement rather than compliance—also left these American plans for a post–Second World War reparations settlement especially vulnerable once the Grand Alliance disintegrated at war's end. After 1945 the escalating Cold War altered the priorities of American and its allies. Together with the struggle to effect recovery in the German zones, these developments altered the Truman administration's perspective on whether the western occupied zones could afford to pay reparations. This is not to say that the United States did not take reparations from Germany and Japan, as it later claimed. As recent research by Martin Lorenz-Mayer eloquently demonstrates, the United States did very well out of confiscating German assets held both inside the United States and in neutral countries. German assets seized in the United States amounted to $98.6 million and were added to around $12.6 million secured from the neutral countries to whom Nazi Germany had economic and financial ties: Sweden, Portugal and Spain, Afghanistan, Tangiers, and Ireland. The most valuable assets were held in the first three countries, which participated in Allied agreements to varying degrees—Sweden alone liquidated all German assets in its country—but Switzerland, where extensive German assets were known to be held, never complied with this postwar process at all. (Interestingly, the lessons of legal history of 1919 were also extensively applied to inform the Allies' approach to neutral countries who previously had not recognized any Allied measures to expropriate German property in their countries.)[36]

Although some of the lessons drawn by American planners from the history of the post-WW1 reparations settlement during the Second World War were acutely observed, they should not be judged as history. The most recent and best studies of the impact of the reparations, including work by some of the authors also represented in this volume, draw out the very wide-ranging impact that reparations had on German political, social, cultural and economic life. Their studies underline that the real value of history as an explanatory tool lies in the richness of its recovery of the concrete life of the past. The best history does not seek to answer the type of specific questions posed by American policymakers and does not need fall prey to the temptation to oversimplify its conclusions in order to generate proposals for policy that appeal to a specific audience.

It is apparent in the minutes of the American reparation sub-committee that there was a significant pressure, some of it unconscious, to organize the lessons of history around simple and attractive themes that suited the audience for which they were being formulated. The determination to underline the value of an American commitment to internationalism caused these officials to play down the question of German compliance and to largely ignore the implications for reparations should the decision be taken to reconstruct Germany as a liberal democracy within an open international economy. History can provide the larger perspective that helps to understand the present and reshape the future—the broader observations of American planners mentioned at the start of this paper are a case in point. But we should always be cautious of the easy historical analogy used to win support for a particular cause. As propagandists have long recognised, it can so easily be made to serve as an emotive tool designed to captivate the emotion rather than the reason of its audience.[37]

NOTES

1. Conan Fischer, *The Ruhr Crisis, 1923–1924* (Oxford, 2003), pp. 17–18; Gerald Feldman, "Comment" in Manfred F. Boemeke, Gerald D. Feldman, and Elizabeth Glaser (eds.), *The Treaty of Versailles: A Reassessment after 75 Years* (Cambridge, 1998), p. 445.
2. The topic came under the auspices of the European Advisory Committee, which met in London.
3. Quoted in memorandum by Academician Eugene Varga, "Payment of Reparations by Hitler [sic.] Germany and Her Accomplices," *Information Bulletin, Embassy of the USSR*, stored in National Archives 2, Washington DC, Record Group (hereafter NARA RG 59), RG 59.3.8, Economic Committee, 1940–46, Box 49. The only other country to articulate such an open-ended approach to reparations in wartime with regard to both the range of damages sought and the countries they were to be sought against was The Netherlands.
4. The officials with whom Keynes met included: Averill Harriman, Adolf Berle, Dean Acheson and Leo Pasvolsky. For an American assessment of Britain's position, as well as British documentation, see NARA RG 59.3.8, Box 50, State Department memorandum, "British Thought on Reparations and Economic Security," Sep. 1943.
5. NARA RG 59.3.8, Economic Committee, 1940–46, Box 49, "Draft Memorandum on Part One, II, B, 3, of Agenda (Reparation I)," Feb. 18, 1944, authored by and for the Reparation Committee.
6. Ibid.
7. The United States were concerned that "some demand a stripped and prostrated Germany after this war, while others indicate that the primary motives will be the economic and commercial benefits to be derived by each nation from the reparation settlement in contrast with the long-term liberal objectives of those who wish to see a democratic Germany integrated into the economy of the post-war world." NARA RG 59.3.8, Economic Committee, 1940–46, Box 49, "Draft Memorandum on Part One, II, B, 3, of Agenda (Reparation I)," Feb. 18, 1944, authored by and for the Reparation Committee.
8. Patricia Clavin, "Shaping the Lessons of History: Britain and the Rhetoric of American Trade Policy, 1930–60," in Andrew Marrison (ed.), *Free Trade and Its Reception: Freedom and Trade* (London, 1998).
9. For an example of the structural approach, see Thomas Zeiler, *Free Trade. Free World. The Advent of GATT* (Chapel Hill, 1999). For the role of interest-group consetellations see Thomas Ferguson, "Industrial Conflict and the Coming of the New Deal: the Triumph of Multinational Liberalism in America" in Steve Fraser

and Gary Gerstle (eds.), *The Rise and Fall of the New Deal Order, 1930–1980* (Cambridge, Mass., 1992). For the role played by key individuals and ideology see, for example, John Lambert Harper, *American Visions of Europe. Franklin D. Roosevelt, George F. Kennan and Dean Acheson* (New York, 1994).

10. Michaela Hönicke is also right to argue that the "lack of fixed solutions and the multitude of interpretations and plans testify to the procedure of a democratic society and its sincere efforts to understand the problem posed by the enemy nation." See Michaela Hönicke, "Morgenthau's Programme for Germany," in Robert Garson and Stuart Kidd (eds.), *The Roosevelt Years. New Perspectives on American History, 1933–45* (Edinburgh, 1999), p. 168.

11. This particular report was drawn up by subcommittee three, a sub-division of the Interdivisional Committee on Reparation, Restitution, and Property Rights. Its membership comprised, P.S. Sandifer (PS), F.D. Plakias, E.D. Dulles and was chaired by Alger Hiss. It was established on December, 29 1943 and among the history books it consulted was Philip Mason Burnett, *Reparation at the Paris Peace Conference from the standpoint of the American delegation* (New York, 1940), 2 vols.

12. The point is well made simply in the title of Sally Marks recent study of the period: *The Ebbing of European Ascendancy. An International History of the World 1914–1945* (London, 2002).

13. NARA RG 59.3.8, Economic Committee, 1940–46, Box 49, Reparation Memo 11, Subcommittee 3, "The Reparation Problem: Experience after World War 1, Feb., 28 1944, p. 2.

14. For the current view see Arthur Link, *Wilson* (Princeton, 1967); Anthony Lentin, *The Versailles peace settlement: peacemaking with Germany* (Oxford, 2003); and Margaret Macmillan, *Peacemakers. The Paris Conference of 1919 and Its Attempt to End War* (London, 2001). Sally Marks reminds us that the inclusion of these allowances "did not expand the reparations pie but enlarged the British Empire's slice of it." See Sally Marks, *The Ebbing of European Ascendancy. An International History of the World 1914–1945* (London, 2002), p. 93. This was not noticed in State Department assessments of the topic. The committee based their assertions here on the book by Burnett, *Reparation* (reprinted New York, 1965).

15. Their views echoed best-selling historical studies of the day, notably Thomas A. Bailey's two widely read studies of the Paris Peace Conference and the League. Thomas J. Knock, *To End All Wars. Woodrow Wilson and the Quest for a New World Order* (Oxford, 1992), p. 272 notes the "extraordinary recovery" of Wilson's stock after 1941 for a season of three or four years culminating in Truman's announcement in the summer of 1945 that the Charter of the United Nations had at last vindicated Wilson.

16. Steven Schuker, *The end of French Predominance in Europe: The Financial Crisis of 1924 and the Adoption of the Dawes Plan* (Chapel Hill, 1976); Marc Trachtenberg, *Reparation in World Politics: France and European Economic Diplomacy 1916–1923* (New York 1980); and Stanislas Jeannesson, *Poincaré, la France et la Ruhr (1922–1924). Histoire d'une Occupation* (Strasbourg, 1998).

17. For problems this caused in the 1920s, see Frank Costigliola, *Awkward Dominion: American Political Economic and Cultural Relations with Europe, 1919–1933*

(Cornell, 1984). For the 1930s, see Patricia Clavin, *The Failure of Economic Diplomacy. Britain, Germany, France and the United States, 1931* (London, 1996); and Patricia Clavin, *Europe and the Great Depression, 1929–1939* (London, 2000), chs. 6 and 7.

18. NARA RG 59.3.8, Economic Committee, 1940–46, Box 49, Reparation Memo 11, Subcommittee 3, "The Reparation Problem: Experience after World War 1," Feb., 28 1944, p. 7.
19. Ibid. p. 8.
20. The Allies' failure facilitated the development of "a spirit of reckless opportunism among German industrial and financial leaders and a feeling of discouragement among the professional classes." See NARA RG 59.3.8, Economic Committee, 1940–46, Box 49, Reparation Memo 11, Subcommittee 3, "The Reparation Problem: Experience after World War 1," Feb. 28, 1944, pp. 8–9. For a modern echo see G. D. Feldman, *The Great Disorder: Politics, Economics and society in the German Inflation* (Oxford, 1993), passim.
21. See Wilfried Mausbach, *Zwischen Morgenthau und Marshall: Das wirtschaftspolitische Deutschlandskonzept der USA, 1944–47* (Düsseldorf, 1996). His work shows how Morgenthau's intervention marked the beginning of an intricate process of negotiations between different government departments.
22. NARA RG 59.3.8, Economic Committee, 1940–46, Box 49, Reparation Memo 11, Subcommittee 3, "The Reparation Problem: Experience after World War 1," Feb. 28, 1944, pp. 8–9.
23. This stands in contrast to assessments by Feldman, Borchardt, Temin, and Ritschl of German economic performance, but echoes *inter alia* the work of Marks, Schuker and Ferguson: Feldman, *Great Disorder;* Knut Borchardt, *Perspectives on Modern German Economic History and Policy* (Cambridge, 1991); P. Temin, *Lessons from the Great Depression* (Cambridge Mass., 1989); Albrecht Ritschl, *Deutschlands Krise und Konjunktur 1924–34. Binnenkonjunktur, Auslandsverschuldung und Reparationsproblem zwischen Dawes-Plan und Transfersperre* (Berlin, 2002). Ritschl's recent work returns to the problem of the transfer conditions imposed by the Dawes plan, the topic of extensive debate between Keynes and Ohlin in the 1930s. His view that the transfer (the means by which wealth could be transferred abroad) mechanism imposed by the Dawes plan was the main trigger for credit withdrawals within Germany is tempered by Balderston's study which emphasises that a mixture of elements triggered the collapse in investor confidence, notably the rise of the political Right, budgetary pressures and German efforts to secure concessions on reparations from the Allies. See: Theo Balderston, *The Origins and Course of the German Economic Crisis, 1928–1932* (Berlin, 1993). For a wartime American view of the so-called transfer problem, see NARA RG 59.3.8, Economic Committee, 1940–46, Box 49, Reparation Memo 11, Subcommittee 3, "The Reparation Problem: Experience after World War 1," Feb. 28, 1944, pp. 9–12. The Americans paid particular attention to Keynes' 1920 assessments as to Germany's capacity to pay in *The Economic Consequences of the Peace* (New York, 1920), pp. 104–46: NARA RG 59.3.8, Economic Committee, 1940–46, Box 49, Reparation Memo 11, Subcommittee 3, "The Reparation Problem: Experience after World War 1," Feb. 28, 1944, pp. 9–12. Scholars deploying a variety of evidence to suggest Germany had the

financial wherewithal to make the payments include, Sally Marks "The Myth of Reparations," *Cental European History*, 11 (1978); Stephen Schuker, *American 'Reparations' to Germany, 1919–1933* (Princeton NJ, 1988), and Niall Ferguson, "Constraints and room for manoeuvre in the German inflation of the early 1920s," *The Economic History Review*, 49(4) (1996).

24. American calculations here were influenced by Russian estimates. See V. Gay, "Certain Estimtes of the Plundering by Germany in Occupied Countries in Europe," *Foreign Trade (Organ of the USSR People's Commissariat of Foreign Trade, 1943)*, Nos. 7–8. Discussed in NARA RG 59.3.8, Economic Committee, 1940–46, Box 49, Reparation Memorandum 5, "First Report of Subcommittee 5 in Reparation, Restitution and Property Rights," Jan. 14, 1944. German wartime production was the basis on which the Americans calculated reparations in 1944: 'The reparation burden to be imposed on Germany should be calculated as a proportion of Germany's estimated national income. As a guide to determining this proportion, regard may be had to the average proportion of her income Germany has devoted to war and preparation for war over an agreed period, to estimates of necessary governmental expenditure and of supportable levels of taxation." NARA RG 59.3.8, Economic Committee, 1940–46, Box 49 Reparation Memo 12, Subcommittee 5, "Revised Report of Subcommittee 5 on the Amount of Reparation," Apr. 20, 1944, p. 1. It is difficult to compare these figures with more modern estimates of German wartime production, although no one would now argue that the German wartime economy was subject to thorough-going totalitarian control. W. Abelshauser in M. Harrison (eds.), *The Economics of the Second World War: Six Great Powers in International Comparison* (Cambridge, 1998) does not offer figures on tribute. Richard Overy, *War and Economy in the Third Reich* (Oxford, 1994), pp. 321–53, reveals that Göring, in particular, sought to condemn "wild confiscation." Instead, German strategy towards occupied Europe was a policy of direct investment in the region, with the expectation that the economic extension of "Germandom" should be properly co-ordinated. Rather than totalitarian control, there were plenty of complaints of "*Intrigenspielen*" over the management of territories.

25. NARA RG 59.3.8, Economic Committee, 1940–46, Box 49, Reparation Memo 12, Subcommittee 5, "Revised Report of Subcommittee 5 on the Amount of Reparation," Apr. 20, 1944, pp. 2–5.

26. NARA RG 59.3.8, Economic Committee, 1940–46, Box 49, Reparation Memo 11, Subcommittee 3, "The Reparation Problem: Experience after World War 1," Feb. 28, 1944, p. 11.

27. American planners treated the causes of the German inflation in a cursory fashion: "The effect of the reparation settlement on the value of the mark was at first ignored and then exaggerated. They recognized that a strong inflationary current was underway in Germany before reparations were imposed but dated it as beginning at war's end." Feldman has shown convincingly it began during the war. See Feldman, *Great Disorder*, pp. 25–98.

28. It was noted "the theories of economists were based mainly on the literature which was written after the Napoleonic wars and had been influenced only slightly so far by more recent books," notably Mitchell's *History of the Greenbacks*. The only economist who was noted by name was Keynes who, they

rightly argued, "had written little and was relatively unknown." NARA RG
59.3.8, Economic Committee, 1940–46, Box 49, Reparation Memo 11, Subcommittee 3, "The Reparation Problem: Experience after World War 1" Feb.
28, 1944, pp. 12–13.

29. NARA RG 59.3.8, Economic Committee. 1940–46, Box 49, Reparation Memo 11,
    Subcommittee 3, "The Reparation Problem: Experience after World War 1,"
    Feb. 28, 1944, p. 21.
30. NARA RG 59.3.8, Economic Committee, 1940–46, Box 49, Reparation Memo 11,
    Subcommittee 3, "The Reparation Problem: Experience after World War 1,"
    Feb. 28, 1944, p. 16.
31. Peter Haas, "Introduction: Epistemic Communities and International Policy
    Co-ordination," *International Organization*, 46(I) (1992), p. 27 and p. 3.
32. I am currently engaged in a sustained study of the work of the Economic and
    Financial Organisation of the League of Nations sponsored by the AHRB
    (Grant number APN 4009/APN12550). See, Patricia Clavin & Jens-Wilhelm
    Wessels, "An Idol of Gold? The League of Nations Gold Inquiry and the Great
    Depression, 1929–32," *International history Review*, XXVI (3) (2004); and
    "Understanding the Work of the League of Nations," forthcoming. Influential
    Economic and Financial Organisation publications included: *The Report of the
    Committee Appointed on the Recommendaton of the London Conference 1931*
    (Basel,1931); *The Transition from War to Peace Economy: Report of the Delega-
    tion on Economic Depressions*, (Part 1, serial no. 1943); *Commercial Policy in the
    Inter-War Period: International Proposals and National Policies. Part 1: An Histor-
    ical Survey; Part 2: An Analysis of the Reasons for the Success or Failure of Interna-
    tional Proposals* (September 1942); *The League of Nations and the Post-War
    Settlement* (Mar. 11, 1944); *The International Currency Experience. Lessons of the
    Interwar Period* (Apr. 1944) For an interesting discussion on US relations with
    the League between British and League officials see: PRO FO371/34519,
    minute of conversation with Loveday by Jebb, Mar. 23, 1943.
33. G.J. Ikenberry, "A world economy restored: expert consensus and the Anglo-
    American postwar settlement," *International Organisation*, 46(1) (1992),
    pp. 290–321. Also worth noting, the role of Vansittartists in shaping American
    perceptions of Germany in Hönicke, "Morgenthau's Programme," pp. 159–60.
    Although members of the Post-War Planning Committee certainly read
    Vansittart they could not be classified as Vansittartist. See their use of Robert
    Vansittart, *Lessons of My Life, by the Rt. Hon, Lord Robert Vansittart* (New York,
    1943), in NARA RG 59.3.8, Economic Committee, 1940–46, Box 49, Repara-
    tion Memo 11, Subcommittee 3, "The Reparation Problem: Experience after
    World War 1," Feb. 28, 1944.
34. NARA RG 59.3.8, Economic Committee, 1940–46, Box 49, Reparation Memo 11,
    Subcommittee 3, "The Reparation Problem: Experience after World War 1,"
    Feb. 28, 1944, p. 10.
35. Here the path-breaking study of the history of reparations by the Italian national
    economist and a former member of the reparations commission, Bresciani-Turroni
    is worthy of mention. First published in Italy in 1931, with its English publication
    in 1937, it was a widely read study of the link between reparations and inflation
    with a foreward by the British economist Lionel Robbins. See Constantino

Bresciani-Turroni, *The Economics of Inflation. A Study of Currency Depreciation in Postwar Germany* (London, 1937). It was reprinted in 1968. See also the commentary in Feldman, *Great Disorder*, p. 7; and Gerold Ambrosius, *Staat und Wirtschaft im 20. Jahrhundert* (Munich,1990), pp. 78–9. Although the first study of the topic was by the Princeton economist Frank D Graham, *Exchange, prices, and production in hyper-inflation: Germany, 1920–1923* (Princeton, 1930), Bresciani-Turroni's work was more popular because its conclusions were palatable. Bresciani-Turroni blamed the fall of the mark almost exclusively on German financial and monetary policy, Graham placed some emphasis on the role of reparations and, therefore, on the balance of payments. Graham also took some account of the international economic and financial architecture under which reparations were levied and his work was consulted by the American advisors.

36. The problem arose when a German company being liquidated by the Allies had offices and assets in a neutral country. I am very grateful to Martin Lorenz-Mayer for sight of an unpublished paper that has emerged from his Ph.D. thesis, "To Avert a Fourth Reich: The Safehaven Program and the Allied Pursuit of Nazi Assets Abroad" (Ph.D., University of Kansas, 2004).

37. Donald Rumsfeld's easy analogy between the resistance faced by troops in Iraq to the "dead-enders" (bands of Nazis who fought on after World War II), made at the end of his speech to the 104th Annual Convention of Veterans of Foreign Wars held in San Antonio 2003 fails to stand up to any serious scrutiny. See speech reported by T.A. Badger, Associated Press, August 26.

DISARMAMENT AND BIG BUSINESS: THE CASE OF KRUPP, 1918–1925

Klaus Tenfelde

I

One of the many lessons the two Iraq wars may have taught between 1990 and 2003 is the difficulties confronted by victorious powers when seeking to enforce disarmament agreements. Unless a complete surrender is achieved, as was the case in Germany 1945, the defeated nation will take action to preserve and reconstruct diplomatic and military power. Such action may include resistance against arms control, evasion or deception of control procedures, secret rearmament, and finally open breach of agreement. As in the case of Prussia in 1806, military defeat simultaneously may result in a major modernisation of military structures. In fact, German officials in 1919, during the Armistice and Versailles peace talks, remembered the consequences of the defeat against Napoleon, and therefore contemplated resisting and evading the arms control measures of the Allied forces.[1]

The following article deals with the consequences of such behavior and attitudes within heavy industry, exemplified by the case of the Krupp steel plant in Essen, and to a much lesser degree, the plants in Magdeburg and Kiel. Understandably, recent research on the social history of the Great War and its aftermath has paid much more attention to collective experiences, mental change and political attitudes, including the social and political consequences of demobilization, than to war production ant its transformation to peace industries, including the social and political consequences of disarmament at the end of the Great War.[2] None the less, the sheer mass and value of arms, and the associated manufacturing capacity being abandoned or destroyed in the process of disarmament, were very considerable. This did not concern the defeated nations alone by any means, but disarmament control as decreed by the famous Chapter V of the Versailles Treaty meant an almost complete abandonment of weaponry of all kinds by Germany, and of facilities and capacities to plan and to produce such weaponry. Germany, it should be stressed, was the most heavily armed nation within Europe, whether before or immediately after the Great War. Thus, beside the questions of national pride and honour surrounding the peace conditions in general and Chapter V in particular, the process of restructuring war industries promised to hit the national economy severely at the end of the war. This included the problem of how to deal with huge masses of increasingly obsolete weaponry, and the unavoidable challenge inherent in converting factory halls constructed during the war solely for the sake of production of large cannons or submarines. Among the many private business companies that had served war needs, weapons producers needed to undergo fundamental changes in their production, employment, and market strategies.

Research on the process of disarmament, and on Allied control mechanisms, was carried out back in the 1960s when Michael Salewski published a ground-breaking study; a decade later, Ernst-Willi Hansen investigated the role of heavy and armaments industries in the reconstruction of German war capacities between 1923 and 1932.[3] Both authors made intensive use of diplomatic and administrative sources, but did not consult company records. To my knowledge, a case study of the reactions of private enterprise based on company records does not exist.[4] Such a study would of course have to select from among those company records that have become available, particularly from enterprises that were involved almost exclusively in armaments and ammunition production, such as Krupp, but would have to take into account related industries such as Daimler, Bosch, or Siemens. We do have studies of these companies, but the disarmament question is largely neglected. Within recent comprehensive studies of the Weimar Republic disarmament is mentioned at best, rather than treated in detail. Thus, for instance, within the most recent exploration of German history between 1914 and 1949, Hans-Ulrich Wehler's *Deutsche Gesellschaftsgeschichte*, the problem is not mentioned at all.[5]

The following article seeks to address this deficit, beginning with an abbreviated outline of the role of Krupp in Germany's armament industry at an early stage. I shall then deal very briefly with the process of demobilisation and the so-called "rearrangement" (*Umstellung*) of production at company level between November 1918 and the mid-1920s. A further section will deal with the Inter-Allied Military Control Commission (IMCC) and its sub-department within the Krupp steel plant in Essen. Thereafter I shall attempt to outline the measures of deception and evasion practiced at company level, while also considering the influence of government policy and the company's responses to this. This account relies heavily on company records, but despite of the richness of such records in general, and in the case of Krupp in particular, source material on disarmament and on attempts to deceive and evade control measures, are scarce for obvious reasons.[6] There is no compact body of relevant archival material available, necessitating the reconstruction of the story from a very diverse range of sources.[7]

II

Salewski notes that early in 1919, during Armistice negotiations and during preparations for the peace conference, Lloyd George asked Marshal Foch whether the destruction of the Krupp works would suffice to meet French desires for security against a German military recovery.[8] Salewski believes that this may have been meant "rhetorically" but from here it becomes understandable that French and Belgian occupation of the Rhineland and, in 1923, of the Ruhr industrial district, aimed not only at the enforcement of reparations, but also had in mind the control of the heart of Germany's armament industries.[9] During the exercise of disarmament controls, military occupation in case of non-compliance was considered by the Allies, and feared by Germany, on several occasions, and it may be recalled that the disarmament issue was prominent among the motifs and aims of the notorious Kapp *Putsch* in March 1920. In fact, the British occupation forces during and after 1945 remembered all too well the role of Krupp during the Great War, and for many years blocked the reconstruction of the large Krupp plants by a varied range of decisive measures.[10]

At the outbreak of war in 1914, Krupp had some 42,000 employees in Essen and 81,000 employees in total, including those at the Grusonwerk in Magdeburg and the Germaniawerft in Kiel as well as in several minor operations elsewhere. Magdeburg had been taken over in the 1890s to ensure Krupp's monopoly position in the production of armoured plate (*Panzerplatten*), whereas in Kiel, Krupp intended to play a decisive role in shipbuilding and thereby take advantage of the imperial fleet construction programme.

All in all, from the 1860s the company became an increasingly significant force within the German and international armaments industries.

Krupp took pride in convincing the Prusso-German military establishment that canons produced from a special brand of steel, the production of which was considered to be a company secret, was very much superior to weaponry made from bronze, or any kind of lower quality steel. While this kind of steel (*Tiegelstahl*) had laid the foundations of the steel casting works, providing high quality materials especially for specialised tools and for the railway system, war production increased from 1870 and made up a considerable part of the company's overall output prior to 1914. In terms of exports, too, Krupp came to be regarded to be one of the four or five major European producers of large-scale weaponry in the pre-war period. Others included Schneider-Creuzot, Vickers, Armstrong, and Skoda.[11]

Internally, the company clearly distinguished between peace and war materials, and drew up its balance sheets accordingly. Within the very high levels of turnover reflected in the balance sheets, the percentage dedicated to war production fluctuated markedly from year to year, from between 53 per cent in the 1880s to 22 per cent at the beginning of the twentieth century. Speaking generally, war material constituted a higher percentage of output in the 1890s than in the immediate pre-war period. That said, it should be noted that the total turnover of the company increased from around 100 million Marks at the turn of the century to some 400 million Marks during the last peacetime business year, 1913/1914. Thus war production also rose considerably between 1900 and 1914 and further significant revenue was generated by the export of weaponry. In addition, profits gained from the production of war materials considerably outweighed those from tracks, engines, or tools and the like.[12] Krupp had decided at an early stage to concentrate on the construction of heavy weaponry, especially large calibre cannons. The company admitted some competition in the field of small calibre armaments, but pistols and rifles or machine guns were not produced by Krupp. Instead, weapon systems such as submarines and fortress defences ranked high. Before 1914 the production of ammunition was of minor importance, but Krupp held an important patent on fuses for grenades, which he even licensed to Vickers before 1914. As a result German soldiers suffered at the hands of German technology, and the royalty payments arising from this dubious business were still being honoured in the early 1920s. Beyond this, it must be kept in mind that the distinction between output for peace and war is unreliable. How, for example, do we categorise strategically significant railway materials? Even the IMCC throughout its existence remained somewhat vague about the very nature of war materials.

During the war, of course, priorities changed fundamentally. It must be said here that the assignments drawn up for the Krupp units in case of war ridiculously underestimated the necessities. In the event of mobilisation,

Krupp was expected to deliver additionally cannons valued at some 13 million Marks, to be produced over a period of no less than twenty-nine months. In addition, some production of ammunition was expected, but without demanding any additional effort on the part of the company. However, the immense need for ammunition became clear even during the first weeks of war, and at the end of the second year of hostilities, Krupp's war production already reached one billion Marks.

After twelve months of warfare, the Krupp management was convinced that the company had managed a successful transformation of the company to war demands.[13] Whereas during the immediate pre-war years, exports of war materials had comprised some 32 percent of the total production of the same, and the export of peace products counted for some 18 per cent of total output, virtually all exports ceased immediately at the beginning of the war because of the allied blockade. From then on, exports amounted to less than one per cent of output, and were delivered exclusively to German allies. Interestingly, the company's capacity for war production prior to 1914 far exceeded peacetime demands. Less than 30 per cent of cannon production facilities were utilised prior to 1914, less than 50 per cent of ammunition capacity, and less than 25 percent for the production of fuses. Considering the enormous profits the company as a whole had made prior to 1914, it is noteworthy that such profits were obtained despite low levels of capacity utilisation. This is not the place to embark on a discussion of war profits which, as is well known, played a significant role in Reichstag debates during the war and thereafter.[14] Yet it is clear that in the case of Krupp, war dividends were kept at a politically acceptable level, which provided the company with enormous sums for reinvestment. Contrary to other industrial companies, or institutions such as the big cities, investment in new company facilities, in company housing and even in real estate was continued and perhaps even increased during the war. Krupp was confronted by the need somehow to conceal war profits.

With regard also to raw materials, the company was well equipped to meet war demands. Considerable sums had been invested to stockpile ores that the company was able to maintain even during the war; during the final days of hostilities supplies were sufficient to maintain war production at least for one more year. This even applied to precious metals, which were indispensable for steel refining. In addition, the company gained a privileged position when, in 1915, a controlled raw materials economy was introduced. Certainly shortages occurred, particularly in fields where they had not been expected. This was especially true in the case of lubricating oil. Beyond this, extraordinary measures were called for to ensure supplies of rubber and manganese ore, the first being transported from the United States by an especially constructed freight submarine, the latter transported by rail and routed in conspiratorial manner through southern France.

Thus the Krupp factories were certainly well prepared for a complete transformation to the demands of war goods production. This accorded with the conviction of the owner and management (reinforced by Krupp's personal, special relationship to the monarchy and establishment politics) that in case of war the company would have unreservedly to serve the fatherland. Among the war producers, Krupp remained privileged throughout. This became obvious when the company demanded additional labour resources, a problem common to every industrial effort during the war. Krupp was favored repeatedly and even more obviously when the question of wartime food supplies came up. The introduction of the Hindenburg programme in the fall of 1916 was an especially interesting example of the above. Gustav Krupp von Bohlen und Halbach had been informed of the programme well in advance of a meeting of leading industrialists in Berlin in September 1916, and during a railway journey on September 9 met Hindenburg and Ludendorff who personally informed him about future military needs and expectations. Krupp himself apparently consented unreservedly to the developments that ensued and there is no doubt that an agreement concerning the provision of a sufficient work force was reached simultaneously.

The expansion that was set in train following these rather intimate agreements turned out to be gigantic. A massive programme of plant construction was launched to expand output of weaponry and ammunitions. Leaving aside the finer detail of the construction programme, the results were as follows. During the war, Krupp received orders for war materials valued at 4.170 billion Marks, and the company delivered war materials valued at 3.310 billion Marks; thus orders for some 860 million Marks remained unfulfilled—a burden that would have to be dealt with during the post-war years. Recent research estimates the war expenditure of the German Reich at 164 billion Marks, of which some 17 billion Marks were dedicated to war debt services; war expenditure in Germany rose from some 15 percent of the Gross National Product during the first year of war to some 70 percent by the end.[15] It is clear therefore that the Krupp combine received well above two per cent of the Reich's war expenditure.

The efforts to execute the Hindenburg programme provide a valuable insight into the financial conditions of war production in this specific enterprise. Under an agreement signed on January 29, 1917 between Krupp and the Reich government, down payments on war orders were achieved for the first time, thereby securing financial planning and making it possible for payments to reach the company even after the Armistice. The Reich further agreed to support the construction programme on company sites with a subsidy of some 55 million Marks. In addition Krupp, for the first time in decades, raised a bank credit to the amount of 43 million Marks. The costs of the Hindenburg construction programme, which led to a doubling of the company's production facilities between 1917 and 1919, cannot be established precisely, but the programme, obviously, had to be continued even after the end of war just to complete construction projects. These costs were met out of company reserves to an overwhelming extent.

Some figures must be added to shed light on the results of the construction programme. Employment at the company's facilities had doubled by January 1917 to around 83,000 in Essen and 133,000 in total, and peaked in July 1918 at 169,000. Understandably, prisoners of war were employed only to a small extent in the production of war materials, but more significantly within the mines and steel casting works, although conscripted workers from Belgium had to be released in early 1917 because of international intervention with which the Reich government had to comply. Some 105,000 employees crowded the company's sites in Essen during 1918, where, for the first time, Krupp had to employ female workers, especially in the production of ammunition. Krupp was confronted by considerable turnover rates within its workforce, and had to house thousands of workers, necessitating the provision on a grand scale of camp housing, clothing and food. The yearly production of large calibre heavy cannons rose to no less than 6,400 in 1917/18, and the production of ammunition rose from 4.5 million tons to 23.8 million tons during the last year of war. These achievements allowed the German war effort to rely entirely on domestic production throughout the war.

III

These figures make plain the scale of transformation that had to take place following the Armistice. In contrast to most of the large industrial plants during the weeks of transition, Krupp very consciously decided to carry out the demobilization of the company within the shortest possible time period. Keeping the workers at their place of work place was regarded as a contribution to the maintenance of calm during the post-war revolutionary period, but in addition, it was feared that the many foreign workers in Essen might contribute to whatever unrest resulted from the establishment of soldiers' and workers' councils. Following intensive deliberations that began in mid-October 1918, a program of release was set up. This "social" disarmament, was realized within approximately six weeks. Krupp decided to keep those 21,000 workers and white collar employees who had been on the payroll on January 1, 1914, and in addition to reemploy another estimated 6,000 to 8,000 workers including the injured who had been serving in the army during the war. These were the 30,000 people who were considered to form the "core labor force" (*Arbeiterstamm*) of the company in Essen. Therefore, some 70,000 workers had to be released. The company made it attractive for those who wanted to disappear as soon as possible, and put a degree of pressure on those who hesitated, so that as early as spring 1919, a potential demand for skilled workers emerged. To an extent, this renewed need resulted from the introduction of the eight-hour shift as decreed by the November Revolution. All in all, therefore, 42,000 male and 24,500 female workers left the company between November 1918 and January 1920. Many of the male workers went into mining where jobs were offered early in 1919. As a result of the strenuous efforts to scale down the workforce, Krupp successfully kept the revolutionary events somewhat at a remove from company premises.

The transformation to peace industries sometimes proved much more difficult. The shipyards in Kiel went into crisis from which they were not to recover throughout the Weimar Republic. However, in Magdeburg, where prior to 1914 peace production had prevailed, transformation took place rather smoothly, while the iron cast works in Duisburg adapted successfully because of an increase in the demand for steel, not least thanks to inflation which allowed for cheap production costs, and even for the recovery of foreign markets within a surprisingly short time.[16]

Thus it can be said that two important preconditions of a successful transformation into peace production were met. First, the company energetically solved the problem of war-related over-employment, and secondly the ongoing inflation improved market conditions facilitating a successful re-entry into foreign markets. With regard to subsequent developments, four issues must be considered:

First, the Armistice agreement basically decreed the retreat of the German army from foreign territory and the Allied occupation of the western bank of the Rhine, not forgetting the treatment of the German naval forces. Though the Allied forces, of course, were intent on disarming Germany, concrete proposals only emerged during the peace talks and preliminary negotiations that began in February 1919. Thus the extent to which German industry would be affected became increasingly clear only from spring 1919.

That said, decisive steps to restructure the processes of production were called for anyway. During the war, the Krupp management was aware, of course, that were Germany victorious, the level of weapons production within the company would also have to be scaled down once peace returned. Thus, apparently, many of the large factory halls constructed during the Hindenburg program were also expected to serve product lines in peace time. Yet the nature of such products remained completely undecided. As early as December 6, 1918, the management issued a memorandum to the Krupp employees asking for ideas for peace production. Thousands of proposals were submitted, and quite a few of them were realised more or less successfully. Most successfully, Krupp subsequently turned to the construction of trucks of various sizes; plans to construct railway locomotives proved less successful, despite the early encouragement of large orders from the Reichsbahn, and later from the Soviet Union. Though the management correctly expected textile industries to experience a major recovery after the end of war, the attempt to produce textile machinery proved a failure because of a lack of technical experience and market knowledge. The manufacture of agricultural machinery generated some profit, while railway equipment, especially tracks and wagons, became important again. Among the many suggestions could be mentioned Krupp's successful production of mechanised cash registers and film cameras, but when it came to counters for coal production the traditional procedure of counting underground production with the simple help of chalk proved less expensive. Another line of production became highly profitable when Krupp decided to produce dentures from a special steel alloy; the so-called "teeth hospital" that produced such aids became briefly famous.

For all this, however, the company's traditional strengths became dominant again in the post-war years. Iron and steel were badly needed, and thus the Rheinhausen and Essen works soon recovered. A lack of capital postponed important investment in modernized methods of steel production, with the Borbeck steel casting works only coming on stream in 1929. Finally, the transformation led to a rising employment levels as early as late 1919, and in 1922 Krupp clearly worked profitably, though the management knew that an important part of the recovery was due to the market niches provided by inflation.

Secondly, from the time of the Armistice negotiations German industrialists were well informed about the proceedings at the peace conference that led to the famous section V of the Versailles Treaty.[17] In his famous note of January 10, 1919, Marshall Foch informed the Allied forces that military control would have to include control of the German defence budget, of the industrial budget, of the organisation of the general staff and military training, the reduction of military forces and the structure of further recruitment, of surviving war material, and Germany's armaments production capacity. Finally, even ethical guidelines of a sort were envisaged, to include the content of the school curriculum.[18] During the following weeks prolongation of the Armistice became a problem, and the Allied forces became increasingly worried about the continuing threat posed by German war material which provided a potential basis for resuming hostilities. Indeed, war material was continuously manufactured by Krupp well into 1919! To a degree, this seems to have been a consequence of the Hindenburg agreement and the procedure of orders and down payments that demanded completion, but the need to keep factories running may also have played a role. Krupp officials were invited to participate in the various German delegations to negotiate the armistice and peace agreements, and later on those on reparations, but the management hesitated, and Gustav Krupp himself refused several government demands to represent German industries in Spa or elsewhere.[19] That said, sufficient information on forthcoming regulations existed, and throughout 1919 the company had ample opportunity to prepare for the execution of military control and evade its consequences.

Thirdly, during preparations for the above, close contacts existed between the Berlin government and the Essen management. Thus, for example, Krupp asked Berlin how to treat the expected demand to hand over blueprints for the construction of heavy weaponry. Berlin responded that such materials should certainly only be handed over reluctantly. For decades, Krupp had employed a huge establishment dedicated to the construction of war material, which must have been present in abundance, but with plenty of time available to dispose of such material in an appropriate way. Both Berlin and the Krupp management clearly agreed in essence to respond reluctantly to Allied demands. In addition, legislation had to be passed by the Reichstag to define war material, and to prohibit future exports and imports of the same, but such legislation was only approved on December 22, 1920[20]—by which time Allied Control Mission had already been operating for a year.

Fourthly, one of the major problems faced by the company concerned the maintenance and preservation of know-how in the construction of weaponry. Shortly after the war Krupp decided to draft an extensive memorandum, describing and justifying the company's war effort. Through this the company constructed its own "stab-in-the-back" legend to make clear to everybody that Krupp's management and employees had done everything to ensure victory. The wartime civil service, its decision making processes and weak administrative structures were held accountable, whereas the company had completely devoted itself to war aims. The memorandum consisted of some thirty-five type-written volumes, and on several occasions Krupp considered its publication.[21] This huge work maintains throughout that the immense staff hitherto employed in armaments production would have to be re-trained for civil production. Many of these people could have been dismissed, but apparently, Krupp preferred continuous occupation in this or some other way. This accorded with traditional company practice that white collar employees enjoyed a job for life.

For decades before the war, the construction offices (*Konstruktionsbüros*) of the Krupp company had enjoyed an enviable reputation. From the earliest days of the war Krupp cannons such as "Big Bertha" (*Dicke Bertha*, 42 cm) that smashed the Liège fortifications, boosted the pride of the German artillery. Krupp's engineering capacities were reaffirmed when "Long Gustav" (*Langer Gustav*), a cannon of tremendous size, later bombarded Paris from a distance of more than 100 kilometres. The archives provide no clue regarding the fate of the enormous volume of construction materials that must have been kept within the Essen offices, or at the shooting range in Meppen where, since the 1860s, the company had tested the penetrative power of grenades as well as the strength of armoured plate.

IV

An advance commission of the International Military Control Commission arrived in Berlin on September 15, 1919, and the main commission started work in January 1920. The staff included 291 officers, 88 interpreters and 654 additional personnel. The commissions on naval and aviation control worked relatively autonomously, whereas the IMCC set up district commissions that came into being no earlier than May 1920. Krupp had to deal with such district commissions in Kiel, Münster, and later in Essen where the body comprised eight control officers, six of whom were British, two French.[22] Over the following five years, the Essen commission, which in effect enjoyed unlimited powers of control, remained within the huge company district. Krupp responded with relatively detailed instructions on how to deal with unannounced inspections as early as January 13, 1920. The commissioners would be met with delaying tactics, if possible, until the company's central offices had approved compliance. Additionally it was recommended that senior personnel should only respond to questions within the area of their immediate responsibility. Within individual factories and offices, lists of all kinds of machines and items that could be covered by the term "war material" were to be kept available. Such lists were demanded by the IMCC in general, to include raw materials "which have been prepared specifically for the manufacture of war goods"—a broad notion. Yet an important distinction could be made: the lists were to include material possessed by the company; while other lists would include material possessed by third parties, such as material or products already sold.

Particular attention was paid by the IMCC to machines that could, potentially, be used to manufacture weapons. It seems that the company took some advantage of the fact that the responsible IMCC sub-commission mainly consisted of British officers. In February 1920, Colonel Longhorne informed the company that the commission would disregard the previous sale of machinery, whatever the destination, but would have to control future sales. In spring 1920 the IMCC formulated demands for all construction blueprints relating to naval warfare, in an extensive list that was translated by the press office of the War Ministry (*Nachrichtenstelle des Reichswehrministeriums*). As the Ministry observed appositely, it had been anticipated that the Entente would pursue demands for the submission of blueprints "to the utter limits," but now, an "unconditional disclosure of our whole intellectual property" was demanded. It could therefore be "reasonably assumed" that the Allied forces, under "the pretext of the peace agreement, wanted to appropriate our intellectual property so as to catch up effortlessly with Germany's technological lead in specific areas." This consideration lay at the heart of German resentment regarding the activities of the IMCC, over and above any injury to national pride.

When the Essen sub-commission came into being during May 1920, Colonel Everett was appointed executive officer. It remains unclear to what extent the members of the sub-commission exerted their rights of control, but in fall 1920, "because of unpleasant events," Krupp's management was obliged to instruct all factories to take pains to locate war materials previously abandoned and forgotten within the huge factory district. Unfortunately only fragmentary evidence exists regarding visits by the control officers to the various facilities located inside and outside the company district, including the Annen and Rheinhausen works, and the shooting range in Meppen. The management apparently sought to ensure that the control officers discovered what could not be hidden, whilst overlooking what could be concealed within the factories or elsewhere. Of course the commission met with distrust and rejection wherever they made their appearance, added to which public opinion was unanimously hostile and bolstered by official German protest notes, appeals to the public within Germany and abroad, and memoranda drafted by the industrialists' associations and trade unions.

The commission also supervised the destruction of weaponry, ammunition, any other war materials, and any machinery capable of producing armaments. The intensity of such activity bordered on the ridiculous. The little museum of artillery that had been established in the time of Alfred Krupp, and extended on the occasion of the anniversary celebrations in 1912, fell victim when inspections were resumed in the fall of 1924. Colonel Everett protested repeatedly that the collection was much too extensive, the partial destruction of the guns exhibited was insufficient, and that an imminent visit from the Berlin commission—"mainly French people"–would certainly demand further measures. Thus all barrels (*Geschützrohre*) would have to be rendered completely unusable by an incision of at least eighteen inches. Also, in late 1924, there was fierce debate over what kinds of machinery and in particular how many machines would be needed to produce heavy calibre guns for the German army within the parameters of the Versailles Treaty. The latter permitted the manufacture of four artillery pieces below and four above a calibre of 30.5 cm per year. Finally, compensation for the destruction of assets on government orders remained on the agenda. Apparently, Krupp officials had to be persuaded that these assets had of course become so devalued that complete compensation was out of the question.

From all these measures it is possible to discern the volume and range of Germany's armaments at the end of the Great War. The IMCC oversaw the destruction in total of six million rifles, 105,000 machine guns, 28,000 mine mortars, 55,000 artillery pieces, 39 million shells and related ammunition, 490 million rounds of rifle and pistol ammunition, 14,000 aircraft and 28,000 aircraft engines.[23] At the Krupp company sites in Essen, of course, guns and cannons of any kind were destroyed, including 159 that were used for artillery trials. In addition, 379 large pieces of equipment such as cranes, ovens and containers, ten thousand machines, and 800,000 tools and minor pieces of equipment were destroyed. In addition 120,000 cubic metres of concrete fabrications were demolished. Special machinery had to be constructed to carry through this programme, not to forget the considerable number of workers it must have employed.

The IMCC delivered a final report in February 1925, which demanded the destruction of no less than an additional forty-eight huge lathes (in the course of discussions the number was reduced to some twenty-four) that had been used to prepare and refine cannon barrels. These lathes were among the biggest ever constructed. Krupp maintained that they were now used to produce hollow cylinders to store chemicals, but it was well known that other than Krupp, only Armstrong in Britain could produce such cylinders. Thus it was suspected that the IMCC demanded destruction under the pretext of disarmament, but in fact again wished to undermine German industrial competitiveness. Accordingly, the charge of industrial espionage passed from within industry into wider public opinion, leading dubious people, such as Vivian Stranders,[24] to try and prove such accusations. However, the lathes could easily be redirected to their original purpose, and they were therefore destroyed. The company may even have welcomed this measure because new tools could be constructed, and the government asked to compensate.[25] Indeed, such compensation was granted, but essentially in response to the deep financial crisis that hit the company during the stabilisation crisis of 1924 and 1925.

V

Issues surrounding industrial competition may have played a role in the above, but the Krupp company simultaneously tried to evade the IMCC's demands and control procedures, and even to violate disarmament regulations as they had been laid down by Chapter V of the Versailles agreement. It is this aspect of arms control that I shall consider in conclusion.

Apparently, Gustav Krupp did not tolerate any kind of arms production in Essen beyond what was allowed by the peace agreements. He reacted cautiously to the presence of the sub-commission of the IMCC, and above all, the company's location itself seemed vulnerable following the occupation of the Rhineland by French troops. Berlin officials repeatedly suggested transferring parts of the Essen operation to the heart of Germany where, in Magdeburg, an appropriate site already existed. Such suggestions became the more urgent when the Ruhr was occupied in 1923, leading to the military imprisonment of Gustav Krupp and several of his company managers. Apparently, Krupp decided in favour of family traditions which maintained that Essen should be the major site of production. Despite many suggestions completely to reorganise the company along more modern legal and structural lines, Krupp therefore adhered also to the old and hardly efficient family structure of the company as a whole. Only during the occupation in 1923 was a formal legal subdivision invoked that made Berlin a company site so that in case of expropriation by the occupation forces, legal titles could be kept.[26]

We can discount entirely another possible means of continuing arms production. Though Krupp invested modestly in the Soviet Union, and received an order from Moscow to manufacture a substantial number of locomotives, the company did not relocate there any kind of arms production. Zeidler's investigation of the relations between the German and Red Armies in the 1920s found no such evidence, and while the Krupp records may indicate some deliberation, it is clear that no substantive agreements followed.

However, Krupp remained or became active elsewhere.[27] First, there was the longstanding relationship with the Netherlands, be it through the export of weaponry, or through trade and financial relations. During the war, the Dutch had ordered new cannons and blueprints for a major new warship; contracts which demanded completion. The Netherlands had also granted refuge to the Kaiser, to whom the Krupp family had displayed strong loyalty. The culture of the two countries was alike, and many personal ties had existed prior to 1914. Though no clear indication of such activities appears in the records, it is quite obvious that Krupp used the months between the Armistice and the point when the Versailles Treaty came into force to relocate weaponry, construction plans and machinery from Essen to the Netherlands. Thanks to a strong Dutch currency, the Netherlands also served as a depository for financial assets during the inflation. Since the construction of submarines was prohibited, Krupp sold construction plans to Japan, and sent his chief engineer from Kiel to Amsterdam where a shipyard company was established. This proved relatively unsuccessful, but it seemed important to preserve the relevant know-how in any way possible. An outstanding order to construct a number of guns for the Dutch army was shifted to production facilities in Sweden. Additional equipment required to fulfil this order was produced in the Netherlands by a Siemens company established precisely for this purpose.

Secondly, Sweden was to become a prominent location for investment. Once again, Krupp relied on traditional relations, here to AB Bofors, a leading steel and arms producer in Stockholm. Iron ore interests had long since existed, and after 1918, Krupp hurried to compensate for the so-called "Swedish debt" that had piled up during the war. Sweden had purchased Krupp cannons prior to 1914 because of their superior quality, and the request by Krupp in 1919 to fulfil the Dutch gun order in Sweden led to an exchange of interests and ideas. From 1920 onwards, by way of private agreements, Krupp provided Bofors with metallurgical and construction expertise, along with the appropriate personnel, thereby allowing the Swedish company temporarily to become a leading European arms producer. These experts were now even able to carry out gunnery trials in Sweden. Krupp secured his Swedish activities through capital investment in Bofors, and for a time, he may have been the majority shareholder, through a Swedish nominee holding held by a Krupp confidant.

Thirdly, and within Germany's borders, it should be noted that as early as 1922, Krupp concluded an agreement with the government that ensured the mutual exchange of expertise, production plans, and strategies relating to the metal market as a whole and to new arms technologies. This of course was a major violation of the Versailles agreement although, apparently, no material consequences resulted. However, the advantage derived by Krupp became clear since the defense ministry (*Reichswehrministerium*) bound itself to deliver information on competitors. Krupp agreed to provide Berlin with appropriately qualified leading personnel, where a secret, if small-scale, construction office, Koch & Kienzle, was established. It is remarkable that the agreement was reached prior to the occupation of the Ruhr, though with limited practical results. However, activity increased from 1925, and especially after 1927 when the IMCC ceased operations.

Fourthly, it must be added that, after 1918, Krupp even broadened his range of interests in arms production, although admittedly this was not particularly important. Prior to 1914, one strategy for fending off unwelcome competitors had been to buy their shares. Rheinmetall, located in Düsseldorf, was among these relatively successful competitors. Krupp decided silently to buy shares and rely on a confidant on Rheinmetall's board to garner sufficient intelligence regarding its production strategies. Apparently, this strategy was pursued with greater vigour after the war.

Krupp even gained a majority holding in Rheinmetall, thereby leaving Krupp Essen as the proprietor of a Rheinmetall subsidiary located in Sömmerda in Thuringia. During the war, Sömmerda had been a significant arms producer, and thereafter the location seemed appropriate for further development of light weaponry such as machine guns, quite contrary to the peace agreements. Although Krupp's influence here apparently remained a secret, it nonetheless indicates that the company remained active as a major arms producer.

In 1968 William Manchester published a monumental and controversial, largely unreliable, history of the Krupp family and company, in which he maintained that during the Weimar era the enterprise remained a "suspended arms forge." My own findings would suggest that this particular claim is apposite.[28] The company sought to preserve construction expertise and experience, and await better political times. This was considered by company headquarters as service to the fatherland, to which the Krupps had dedicated themselves for over a hundred years. This was more than lip service; the company did not hesitate in spending considerable sums to maintain capacity, and further develop expertise. Arms control seriously hampered such strategies, but in spite of these legal constraints Krupp resumed its activities step by step from around 1927, long before Hitler's rise to power.

NOTES

1. See Michael Salewski, "Der böse Staat. Entwaffnung und Militärkontrolle in Deutschland," in *Frankfurter Allgemeine Zeitung*, 70, Mar. 24, 2003, p. 13.
2. See Gerhard Hirschfeld, "Der Erste Weltkrieg in der deutschen und internationalen Geschichtsschreibung, "in *Aus Politik und Zeitgeschichte*, 29–30(2004), July 12, 2004, pp. 3–12; Robert L. Nelson," "Ordinary Men" in the First World War? German Soldiers as Victims and Participants," in *Journal of Contemporary History* 39(3) (2004), pp. 425–35. On demobilization, see especially Susanne Rouette, *Sozialpolitik als Geschlechterpolitik. Die Regulierung der Frauenarbeit nach dem Ersten Weltkrieg* (Frankfurt am Main, 1993).
3. Michael Salewski, *Entwaffnung und Militärkontrolle in Deutschland 1919–1927* (Munich 1966); Ernst Willi Hansen, *Reichswehr und Industrie. Rüstungswirtschaftliche Zusammenarbeit und wirtschaftliche Mobilmachungsvorbereitungen 1923–1932* (Boppard am Rhein, 1978).
4. Egbert F. Schwarz, *Vom Kriege zum Frieden. Demobilmachung in Zeiten des politischen und sozialen Umbruchs* (Frankfurt am Main, 1995), uses company records to a certain degree, especially from the Ruhr, but limits himself to the processes and social consequences demobilisation. Michael Gaigalat and Joachim Schaier, *Krisenbewältigung nach 1918, in: Schwerindustrie* (Essen, 1997) (exhibition catalogue), pp. 122–39, make some use of company records including Krupp and Rheinmetall. This all too short article includes some photographs of destroyed war materials.

5. Hans-Ulrich Wehler, *Deutsche Gesellschaftsgeschichte, 4. Band: Vom Beginn des Ersten Weltkriegs bis zur Gründung der beiden deutschen Staaten 1914 bis 1949* (Munich, 2003). Wehler pays extensive attention to the economic conditions of reconstruction in the post-war period, but does not mention the destruction of assets by disarmament.

6. See Klaus Tenfelde, "Krupp in Krieg und Krisen. Unternehmensgeschichte der Fried. Krupp AG 1914–1924/25," in Lothar Gall (ed.), *Krupp im 20. Jahrhundert. Die Geschichte des Unternehmens vom Ersten Weltkrieg bis zur Gründung der Stiftung* (Munich, 2002), pp. 15–165.

7. In general, the materials of the Krupp Archive (Villa Hügel, Essen: Historisches Archiv Krupp (HAK)) divide into the Family Archives (FA) and the Works Archives (WA). There is one single file that includes scattered information on the Essen Branch of the IMCC: WA 4/1694. As a typical illustation of the problems inherent in collecting further information, see FAH 4 c 152: This file contains only one sheet, a personal note by Gustav Krupp von Bohlen und Halbach on the visit of a Dutch naval officer, Baert, to the Krupp factories for talks "on measures to safeguard materials against interference by an Allied commission" that had not yet come into being, Jun. 20, 1919. At this time, Krupp managers obviously already contemplated a formal transfer of properties of war materials to Dutch citizens or companies and, maybe, even to Dutch military institutions, but it was realized that the Dutch Naval Inspectorate had reacted somewhat "nervously." Apparently a compromise was reached, the content of which is not recorded. There is a collection of photographs of destroyed war materials that in itself tells a story of annoyance and regret: HAK XVI z 87, XVI 7 98, and XVI z 99.

8. *Foreign Relations of the United States, Paris Peace Conference*, Vol. III, pp. 711, 713; Salewski, *Entwaffnung und Militärkontrolle*, p. 23.

9. See Conan Fischer, *The Ruhr Crisis, 1923–1924* (Oxford, 2003) pp. 5–28; Georges-Henri Soutou, "Vom Rhein zur Ruhr: Absichten und Planungen der französischen Regierung," in Gerd Krumeich and Joachim Schröder (eds.), *Der Schatten des Weltkriegs: Die Ruhrbesetzung 1923* (Essen 2004), also other articles in this volume.

10. See Marion Heistermann, *Demontage und Wiederaufbau. Industriepolitische Entwicklungen ind er "Kruppstadt" Essen nach dem Zweiten Weltkrieg (1945–1956)* (Essen 2004).

11. See, among others, Heinz-J. Boutrup and Norbert Zdrowomyslaw, *Die deutsche Rüstungsindustrie. Vom Kaiserreich bis zur Bundesruplik. Ein Handbuch* (Heilbronn, 1988); Michael Geyer, *Deutsche Rüstungspolitik 1860–1980* (Frankfurt am Main, 1984); Zdenek Jindra, *Der Rüstungskonzern Fried- Krupp AG 1914–1918. Die Kriegsmateriallieferungen für das deutsche Heer und die deutsche Marine* (Prague, 1986); Michael Epkenhans, *Die Wilhelminische Flottenrüstung 1908–1914. Weltmachtstreben, industrielle Fortschritt, soziale Integration* (Munich, 1991).

12. See Klaus Tenfelde (ed.), *Bilder von Krupp. Fotographie und Geschichte im Industriezeitalter*, 2nd ed (Munich, 2002), pp. 35 f. (English edition in preparation); in more detail on pre-war profits: Tenfelde, *"Krupp bleibt doch Krupp." Ein*

Jahrhundertfest: Das Jubiläum der Firma Fried. Krupp AG in Essen 1912 (Essen, 2005).

13. Figures that follow are taken from Tenfelde, "Krupp in Krieg und Krisen," passim.

14. Among others, see esp. Lothar Burchardt, *Friedenswirtschaft und Kriegsvorsorge. Deutschlands wirtschaftliche Rüstungsbestrebungen vor 1914* (Boppard, 1968); Burchardt, "Zwischen Kriegsgewinnen und Kriegskosten. Krupp im Ersten Weltkrieg," *Zeitschrift für Unternehmensgeschichte*, 32 (1987), pp. 71–122.

15. See Boutrup and Zdrowomyslaw, *Rüstungsindustrie*, p. 29, and Tenfelde, "Krupp in Krieg und Krisen," pp. 51 f.

16. On the effects of inflation upon German industries, see Gerald D. Feldman, *The Great Disorder. Politics, Economics, and Society in the German Inflation 1914–1924* (Oxford, 1997), pp. 255 ff.

17. For the example of Stinnes, see Gerald D. Feldman, *Hugo Stinnes. Biographie eines Industriellen 1870–1924* (Munich,1998), pp. 533 ff.

18. See: Salewski, *Entwaffnung und Militärkontrolle*, pp. 18 f.

19. Otto Wiedfeldt, who in 1919 became senior manager of the Krupp combine, served as an official delegate. See for example: HAK, WA 3/222, memorandum of Adalbert Keil to Otto Wiedfeld, June 10, 1919, on the econmic consequences of the peace agreement.

20. Salewski, *Entwaffnung und Militärkontrolle*, p. 99.

21. On the Krupp memorandum on war effort (*Kriegsdenkschrift*), see Tenfelde, *Krupp bleibt doch Krupp*; on the stab-in-the-back legend (*Dolchstoßlegende*), see Boris Barth, *Dolchstoßlegende und politische Desintegration. Das Trauma der deutschen Niederlage im Ersten Weltkrieg, 1914–1933* (Düsseldorf, 2003). This voluminous study does not consider company records.

22. Unless otherwise indicated, what follows is taken from HAK, WA 4/1694.

23. Salewski, *Entwaffnung und Militärkontrolle*, p. 375.

24. Vivian Stranders, *Die Wirtschaftsspionage der Entente, dargestellt am Wesen und Treiben der Kontrollkommissionen* (Berlin, 1929).

25. See HAK, WA 4/1694, Report of a conference held at the Berlin Foreign Office, Nov. 26, 1924: "It is of utmost importance that we [Krupp] do not suffer from limitations regarding replacement of such lathes. Were this to happen, we would suffer permanent economic impairment, and naturally would have to apply for compensation."

26. See esp. HAK, FAH 23, 500.

27. On what follows, very few archival sources are kept in the HAK: FAH 4 c 177 on relations to Sweden, FAH 4 c 152 concerning the Netherlands; more in WA 0 h 643, WA 7f 1002, WA 42/244. See Tenfelde, "Krupp in Krieg und Krisen," pp. 108–17, and Ehrhard Reusch, "Die Fried. Krupp AG und der Aufbau der Reichswehr in den Jahren 1919-1922," *Archiv und Wirtschaft* 13 (1980), pp. 72–88; Inger Ström-Billing, "Die Behandlung der deutschen Interessen in der schwed-ischen Rüstungsindustrie," *Vierteljahrsschrift für Sozial- und Wirtschaftsgeschichte* 57 (1970), pp. 239–54; Mats Larsson, "Bofors and the Swedish Armament Industry 1875–1939," (Florence, undated [1991, Colloquium Papers of the European University Institute]).

28. William Manchester, *The Arms of Krupp, 1587–1968* (Boston, 1968); HAK, WA 40 B v 352, includes a comprehensive overview of activities 1922–1933

in the field of war materials, apparently prepared to support the defense of Alfried Krupp von Bohlen und Halbach during the Nuremberg trials. The list does not mention relations with and activities in the Netherlands and Sweden, but pays some attention to the construction of guns in Tangerhütte, Kiel, in 1922 and Berlin (see above). It is mentioned here that activities in Essen were resumed in 1926.

MAKING DISARMAMENT WORK: THE IMPLEMENTATION OF THE INTERNATIONAL DISARMAMENT PROVISIONS IN THE LEAGUE OF NATIONS COVENANT, 1919–1925

Andrew Webster

The interwar international disarmament process was, in practical terms, a failure. The British foreign secretary Sir Edward Grey wrote of 1914, "The enormous growth of armaments in Europe, the sense of insecurity and fear caused by them—it was these that made war inevitable."[1] Believing this, many people invested their hopes for lasting peace in disarmament, which became a vital part of the Treaty of Versailles, partly in a sincere attempt to avoid a repetition of the carnage of World War I and partly because of political manoeuvres at the peace conference.[2] Part V of the treaty enforced land, sea and air disarmament on Germany. Its preamble stated that such arms reductions were being made "in order to render possible the initiation of a general limitation of armaments of all nations."[3] The League of Nations was entrusted with international disarmament as a fundamental task. From this sprang initiatives, plans, committees, conferences and even agreements, yet there was a new war in 1939. This failure has led to the condemnation of interwar disarmament efforts, especially those instituted by the League, as a meaningless cul-de-sac. Scholars have investigated the critical period of the early 1930s, and its centerpiece the World Disarmament Conference (WDC) of 1932–34[4] but neglected the League's earlier attempts, immediately after the peace, to reduce and limit national armaments. These diverse and generally modest initiatives seeking only to establish tentative regimes of control over armaments, did achieve results, perhaps requiring a less negative evaluation of the interwar international disarmament process.

The Covenant's eighth article was the first substantive statement of the League's mission and the key declaration of interwar disarmament. Salvador de Madariaga, chief of the disarmament section of the League's secretariat in the mid-1920s, noted: "Disarmament may therefore be considered as the first task entrusted to the League by the drafters of its charter."[5] Article 8 contained six paragraphs. The much-quoted first was a generalized and conditional statement of good intentions recognizing that "the maintenance of peace requires the reduction of national armaments to the lowest point consistent with national safety and the enforcement by common action of international obligations." The five following specific practical directives have been neglected or ignored. The League Council, "taking account of the geographical situation and circumstances of each State," was to formulate plans for such reductions of arms for consideration and approval by member governments (paragraph 2). These plans would be revised at least every ten years (paragraph 3), and states were not to exceed the stipulated limits without Council approval (paragraph 4). The Council should advise on controlling the "evil effects" arising from "the manufacture by private enterprise of munitions and implements of war," bearing in mind the needs of those states not able to manufacture the armaments considered necessary for their own protection (paragraph 5). Finally, member states undertook to exchange "full and frank information as to the scale of their armaments, their military, naval, and air programmes and the condition of such of their industries as are adaptable to war-like purposes" (paragraph 6).

Four other article established additional measures. Article 1 included a provision that future League members must accept "such regulations as may be prescribed by the League in regard to its military, naval, and air forces and armaments." Article 9 specified a "permanent commission" to advise the Council on the execution of the provisions of Articles 1 and 8 "and on military, naval, and air questions generally." Articles 22 and 23 directed that League activity should seek to regulate, not eliminate, the global arms trade. The former required mandatory powers to prohibit "the arms traffic" (along with the slave trade and the liquor traffic) in the former German colonies. The latter established the League's trade responsibilities, including "the general supervision of the trade in arms and ammunition." The word "disarmament" never actually appeared in the Covenant or anywhere in the Versailles treaty. All references were to the "regulation," "reduction," or "limitation" of armaments. "Disarmament" nevertheless became the catch-all term for a wide array of approaches to the issue, a lack of precision that only served to widen the gaps between the vastly differing expectations about the intended outcome of the process.[6]

The League Council in May 1920 created the Permanent Armaments Commission (PAC) required by Article 9.[7] France's delegate Léon Bourgeois emphasized that its main duty was coordinating disarmament: "It is this question, above all others, which interests public opinion. To postpone the discussion of so important a problem would be to disappoint the most confident hopes of the peoples of the world."[8] He qualified this bold statement, insisting it was essential first to complete the disarmament of the ex-enemy powers. The commission, under pressure from Paris, reflected this priority for German disarmament. The PAC was given sole responsibility to plan the reductions of arms specified in Article 8; each Council member was to have three representatives on the commission—military officers expert in land, naval and air questions respectively—who were responsible to their respective governments and general staffs; the commission was to report directly to the Council, not to the Assembly. The PAC, dominated by the representatives of the major powers, thus focused more on national security than on international cooperation.[9] Lord Robert Cecil, the great British disarmament champion, noted sourly, "[these experts] had to do what their professional superiors at home desired, and that was almost invariably that they should do nothing themselves and if possible prevent anyone else from doing anything."[10]

The commission concentrated upon limited highly technical tasks between August 1920 and June 1925. Some meetings were futile—the seventh session in May 1922 could not agree a definition of "war material" after five days.[11] The commission's September 1924 proposal for implementing the Council's right of inspection in the ex-enemy states, specified in Article 213 of the Versailles treaty, to which France attached great importance, was never activated.[12] It established regulations for the military forces of League applicants, compiling statistical surveys of national arms programmes and offering technical assessments of the other League disarmament inivitives.[13] French success in strictly delimiting the PAC's responsibilities conflicted sharply with widespread public hopes for real armament reduction.

In October 1920, the Swedish, Danish, and Norwegian governments asked the Council to establish an "effective limitation of armaments" to be pursued with all speed. Bourgeois insisted that "the Council could not improvise a scheme of disarmament, and that the question could not usefully be considered in detail until after the Treaties of Peace had been executed"—Germany must comply with all its Versailles obligations and the Article 213 mechanisms be in place.[14] At the first Assembly, in November 1920, the British delegate, H.A.L. Fisher, warned the Assembly's disarmament committee: "Disarmament could not possibly be carried out in a hurry . . . [thus] the committee should limit itself to a somewhat narrower sphere instead of attempting a grandiose and comprehensive solution of the whole problem."[15] The larger powers (notably France and Britain) resisted precipitate arms reductions, using the executive authority which Article 8 reserved for the Council to formulate plans for disarmament.

Smaller states (especially the Scandinavian countries) used the Assembly to press for faster progress and greater ambition. Cecil, then serving as delegate for South Africa, expressed their frustration during the 1920 Assembly.

The disarmament committee's report oozed compromise. It desired "in the most solemn way possible to register their belief in the vital necessity of reducing the burden of armaments in the world" but stated "a comprehensive scheme of disarmament based on a thorough feeling of trust and security as between nation and nation, cannot be looked for at once." There could be no real arms reductions before the ex-enemy states had disarmed, the League oversight mechanisms been established and collaboration with the "great military powers" still outside the League agreed. Disarmament would follow in three stages. Firstly states, save in exceptional circumstances, should not exceed their existing levels of armaments. A "proportionate and simultaneous reduction" in either armaments or military budgets would follow. Finally states would undertake "comprehensive reduction of armaments under the supervision of the League to the lowest figure compatible with national security." There was to be "a distinction between limitation of armaments, reduction of armaments, and disarmament"—nothing was to be done too hastily.[16]

The Assembly secured the creation of a parallel, or indeed rival, disarmament body to the PAC. The Temporary Mixed Commission on Armaments (TMC) was composed of independent civilian expert drawn from political, economic, business, and labor spheres with a broad view of disarmament. They would not represent their national governments.[17] Paris and London did not approve: military adviser Colonel Edouard Réquin condemned its "untimely and ill-thought activities," while Foreign Office Permanent Under-Security, Sir Eyre Crowe lambasted its membership as "absolutely irresponsible amateurs."[18] Britain and France ensured that six members of the PAC would also serve on the TMC to curb its potentially dangerous idealism. They made the new commission "temporary." Its mandate was reviewed annually and the French tried, but failed, block its renewal. The commission gained stature and existed until its renaming and reorganization in 1924. Initially its French president, René Viviani, curbed its activities. He delayed its summoning until July 1921 and then concentrated on regulating the global arms traffic and the private manufacture of armaments, drafting plans to collect and exchange data on national armament levels, and implementing the League's "right" of investigation—rather than on ambitious schemes for general disarmament.[19] The TMC's 1921 Assembly report asserted that "immense progress has already been made in the direction desired," but insisted "it is only when security has been obtained that general disarmament can be contemplated and gradually attained."[20]

The 1920 Assembly proposal to limit military budgets produced another clash between smaller and larger states. The League's International Financial Conference at Brussels in September 1920 had emphasized the need for "a general and agreed reduction of the crushing burdens which, on their existing scale, armaments still impose on the impoverished peoples of the world."[21] The Norwegian delegated, Christian Lange, argued strongly that "the peoples will be sadly disillusioned if we leave this hall having given them only a promise—and that a vague one—of studying the question of armaments a long time hence. . . . [W]e must do something tangible today."[22] The Assembly, despite French protests, proposed that League members should not increase military expenditure for the next two financial years, but the French entered a caveat about "exceptional conditions" and established it was merely a "recommendation" to members, not a formal Assembly resolution.[23]

League members received the report in March 1921; twenty-six responses dribbled in between April and August. Most resisted a two-year freeze on military estimates. Some states (Finland, Greece, Poland) rejected it because of their "exceptional" circumstances; others (France, Spain) because it was a flawed method to control armaments; and some (Bolivia, Britain, Denmark) insisted they were already reducing military expenditure. Only China and Guatemala accepted outright and Belgium, Italy and the Netherlands with reservations.[24] The 1921 Assembly tried again but received short shrift in twenty-three replies between January and August 1922. Britain, Czechosolovakia, France, Japan and Poland claimed existing large reductions in defence expenditure and would not commit to a formal budget freeze.[25] At the 1922 Assembly the French delegate, Henry de Jouvenel, anxious to divert an unwelcome British reparations initiative and to emphasize the need for financial and economic reconstruction, proposed all European states should return to their 1913 armaments expenditure.[26]

The Council and the Temporary Mixed Commission squabbled over Jouvenal's proposal for a year. The TMC objected strongly about the states nominated and 1913 as the base year, and, ultimately, it was never put to the members.[27] In 1923 Lange persuaded the Assembly, despite French opposition, to return to his original proposal and recommend that future national defence expenditure should not exceed that of the current fiscal year, with allowance for "exceptional situations."[28] But budgetary controls were not going to work. At the Council meeting of June 1924, Britain, France and Japan refused any further restrictions. Only thirteen governments responded: almost all refused to make any commitment, only Liberia accepted without reservation. The 1924 Assembly decided, lamely, not to pursue the matter since it would be an agenda item at the general disarmament conference anticipated for 1925. That conference never happened but the 1925 Assembly omitted to mention the issue.[29]

The international traffic in arms was the most promising area for control. The regulation or limitation of arms exports for the sake of international security was an innovative idea, though with pre-war roots.[30] The Covenant permitted restrictions on the sale of weapons in areas considered undesirable by the imperial powers whilst not prohibiting major European powers from selling arms to allies. All the major powers signed a Convention for the Control of the Trade in Arms and Ammunition, at St. Germain-en-Laye on 10 September 1919. The preamble did not regard the arms trade as pernicious in itself, but suggested that the instability caused by the war and the resulting increase in world armaments made new regulation necessary. The convention sought to control armaments exports by licenses issued by national governments. Only states that signed the convention could trade in arms. The League would publish an annual statistical report including details on "the quantities and destinations of the arms and ammunition to which the export licenses referred." Certain "prohibited areas" of the world, including most of the African continent and much of the Middle East, were to be embargoed except under much stricter import controls.[31] The convention thus combined imperial desires to prevent arms falling into the hand of "barbarous or semi-civilized people" with elements of an internationalist scheme based on the belief that the fullest publicity was necessary to make disarmament work.[32]

The St. Germain convention was not a League initiative, but became intimately linked to the League's mission. The convention's ratification was on the agenda of the first League Assembly in November 1920; throughout the next two years, the Council pressed for its earliest implementation but few of the signatory states, and none of the major powers, would ratify.[33] Washington was blamed. Secretary of State Charles Evans Hughes rejected the convention in July 1922 which would have slashed American exports to Latin America and undercut the domestic arms industry. The other major powers also demurred. The security of Britain and France's imperial possessions would benefit from control of the arms traffic, but ratification by either state without American adherence would merely result in the loss of trade to US competitors.[34] The League continued, unsuccessfully, to seek a compromise with Washington but the 1923 Assembly abandoned the old convention and initiated a new conference for League members and other states.[35] The American government agreed to participate from February 1924 on condition that the new convention would be formally separate from the League and in the knowledge that its representative could exclude any objectionable provisions.[36] A draft arms traffic convention was ready by mid-1924. It distanced the agreement from the League and permitted arms exports to states outside the convention; such exports still required licences awarded at the discretion of the exporting state and made public through a central bureau (whose relationship to the League was deliberately left ambiguous).[37]

A Conference for the Supervision of the International Trade in Arms and Ammunition and in Implements of War convened in Geneva between May 4 and June 17, 1925 to approved the draft convention. Forty-four nations attended, including the United States, Germany and Turkey. The Soviet Union was the only absent major power. The Geneva debates revealed wide splits between larger, arms-producing states and smaller, non-producing ones. Despite some reservations, the major powers agreed that licensing and publicity were necessary and valuable. The smaller states fought against infringements on their sovereignty, in particular their ability to buy arms from private manufactures, fearing that the requirement for the government of the exporting country to issue a license would leave every purchase vulnerable to veto. El Salvador's J. Gustavo Guerrero, vice-president of the conference, argued it was inadmissible "to render countries which do not produce arms dependent in some sense on the exporting countries and to create, as between equal governments, two groups, one of which would control the other." Vassili Dendramis, the Greek delegate, complained that publication of arms imports would mean that "the secrets of the national defence force of the small states will be compulsorily revealed, whilst the producing states will maintain complete secrecy as to their armaments." Eastern European states, such as Poland and Romania, were anxious not to reveal their military strength to the Soviet Union. The convention signed on June 17, left these grievances unresolved. The non-producing states would have their purchases made public (though not through a central international bureau), those purchases would still require approval from the exporting government, and exports to certain "special zones" in Africa and the Middle East remained much more tightly restricted.[38] The agreement was still perceived as "an exceedingly important piece of work," helping to establish the wider system of international agreements necessary to implement the disarmament called for by the Convenant.[39]

The global arms trade was very closely linked to the private manufacture of armaments whose "evil effects" were specifically criticized by the Covenant. The 1921 TMC report, commissioned by the 1920 Assembly, asserted that arms firms fomented war scares, bribed government officials, stimulated arms production by spreading false reports about the military and naval spending of other countries, sought to influence public opinion through control of newspapers, organized international arms rings which enabled them to accentuate the arms race by playing one country off against another and, finally, established international arms trusts so as to push up the price of armaments sold to governments. The report proposed an international conference, open to both League members and non-League states.[40] Cecil and the Assembly pressed each year between 1921 and 1924 for such a conference, but the non-involvement of the United States and failure to ratify the St. Germain convention prevented progress.[41] Unless the United States participated, the major European powers believed any agreement would be meaningless, with Britain and France reluctant to undermine their arms industries or to impair the effectiveness of their armed sevices.[42]

The League continued with its preparations. In July 1924 a further TMC study reflected continuing divisions with majority and minority reports. The former concluded that control of private armaments manufacture should be through common principles applied at a national, not international, level. These principles were similar to those of the new draft arms traffic treaty being simultaneously prepared. Governments should license all arms manufactures and the licenses should be made public; manufactures were to supply their national governments with full details of their operations, though each government could determine how to verify the information and how much publicity to give it; license holders would be forbidden from engaging in propaganda and from owning or influencing newspapers, nor could they hold political office; a central international office would publish a list of all national licenses. The minority report was even more was ambitious, insisting that, even if the ideal of absolute prohibition of private manufacture was unachievable, all control and supervision must be international.[43]

The 1925 treaty to regulate arms traffic reinvigorated the attempt to control private armaments manufactures. The Geneva conference's final protocol explicitly called for its "early consideration" and the 1925 Assembly requested the Council to prepare a draft convention for an international conference within the year. Ominously, as Edouard Benes, the ubiquitous Czechoslovak delegate, reported to the Council, the smaller states again agitated for "equality" between the arms-producing and non-producing states. They insisted that, as the 1925 Geneva convention "subjected the purchase of arms to the regime of publicity, the producing states must, in order to re-establish equality, accept the same principle of publicity by concluding a convention on the supervision of manufacture."[44] The major powers would never reveal confidential details about their own arms production and defence preparations and the idea made no progress.

Article 8 required member states to exchange information on the scale of national armaments, military programmes and industrial production with wartime applications. Even such an apparently innocuous idea aroused significant resistance. The French military was not alone in its opposition to divulging sensitive information about its force strengths and mobilisation preparations. During 1920, French delegates ensured that the Permanent Armaments Commission merely drew up a model questionnaire on troop numbers, war material and national defence expenditure for League members to complete—information that was all publicly available. The commission's report to the Council asserted that it was not "opportune" to carry out any full exchange of information, given that not all the great powers were members of the League and stable conditions of peace were not yet restored throughout the world. The Council agreed and in December 1920 shelved the questionnaire.[45] The exchange of information issue became a focal point for fruitless attempts, particularly by France, to extend the Council's powers of supervision and inspection. Several amendments to the Covenant were proposed during 1920–21 to permit the Council to verify information on national armaments and to establish a formal system to check that states were not exceeding the armaments levels it had established. None of these amendments made any headway and were tacitly abandoned after the 1921 Assembly.[46]

The initial conception of the PAC's draft questionnaire as a mandatory submission by each country of specific data on its military and industrial readiness became, over the next three years, a much less intrusive process, whereby the League would independently collect data on each country from official and public sources. State cooperation was encouraged, but not required. The Italian delegate, Carlo Schanzer, at the first Temporary Mixed Commission meeting in July 1921, proposed that the League secretariat undertake a "statistical enquiry" on the exact state of national armed forces and military expenditure before and since the war. "Reliable statistics," he argued, were the essential preliminary for any study of armament reduction. Viviani, however, persuaded the commission to link its statistical questionnaire to a request that states should also report on "the requirements of their national security, international obligations, their geographical situations, and their special circumstances." This obvious ploy to allow states to justify retaining existing arms levels was confirmed when the first data was published in 1922, the TMC's report noting "the especial importance attached by all governments to political factors."[47] The 1922 Assembly narrowed the scope of the statistical inquiry for the next year to peace-time armaments and defence spending. The 1923 Assembly received two volumes of data. The first, based upon replies from twenty-five governments, provided details of national armed forces. The second was the Secretariat's report, compiled from official and public documents, on national defence expenditure in seventeen countries.[48]

The League adopted the model of the second volume for its future enquiries. The TMC suggested that the annual publication of such surveys "might prove one solution of the problem of exchanging information as defined in Article 8." The Council agreed and directed the Secretariat to publish an experimental comprehensive yearbook, compiled from open sources, describing the strength and equipment of each state's armed forces, its defence budgets and its industrial production in materials of military use.[49] The result was the mid-1924 *Armaments Year-Book*, covering thirty-seven countries. The disarmament committee at that year's Assembly identified this as "a genuine step" towards fulfilling the League's obligations and approved its on-going publication.[50] In preparation for the 1925 Geneva arms traffic conference the Secretariat had also compiled information on the global arms trade, in an unsystematic fashion, hoping that such data "might contribute to the discovery of an international solution of the problem." This survey was also very well-received by the Assembly, which directed its continuation.[51] All this reflected a belief that publicity and transparency in international dealings, especially over national armaments, could have a powerful, confidence-building effect on international relations. As one commentator reflected, it was hoped "that even this modest element of publicity would do something to check Press scares regarding the armaments of possibly hostile nations."[52]

Article 171 of the Versailles treaty prohibited Germany from possessing "asphyxiating, poisonous or other gases and all analogous liquids, materials or devices," an implicit recognition that the employment of poisonous gases during the Great War had been one of that conflict's greatest horrors. The 1899 and 1907 Hague conventions had also banned poison weapons.[53] There was no post-war consensus for dealing with chemical weapons despite widespread repugnance. Most major powers—including Britain, France, the United States and even, illegally, Germany—studied chemical warfare, claiming they needed to know how to deal with poisonous gases (both defensively and offensively) given their potential importance in future conflicts.[54] At the international level, there were persistent and well supported efforts within and outside the League to impose a universal ban upon the use of gas in warfare.

The Permanent Armaments Commission, instructed to consider the issue of chemical warfare as one of its first tasks, concluded in October 1920 that position gases were "fundamentally cruel" and "barbarous" because of their indiscriminate nature, which could affect civilians as well as combatants. However the commission believed that a peacetime ban on gas manufacture would not restrict its wartime use.[55] Discussions over condemning the use of gas in war at the Council and the 1920 Assembly produced no results before the 1921 Assembly.[56] A 1922 legal commentary expressed well the perceived difficulties of effective prohibition:

> The possible advantages to be gained by a sudden gas attack upon an enemy who is unprotected against it are so great that a prohibition

which cannot be relied upon may well be worse than no prohibition at all, and as the technical processes involved in the production of poison gas are to a large extent identical with those employed in the manufacture of harmless substances in daily use, it is impossible to ensure that a gas attack might not be secretly prepared by the conversion of ordinary commercial plant.[57]

The 1921 Assembly's disarmament committee, driven by Cecil's energy, adopted a resolution seeking to use publicity to control "these fiendish devices." It appealed for all scientists to publish their discoveries in chemical weaponry to minimize the likelihood of their future use in war. The rationale was essentially the same as later Cold War theories of nuclear deterrence through "mutually assured destruction." As Cecil put it to the Assembly: "If one nation, tempted to use some horrible gas of this kind, knew that another nation could easily respond, and that if one set of the population was wiped out the other set would be wiped out also—it was hoped that, even in the madness of war, they might pause before entering upon such a terrible competition."[58] The idea did not catch on. The Committee on Intellectual Cooperation and the Temporary Mixed Commission rejected it as both impractical and ineffective. Instead, the TMC adopted another of Cecil's proposals, appointing a special commission to investigate the "probable effects of chemical discoveries in future wars" to educate public opinion about the full horrors of such weapons. The 1922 Assembly urged "the fullest publicity" for the commission's eventual report.[59] After extensive consultation with scientific experts on the known effects of chemical warfare and the possible effects of bacteriological warfare, the report (written by Réquin, the French delegate) was finally delivered to the Council in late 1924. A catalogue of terrors, based upon the opinions of eight leading scientists from Europe and North America, it concluded only that "all nations should realize to the full the terrible nature of the danger which threatens them."[60]

Other efforts occurred beyond the League. The Washington naval treaty signed by the five chief maritime powers in February 1922 prohibited the wartime use of submarines against merchant vessels and, at the behest of former secretary of state Elihu Root, banned "asphyxiating, poisonous or other gases, and all analogous liquids or materials or devices." Declaring that such weapons had been "justly condemned by the general opinion of the civilized world," the five signatories accepted poison gas was illegal, agreed not to use it as between themselves, and invited all other "civilized nations" to adhere to this prohibition as a binding rule of international law. The 1922 Assembly adopted an Australian proposal urging all League members to adhere to the protocol. France, however, objected to the restrictions on the use of submarines, refused to ratify the treaty and hence none of its provisions came into force.[61] An American-sponsored conference the following year between five Central American states was more successful, producing a convention which, among other arms limitations, bound them not to use poison gas during war.[62]

At the 1925 Geneva conference on the traffic in arms, the Americans proposed that the convention should prohibit the export of materials and implements intended for chemical warfare. Believing this impractical, the conference instead decided to seek an absolute ban on the use of poison gas. The American delegate, Theodore Burton, thus proposed a separated protocol, extended at the behest of the Polish delegation to cover bacteriological warfare, which was unanimously adopted and signed by thirty states at the conference's conclusion on June 17, 1925.[63] The Protocol for the Prohibition of the Use in War of Asphyxiating, Poisonous or Other Gases, and of Bacteriological Methods of Warfare was not a complete ban on such weapons. It prohibited "the use in war of asphyxiating poisonous or other gases, and of all analogous liquids, materials or device," as well as "the use of bacteriological methods of warfare," but not their study, production or storage. It made no provision for verification or enforcement. Several states (most notably Britain, France and the USSR) attached two important reservation to their ratifications: while they would pledge not to make first use of such weapons in war, they would hold themselves free to use them in retaliation; and they would only consider the treaty's prohibitions as binding in regards to other signatory states.[64]

The League's efforts up to 1925 to control and reduce armaments through specific and limited measures were extensive. The limitation of budgetary expenditure on defence, the control of the international arms traffic and the private manufacture of arms, the open publication of data on national armaments, and the prohibition of poison gas in wartime—all attempted to put disarmament into practical form. From 1922 onward, there was also a parallel yet radically different pursuit of "general disarmament"—a vastly ambitious attempt to achieve extensive worldwide armament reductions through the concomitant provision of new international security systems. The ideal was embodied in Resolution XIV of the 1922 Assembly, the 1923 draft Treaty of Mutual Assistance, the 1924 Geneva Protocol for the Pacific Settlement of International Disputes, and the 1925 Preparatory Commission for a World Disarmament Conference. General disarmament increasingly dominated the League's focus and by 1926 became its main approach, but the earlier disarmament initiatives were marginalized rather than disappearing entirely.

Since the Permanent Armaments Commission was established by the Covenant it was never formally dissolved. Even though its twenty-first and last session occurred in May 1932 it remained in the League's budget calculations for 1939.[65] Budgetary limitation and the pursuit of transparency for the "publicity of expenditure" formed a central element of the land and air clauses in the PAC's eventual draft convention of December 1930. National defence expenditure publicity was one of the few ideas to survive the collapse of the WDC in 1934. The 1938 Assembly was still discussing a draft convention on the subject.[66] States submitted no formal data and there was no process of international supervision but the League's *Armaments Year-Book*, with its independently-compiled statistics, became an essential and well-respected source. It was published annually from 1926 to 1938, regularly covering over 60 countries, with its fifteenth and final edition (for 1939–40) appearing in June 1940–the very last League publication under the heading of "disarmament" (category 'IX').[67] The League published annual reports on the world traffic in arms, running from 1926, with data on 38 countries, to 1938, by which time its *Statistical Year-Book of the Trade in Arms and Ammunition* contained data on 60 countries and 64 colonies, protectorates and mandated territoties.[68] These annual surveys were often approximate, incomplete and non-comparable and Cecil disparaged international efforts to fulfil the information of Article 8, stating that it never went beyond "communicating to the League information that was already public property." Nonetheless the League's massive effort produced a remarkable collection of data.[69]

Eighteen states, including the United States, Britain, France, Italy, and Japan, signed the 1925 Geneva arms traffic convention but few ratified it. Major and minor powers retained their objections. The former would not ratify before other arms-producing states had done so, the latter remained suspicious of schemes perceived to benefit only the arms producers. Britain and France eventually ratified, but at the end of 1932 it was still one short of the fourteen ratifications it required to come into force and several of the ratifications were subject to such reservations as to be meaningless.[70] The 1925 Geneva convention thus suffered the same fate as its 1919 predecessor. The convention to regulate the private manufacture of armaments was, by 1929, only a weak and disputed plan adopted by majority vote. The problem was over the publication of state arms production and the major powers sidelined the issue, arguing that further progress depended on a general disarmament agreement.[71] The twin issues of the global arms traffic and the private and state manufacture of arms were resurrected by the WDC but the old problems remained and no agreement resulted.[72] A Committee for the Regulation of the Trade in, and Private and State Manufacture of, Arms and Implements of War, another surviving remnant of the WDC, adjourned in mid-1935 after months of intensive work without an agreed convention.[73] The Scandinavian countries secured the passage at the 1937 Assembly of a resolution calling on League members, as "a first step" towards the conclusion of a general disarmament agreement, to "examine the possibility of adopting internal measures" to supervise the manufacture of and trade in arms. This was the last stitch of this very lengthy thread.[74]

The 1925 Geneva protocol banning poison gas in war was one of the League's most obvious disarmament successes. France was the first to ratify in May 1926, fearing the superiority of Germany's chemical industry. The second ratification (by Venezuela, in February 1928) enabled the protocol to enter into force. Thirty six states, including Italy, the USSR, Germany and Britain but not the US or Japan had ratified by the end of 1932[75] American opposition was so strong that Senator William Borah, chairman of the Senate Foreign Relations Committee which had recommended its ratification, withdrew it from consideration in December 1926. The US ratified only in 1975.[76] There have been significant violations of the ban—by Italian forces in Ethiopia during 1935–36 and by both sides during the 1980s Iran-Iraq war—but it has mainly been observed. Poison gas was not used during the Second World War or the two recent Gulf Wars.[77] The ban remains in force today.

The Treaty of Versailles had manifest defects and the League has been heavily criticized but easy disparagement is often thoughtless, particularly as we grapple unsuccessfully with many of the same issues today.[78] The pursuit of disarmament after 1919 was perhaps the most important and prominent single issue in international diplomacy for over a decade. The League's tenth anniversary volume in 1930 avowed: "None of the League's activities has aroused so much interest in the world as its work for the limitation and reduction of armaments, and none has so closely or so continuously engaged the attention of the League."[79] That volume focused almost exclusively on plans for general disarmament but the earlier years from 1920 to 1925, saw much of the disarmament effort focused upon more limited gains, trying to establish tentative regimes of control over armaments, rather than immediate and large reductions. It was vital to establish the principle that arms could be limited. Perhaps such limited efforts had more chance to make disarmament work than the grander, but unsuccessful, ambitions of general disarmament. They established the idea that disarmament was an international process requiring national participation. States did accept (with varying degrees of commitment) that their armaments levels could (even should) be limited by international negotiation. Policy-makers understood that they could not simply ignore the process. Disarmament thus remains one of the clearest demonstrations of the new internationalist urge of the 1920s, the positive accomplishments of which are too often swamped by the disasters of the 1930s.

NOTES

1. E. Grey, *Twenty-Five Years, 1892–1916* (2 vols., London, 1925), I, p. 90.

2. On disarmament at the Paris Peace Conference, see: L.S. Jaffe, *The Decision to Disarm Germany: British policy towards post-war German disarmament, 1914–1919* (Boston, 1985); David Stevenson, "Britain, France, and the origins of German disarmament, 1916–1919," paper presented to the International Studies Association, Montreal, March 2004.

3. For all quotations from the Versailles treaty, see: *Treaty of Peace between the Allied and Associated Powers and Germany, signed at Versailles, June, 28, 1919,* in *The Treaties of Peace 1919–1923* (New York: Carnegie Endowment for International Peace, 1924).

4. On 1930s disarmament, different perspectives can be found in: Edward Bennett, *German Rearmament and the West, 1932–1933* (Princeton, 1979); Carolyn Kitching, *Britain and the Geneva Disarmament Conference* (Basingstoke, 2003); Maurice Vaïsse, *Sécurité d' abord: La politique française en matière de désarmement Décember 9, 1930–Avril 17, 1934* (Paris, 1981); Andrew Webster, "An argument without end: Britain, France and the disarmament process, 1925–1934," in Martin S. Alexander and William J. Philpott (eds.), *Anglo-French Defence Relations Between the Wars* (Basingstoke, 2002).

5. Salvador de Madariaga, *Disarmament* (London, 1929), pp. 12–13.

6. Speech by Lafontaine (Belgian delegate), Nov. 20, 1920, League of Nations, *Records of the First Assembly* (3 vols., Geneva, 1920), I, pp. 162–6. On the various contemporary meanings of "disarmament," see Kitching, *Disarmament Conference,* pp. 7–12.

7. Sometimes called the Permanent Advisory Committee on Military, Naval and Air Questions

8. *League of Nations Official Journal* [hereafter *LNOJ*], 1, 4 (Jun. 1920), pp. 131–6. Bourgeois would win the 1920 Nobel peace prize, in recognition of his work as one of the spiritual fathers of the League.

9. See: Edouard Réquin, *D'une guerre à l'autre* (Paris, 1949), pp. 13–14, 23–27; John L. Hogge, "Arbitrage, Sécurité, Désarmement: French security and the League of Nations, 1920–1925" (Ph.D. thesis, New York University, 1994), pp. 93–101; F.P. Walters, *A History of the League of Nations* (London, 1960), p. 121.

10. Lord Robert Cecil, *A Great Experiment* (London, 1941), pp. 78–9.

11. *Monthly Summary of the League of Nations* [hereafter *MSLN*], 2, 5 (May 1922), p. 95.

12. *MSLN,* 4, 9 (Oct. 1924), pp. 174–6; J.W. Wheeler-Bennett, *Information on the Reduction of Armaments* (London, 1925), pp. 45–7.

13. See reports in *MSLN,* 1920–25, *passim.*

14. League of Nations, *Procé-Verbal of Meetings of the Council of the League, 1920,* League of Nations Document [hereafter LND] 20/29/16, 8–9. See also: Hogge, "French security," pp. 121–2

15. *Records of the First Assembly,* III, p. 255.

16. *Records of the First Assembly,* I, pp. 515–20.

17. *Records of the First Assembly,* I, pp. 503–9; Wheeler-Bennett, *Reduction of Armaments,* p. 34.

18. Réquin to Bourgeois, Oct, 22, 1921, quoted in Hogge, "French security," p. 104; Crowe minute, Mar. 1, 1924, quoted in G.A. Silverlock, "Issues of disarmament in British defence and foreign policy, 1918–1925" (Ph.D. thesis, King's College, London, 2000), p. 52.

19. *MSLN,* 1, 4 (Aug., 1921), pp. 56–9; *MSLN,* 4, 10 (Nov. 1924), p. 222; Walters, *League,* pp. 219–20; Marie-Renée Mouton, *La Société des Nations et les intérêts de la France, 1920–1924* (Bern, 1995), pp. 268–78.
20. "Report of the Temporary Mixed Commission" (Geneva, Sep., 15, 1921), LND A.81.1921.IX, pp. 2,8.
21. League of Nations, *International Financial Conference, 1920* (3 vols., Brussels, 1920), I, p. 14.
22. *Records of the First Assembly,* I, pp. 524–6. Lange won the 1921 Nobel peace prize jointly with Karl Branting of Sweden, largely in recognition of their disarmament work at the League.
23. *Records of the First Assembly,* I, pp. 532–5; Mouton, *La Société des Nations,* pp. 196–9.
24. "Reduction of National Expenditure on Armaments: Replies from governments" (Geneva, Aug. 22, 1921), LND A.13.1921.IX.
25. League of Nations, *Records of the Second Assembly* (3 vols., Geneva, 1921), I, pp. 647–9; "Report of the Temporary Mixed Commission" (Geneva, 7 Sep. 1922), LND A.31.1922.IX, annex I, pp. 28–32. See also: "Budget Expenditure on National Defence, 1913 and 1920–22" (Geneva, Sep. 1922), LND A.31(a).1922.IX.
26. League of Nations, *Records of the Third Assembly* (2 vols. Geneva, 1922), I, pp. 253, 287.
27. *LNOJ,* 4, 3–8 (Mar.–Aug. 1923), pp. 210, 427, 587, 719, 872; "Report of the Temporary Mixed Commission," part II (Geneva, Aug. 15, 1923), LND A.35.(part II).1923.IX, pp. 1–2.
28. *LNOJ special supplement* [hereafter *LNOJ ss*] #13 (1923), p. 154; *LNOJ ss* #16 (1923), pp. 66, 76.
29. *LNOJ,* 5, 7 (July., 1924), pp. 912–13; "Limitation of National Expenditure on Armaments: Replies from Governments" (Geneva, Sep. 4, 1924), LND A.40.1924.IX; *LNOJ ss* #23 (1924), p. 181; *LNOJ ss* #26 (1924), p. 83. The Geneva Protocol for the Pacific Settlement of International Disputes, adopted at the 1924 Assembly, envisaged a general conference on disarmament by June 1925.
30. Jozef Goldblat, *Agreements for Arms Control: A critical survey* (London, 1982), p. 4; David R. Stone, "Imperialism and sovereignty: The League of Nations' drive to control the global arms trade," *Journal of Contemporary History,* 35(2) (2000), pp. 216–7.
31. *League of Nations Treaty Series,* 7, 1–3 (1921–22), pp. 331–59. Signatories included Britain, the US, France, Italy and Japan. Britain already had a licensing system regulating the export of war materials, a product of the wartime export controls. See: Elton Atwater, "British control over the export of war materials," *American Journal of International Law,* 33(2) (1939), pp. 297–9.
32. TMC report (1921), pp. 13–16.
33. *MSLN,* 2, 7 (July 1922), p. 145. By July 1922, only ten states had ratified the St. Germain convention: Central and South American (Brazil, Chile, Guatemala, Haiti, Peru and Venezuela), Asian (China, Siam) and minor Europeans (Finland, Greece).
34. Stone "Imperialism and sovereignty," pp. 219–20; Silverlock, "Issues of disarmament," pp. 43–7; Mouton, *La Société des Nations,* pp. 164–7, 272–4.

35. *MSLN*, 3, (March 2, 1923), pp. 6–7; *LNOJ ss* #13 (1923), pp. 154–5; *Survey of International Affairs, 1920–1923* (London, 1925), pp. 390–3.

36. *MSLN*, 4, 2 (Mar. 1924), pp. 32–3; Warren f. Kuehl and Lynne K. Dunn, *Keeping the Covenant: American internationalists and the League of Nations, 1920–1939* (Kent, Ohio, 1997), p. 149.

37. "Report of the Temporary Mixed Commission" (Geneva, Jul. 30, 1924), LND A.16.1924.IX, pp. 2–5, and annex IV (draft arms traffic convention).

38. League of Nations, *Proceedings of the Conference for the Supervision of the International Trade in Arms and Ammunition and in Implements of War, Geneva, 4 May to 17 June 1925* (Geneva, Sep., 1925), LND A.13.1925.IX: pp. 29–67 (text of Convention for the Supervision of the International Trade in Arms and Ammunition and in Implements of War); p. 130 (Guerrero); p. 137 (Dendramis); pp. 138–9, 190–1 (Polish delegate); pp. 147, 192–3 (Romanian delegates). Estonia, Finland, Latvia, Poland and Romania obtained the suspension of the articles on publicity for their arms imports until the Soviet Union acceded to the convention. On the debates at the 1925 conference, see: Stone, "Imperialism and sovereignty," pp. 222–9.

39. *Survey of International Affairs, 1925* (2 vols., London, 1928), II, p. 69.

40. TMC report (1921), 11–13. Also see: Clive Trebilcock, "Legends of the British armament industry, 1890–1914: A revision," *Journal of Contemporary History,* 5(4) (1970).

41. *Records of the Second Assembly,* I, pp. 647–9 and II, pp. 322–8; "Report of the Third Committee to the Third Assembly" (Geneva, 22 Sep. 1922) LND A.124.1922.IX, pp. 5–6; *LNOJ ss* #13 (1923), pp. 154–5; *LNOJ ss* #23 (1924), p. 181.

42. Silverlock, "Issues of disarmament," pp. 67–74; Mouton, *La Société des Nations,* pp. 317–20.

43. TMC report (1924), pp. 20–23. See also: "Work of the Economic Committee" (Geneva, Sep. 5, 1924), LND A.52.1924.II.B, pp. 38–9; *MSLN*, 5, 2 (Mar. 1925), pp. 41–2.

44. "Final Act" of Geneva arms traffic conference, LND A.13.1925.IX, p. 109; *LNOJ ss* #33 (1925), pp. 133–4; Benes report, Sep. 26, 1925, LND C.571.(1).1925.IX.

45. Specimen questionnaire to be forwarded to States concerned for the exchange of information regarding armaments, "*Procès-Verbal of Meetings of the Council, 1920,* LND 20/29/17, pp. 121–32; Hogge," French security, pp. 124–8; *LNOJ,* 2, 1 (Jan.–Feb., 1921), pp. 29–41; *LNOJ,* 2, 7 (Sep. 1921), p. 752.

46. TMC report (1921), pp. 9–10; Committee on Amendments to the Covenant, "Second Report of the Committee to the Council" (Geneva, Sep. 9, 1921), LND A.24(1).1921.V, p. 7; "Report on the Work of the Council," *Records of the Second Assembly,* I, pp. 147–55; *LNOJ,* 2, 10–12 (Dec. 1921), pp. 1137–8.

47. TMC report (1921), pp. 5–8; "Statistical Enquiry on Armaments: First series of data" (Geneva, 1922), LND A.21.1922.IX; TMC report (1922), pp. 5–10, and annex II (replies by governments).

48. Third Committee report to Third Assembly (1922), pp. 4–5; TMC report (1923), pp. 2–3; League of Nations, *Statistical Enquiry into National Peace-Time Armaments. Part I* (Geneva, Aug. 30, 1923), and *Statistical Enquiry into National Armaments. Part II: Budget Expenditure on National Defence, 1921–1923* (Geneva, Sep. 1923), LND A.20.1923.IX.

49. TMC report (1923), pp. 7–9; "Report of the Third Committee to the Fourth Assembly" (Geneva, Sep. 27, 1923), LND A.111.1923.IX (second part), pp. 2–3; *LNOJ*, 4, 8 (Aug. 1923), pp. 873–4, 929–30.

50. League of Nations, *Armaments Year-Book: General and Statistical Information*, First year (Geneva, 1924), LND A.37.1924.IX; "Report of the Third Committee to the Fifth Assembly" (Geneva, 27 Sep. 1924), LND A.122(1).1924.IX, p. 3.

51. League of Nations, *Statistical Information on the Trade in Arms, Ammunition and Material of War* (Geneva, Sep. 1924), LND A.30.1924.IX, p. 4; "Report of the Third Committee to the Fifth Assembly" (Geneva, Sep. 26, 1924), LND A.115.1924.IX, pp. 1–2.

52. H. Wilson Harris, *What the League of Nations Is* (London, 1927), p. 60.

53. Goldblat, *Arms Control*, pp. 81–2, 121–4.

54. Silverlock, "Issues of disarmament," pp. 78–93, 98–104; Mouton, *La Société des Nations*, pp. 167–9; F.J. Brown, *United States Chemical Warfare Policy, 1919–1945: A study of restraints* (Geneva, 1967), pp. 92–111; Rolf-Dieter Müller, "World power status through the use of poison gas? German preparations for chemical warfare, 1919–1945," in Wilhelm Deist (ed.), *The German Military in the Age of Total War* (Leamington Spa, 1985).

55. "Report of the Permanent Advisory Commission" (Brussels, October 22, 1920), LND 20/48/84.IX.

56. *Procès-Verbal of Meetings of the Council, 1920*, LND 20/29/16, p. 37; *Records of the First Assembly*, I, p. 517, and III, pp. 249, 256.

57. H.W. Malkin, "The Washington Conference," *British Year Book of International Law, 1922–23*, III (London, 1922), p. 181.

58. *Records of the Second Assembly*, I, pp. 627–31. (Cecil speech); "Report of the Third Committee to the Second Assembly" (Geneva, Sep. 27, 1921), LND A.158.1921.IX, p. 6.

59. *MSLN*, 2, 8 (Aug. 1922), pp. 176–8; TMC report (1922), pp. 19–21; Third Committee report to Third Assembly (1922), pp. 7–8.

60. *MSLN*, 3, 5 (June 1923), pp. 100–1; TMC report (1924), pp. 24–30 (report of the Special Commission). See also: Wheeler-Bennett, *Reduction of Armaments*, pp. 48–57.

61. Emily Goldman, *Sunken treaties: Naval arms control between the wars* (University Park, Pennsylvania, 1994), pp. 293–6 (Treaty relating to the Use of Submarines and Noxious Gases in Warfare, Feb. 6, 1922); Thomas H. Buckley, *The United States and the Washington Conference, 1921–1922* (Knoxville, 1970), pp. 118, 123–5; *Records of the Third Assembly*, I, pp. 287–9. Britain, the United States, Japan, France and Italy signed the Washington treaty.

62. Wheeler-Bennett, *Reduction of Armaments*, p. 50; Goldblat, *Arms Control*, pp. 6–7, 134–5; *Survey of International Affairs, 1925*, II, p. 415. Article 5 of the Convention on the Limitation of Armaments of Central American States (Feb., 7 1923) also employed similar wording to Article 171 of the Versailles treaty. The five signatory states were Costa Rica, El Salvador, Guatemala, Honduras, and Nicaragua.

63. *Conference for the Supervision of the International Trade in Arms*, 13, pp. 161–2, 306–16, 33–42, 364–5.

64. *League of Nations Treaty Series*, 94, 1–4 (1929), pp. 65–74.

65. *LNOJ*, 13, 7 (Jul., 1932), pp. 1199–1201; *LNOJ*, 19, 10 (Oct. 1938), pp. 748–9.
66. *Survey of International Affairs, 1930* (London, 1931), pp. 91–125; *LNOJ*, 19, 11 (Nov. 1938), p. 876.
67. League of Nations, *Armaments Year-Book: General and Statistical Information,* Second year (Geneva, Jan. 1926), League of Nations Publication [hereafter "LNP"] 1926.IX.1: League of Nations, *Armaments Year-Book: General and Statistical Information,* Fifteenth year (Geneva, June 1940). LNP 1940.IX.1.
68. *Statistical Information on the Trade in Arms, Ammunition and Implements of War* (Geneva, Jan. 1926), LNP 1926.IX.2; *Statistical Year-Book of the Trade in Arms and Ammunition* (Geneva, Oct. 1938), LNP 1938.IX.4.
69. Cecil, *Great Experiment,* p. 79.
70. *Survey of International Affairs, 1932* (London, 1933), p. 295, n. 3; *LNOJ*, 14, 1 (January, 1933), p. 47. The thirteen states to ratify the convention by 1933 were: Australia, Britain, Denmark, Egypt, France, Latvia, Liberia, Netherlands, Poland, Spain, Sweden, and Venezuela. French ratification was contingent upon ratification by Belgium, Czechoslovakia, Italy, Japan, Sweden, and the United States; British ratification upon the same powers plus Austria, Germany and Spain as well. The US also finally ratified the convention, in 1935, but this had no effect on it coming into force.
71. *MSLN*, 9, 8 (Sep. 1929), pp. 256–7; *LNOJ*, 10, 11 (Nov. 1929), pp. 1456–8, 1597–1642.
72. *Survey of International Affairs, 1932,* pp. 295–8; *Survey of International Affairs, 1933* (London, 1934), pp. 288–9.
73. *Survey of International Affairs, 1935* (2 vols., London, 1936), I, pp. 47–58.
74. *LNOJ ss* #169 (1937), p. 92. On the new uprising of public revulsion with "the merchants of death" in the mid-1930s, see: David G. Anderson, "British rearmament and the "Merchants of Death": The 1935–36 Royal Commission on the Manufacture of and Trade in Armaments," *Journal of Contemporary History,* 29(1) (1994).
75. *League Treaty Series,* 94, 1–4 (1929), pp. 65–74; *LNOJ*, 14, 1 (Jan. 1933), pp. 48–50
76. Hugh R. Slotten, "Humane chemistry or scientific barbarism? American responses to World War I poison gas, 1915–1930" *Journal of American History,* 77(2) (1990), pp. 487–91; Daniel Jones, "American chemists and the Geneva Protocol," *Isis,* 71(3) (1980). Japan only ratified the Geneva gas protocol in 1970.
77. Richard Price "A genealogy of the chemical weapons taboo," *International Organization,* 49(1) (1995), pp. 76–8, 96–102; John Ellis van Courtland Moon, "Chemical weapons and deterrence: The World War II experience," *International Security,* 8(4) (1984), pp. 9–35.
78. On the contemporary lessons of interwar disarmament, see: Andrew Webster, "Piecing together the interwar disarmament puzzle: Trends and possibilities," *International Journal,* 59(1) (203–04).
79. League of Nations, *Ten Years of World Cooperation* (Geneva, 1930), p. 49.

FROM LOTHRINGEN TO LORRAINE: EXPULSION AND VOLUNTARY REPATRIATION

Carolyn Grohmann

In the weeks following the armistice, Lorrainers of German origin feared for their future. As one resident of Pfalzburg (Phalsbourg) wrote: "The expulsions have also commenced here; the first twelve victims left last Saturday. You can imagine the state of those who remain, and since it is impossible to obtain a travel permit, one is quite literally a prisoner."[1] Alfred Wahl, however, one of very few historians to have addressed the issue of French policy towards Germans in Alsace and Lorraine (the Moselle), disagrees.[2] All in all, he maintains, France's post armistice policy was altogether more liberal than than adopted by Germany in 1871. The new rulers, Wahl continued, allowed Germans born outwith the provinces to remain and to chose between retaining German nationality or, through naturalisation, becoming French.[3] What, then, was the reality of the situation faced by German residents in the months and years following the conclusion of hostilities?

I would like to acknowledge the help and encouragement I have received from Conan Fischer in the preparation of this article. Any mistakes, however, are my own.

EPURATION

During the initial years of peace thousands of inhabitants left the Moselle region, hitherto the Imperial territory of Lothringen. Although their departure was often voluntary, it none the less formed part of the process of *épuration* initiated by the French authorities and also by many local residents. *Epuration* constituted the cleansing or purification of the region and its population of all German or enemy elements. Although translatable as "ethnic cleansing," the process of *épuration* was largely devoid of the violence and certainly devoid of the mass murder and rape that have characterised many recent examples of this process. Instead, its objective was to erase all effects of Germanisation and carry on as if the half century of German rule had never actually taken place. This, however, was to ignore the multiplicity of linguistic, religious, educational, and legislative hurdles such a strategy faced. Indeed, the policy itself lacked initial coherence, instead emerging from a series of uncoordinated and fluctuating responses to a set of practical problems; similarly the very term *épuration* only crept into use during the months following the war. On some levels the policy sought to make a visual impact, for example through the replacement of street signs and shop hoardings by their French equivalents,[4] but population change was inevitably part of the game. Not all German-born residents wished to leave, and often it was the arrival of an expulsion order which forced individuals to make the journey across the new Franco-German frontier with little more than a suitcase and some small change. Others left voluntarily, either to pre-empt expulsion or from a realisation that there was no future for them in the region.

CLASSIFICATION OF THE POPULATION

As early as 1915, it was decided that following victory, each and every individual in Alsace and Lorraine should be classified according to their "blood origins" rather than by place of birth.[5] Classification of the population in this way, through the issue of identity cards, would facilitate the exclusion of "unreliable" elements in the event of a plebiscite and also the expulsion of German civil servants. There were precedents for such a process, for refugees from the territories who had made their way to France during the war, had been classified by special commissions which accorded the "tricolour card" to those of sound pro-French sentiments. Similarly, inhabitants in the French-occupied corner of Alsace around Altkirch had from 1914 been subjected to a system of military controls involving the use of cards.

Four different categories of card were created. The first, card A, was given to those who had held French citizenship, or whose parents had held French citizenship prior to 1870, but had become German by virtue of the Treaty of Frankfurt (1871). Card B was issued to those born in Alsace-Lorraine and with one parent entitled to card A. Foreign subjects of non-enemy states were issued with card C and card D was issued to those who had originated from enemy countries (Germany, Austria, Hungary, Turkey, and Bulgaria) as well as their children, even if the latter had been born in Alsace-Lorraine.[6] Card A was adorned with stripes in the colours of the French tricolour, B with two red stripes in the shape of a cross, C with crossed blue stripes in the form of a saltire, and D plain white.[7] Once this exercise was completed in December 1918, Alsace-Lorraine contained 1,082,000 card A holders, 183,000 card B holders, 53,000 card C holders and 513,000 card D holders.[8]

This system facilitated the administration of a region that remained under military occupation between the armistice and peace treaty (June 1919), not least by quantifying and making readily identifiable the German element within the population. It also allowed those Alsace-Lorrainers anxious to distinguish themselves from the "Boches" with a ready means of so doing, given that most were German speaking. The cards also served as travel permits, allowing passage through the network of military posts that covered the region, but also helping the French authorities to maintain a tight grip on the population. However, despite the obvious advantages for a government seeking to deal with a seemingly unstable, ethnically and culturally complex population, the system simultaneously created a host of problems which generated anger, disillusionment, and frustration among the elements of society which did not fall neatly into category A.

As theory was translated into practice it emerged that even husbands and wives could find themselves in different categories, the woman, perhaps, a Lorrainer born of Lorrainer stock and thus entitled to card A, but the man the child of parents from metropolitan Germany and thus falling into category D. The classification of children from such "mixed" marriages became little short of nightmarish although most emphasis was placed in the father's origins when deciding which category of card a child should receive.[9] Men, after all, were full citizens in the France of 1918, whereas women were not. This, however, was rather at odds with the reality of a male population which in no small measure had fought in the war as German soldiers and were treated with great suspicion by the French authorities upon their return to the region.

Pierri Zind ranks among the fiercest critics of this system of classification which, he contends, superimposed the artificial unity of France upon regions whose cultural and ethnic ties stretched to the north and east than to the west.[10] Parisians, Zind continues, appeared more foreign to the populations of the Moselle and Alsace than did the residents of Baden, the

Saarland, or the Palatinate. However, these ethnic realities did not necessarily accord with popular sentiment. Many Lorrainers in particular were
overjoyed to receive their red, white, and blue identity cards, particularly
in francophone rural areas where there had been very little German immigration and identity was a clear cut matter.

However, not everyone appreciated having to prove that their origins
were purely "French."[11] Mixed marriages were considerably more common in urban Lorraine and as one exasperated resident complained: "You
quite literally have to produce a family tree merely to obtain an identity
card."[12] Those in the grey area of categories B and C were most likely to
regard the system as unjust and fundamentally flawed. Neighbors,
friends and even relations might easily qualify for category A cards
despite having great grandparents who came from the Saarland, Bavaria
or Prussia. Furthermore, although these identity cards did not grant their
holder any particular nationality, national blood origins rather than
national sentiment determined the type of card issued. As a result a rogue
parent of foreign origin could deny a staunch French patriot full integration into their beloved *patrie*, whilst, across the street, a neighbour, who
had previously denounced fellow Lorrainers to the German administration, was reintegrated as of right with no questions asked.[13] Similarly, residents of Sarreguemines (Saargemünd), hard up on the border with the
Saarland, were reportedly unhappy with conditions for obtaining card A,
laid out in an edict of December 14, 1918. Local women who had married
Germans (possibly born just three miles up the road) were considered by
pro-French residents as unworthy of the tricolour card which, these locals
insisted, should only go to "real" Alsace-Lorrainers.[14]

All in all the cards, intentionally or otherwise, crudely denoted sentiment, segregated the population, and interfered with the everyday lives of
those who carried them. Holders of card A and D, for example, received
radically different rates for their German marks when they sought to
exchange them for francs; 1.25 francs and 0.74 francs, respectively.[15]
Holders of a card B, meanwhile, experienced difficulties in securing positions in the public services, despite protestations from French administrators that there was no legal impediment to such employment.[16] Not
surprisingly, mayor's offices regularly received enquiries from individuals seeking to exchange their cards B for cards A, many even fearing that
only those in category A would be allowed to remain in the regions.[17] All
offices were instructed to turn away such enquiries.

Before long counterfeit identity cards were being sold on the black
market to Germans. One such case was reported in Algrange (Algringen),
where the secretary of the mayor was accused of selling cards A to a
German and his father for 20 francs.[18] The newspaper, the *Lorrain*,
reported that cards were being forged in the German town of Offenburg

and then sold in the Moselle for between 50 and 200 francs.[19] This black market in identity cards was entirely predictable in view of the benefits of card A and the punitive nature of card D. The disadvantages went beyond the financial, or employment difficulties. From the very earliest stages it became obvious that the main reason for classifying the population was to sift out those elements who were deemed "Boche," "suspect," or "undesirable." Ultimately, those in possession of a card D were not expected by the French authorities to remain within the provinces.[20] Classification was the first step in the *épuration* process, which sought to identify the enemy, set them apart, then drive them out, either by persuasion or by force.

EXPULSION OR VOLUNTARY REPATRIATION?

Within the returned provinces card D holders fell into three categories: those allowed to remain for a fixed term; those authorised to leave voluntarily; and those obliged to leave and issued accordingly with expulsion papers. Much has been made of the part played by the *commissions de triage* in the expulsion process,[21] but in fact their expulsion of Germans, as well as Mosellans and Alsatians, from the regions accounts for only a fraction of the overall departures.[22]

The first expulsions date from December 23, 1918, long before the Treaty of Versailles and the legal transfer of the territory to French sovereignty permitted such actions. The last took place in July 1921. Article 7 of the law of November and December 1849 was invoked to this end, which empowered the Interior Ministry to apprehend and expel any foreigner resident or travelling in France.[23] The Ministerial Circular of January 23, 1919 set out the conditions under which a person's presence in the provinces could no longer be tolerated. These conditions were as vague as possible, in other words providing a "licence to expel." Drunkenness, rowdiness, immoral behaviour, or singing loudly in German all fitted the bill. However, as far as the question of *épuration* was concerned, this method was rather haphazard, for it could only affect those who actually stepped out of line. Thus, the French authorities set about establishing which groups in society should formally be invited to leave. Under the terms of the November armistice all military personnel were obliged to leave the regions within two weeks. It was also anticipated by the French authorities that all German civil servants would leave as soon as their positions had been filled by locals or by the incoming French. This involved all levels, including senior administrators, teachers, clerical staff, postal staff and railway workers. Civil servants were regarded as "agents" of the state and, in the case of the Moselle, the vast majority of senior and middle ranking posts had been held by Germans. Many of these had filled posts vacated in the 1870s by *Mosellans* who had opted for French nationality and departed the region.

As well as civil servants, other specific categories of person were expected to leave. On February 25, 1919 the Regional Administrator in Metz, Léon Mirman, echoed a desire by central government to see the expulsion and repatriation of "boches" accelerated in Lorraine.[24] Whether this was intended to appease local sentiment or to free up jobs in an increasingly sluggish local economy is unclear. Whatever the reason, Mirman urged the expulsion not only of overt troublemakers, but also those "liable to exercise a German influence by virtue of their social position: intellectuals, the propertied, industrialists, merchants etc." The higher up the social ladder these people were, the more desirable was their departure. The Administrator for Metz-Campagne also stressed the need to expel factory owners and directors who, he claimed, were "in general very German, anti-French."[25] Mirman was less concerned about the "little people," but all in all senior French officials displayed an aggressive tone as they invoked "preventive measures" against those reckoned most likely to pose a nationalist, political threat.

In May 1919, further groups were identified by the new regime for expulsion, and this time they included the unemployed and the poor. These groups, it was claimed, posed both a political and a social threat to the stability of the region. Bolshevism and poverty allegedly went hand in hand, whilst the expulsion of the poor would relieve the regions of a major potential financial burden. In September, therefore, it was decided that all unemployed Germans who had not yet requested their repatriation should be expelled.[26] Unfortunately, no figures exist for exactly how many were "disposed of" in this way.

The indignity and misery of expulsion from the Moselle region could, supposedly, be lessened by opting for voluntary repatriation. In fact, even before the armistice had been signed, many families had chosen not to remain and attempted to sell as much of their property as possible, and carry with them whatever money and remaining material possessions they could. However, once the French authorities arrived the only way to depart legally was to opt for voluntary repatriation. Regular notices appeared in the Moselle's press informing Germans wishing to leave of the repatriation procedure. After submitting a Request for Repatriation, the individual was obliged to produce identification papers, a certificate of nationality, a receipt stating that payments of all taxes were up to date, and a favourable report from the relevant mayor.[27] All of the above documents were examined by the Special Repatriation Bureau—Germany, which was run in Metz by the military. Once permission had been granted, the applicant was instructed when and where to present themselves.[28] Thus Frau S . . . and her six children, resident near Thionville

(Diedenhofen) were to present themselves at 8 am on April 22, 1919 at the station buffet for examination and a baggage search. Each traveller was permitted a baggage allowance of 30 kilos, two days rations and no more than 2,000 marks in German banknotes (or 500 marks per child).[29] Each refugee was obliged to purchase a railway ticket which was obtained the night before travelling. Gold, coins of any kind, and French or allied money was forbidden. All property left behind, by those expelled or repatriated, was liable for sequestration and subsequent liquidation by the French authorities.[30] Not surprisingly, families reached Germany destitute, for those choosing to leave did so on exactly the same terms and subject to the same restrictions as those expelled. Perhaps only those prevented from leaving, perhaps due to outstanding debts, could consider themselves less fortunate.[31]

Calculation of the numbers affected requires some care. Sources in the *Archives départementales de la Moselle* suggest that between 1918 and 1921 4,389 expulsions were made from the Moselle department, that is the former German Lorraine or Lothringen.[32] The figure may be slightly distorted, as in some cases only the head of the family was listed, even if the whole family was affected. Another, hand-written list includes 5,740 individuals considered to be "undesirables;" a type-written list gives more information about the 2,678 individuals expelled from the city of Metz.[33] They included nuns, lawyers, doctors, shopkeepers, domestic servants, and hairdressers, to name but a few.

Overall, though, the total number of expulsions indicated by these lists does not account for the dramatic reduction in the size of the German community indicated in the census figures of 1910 and 1921. In 1910 164,502 Germans lived in the Moselle, but only 44,899 by 1921, a drop of 119,603 (72.7 percent). In addition almost 3,200 (83.8 percent) of native Austrians and 104 (53.2 percent) of native Hungarians left the region.[34] The additional numbers can largely be accounted for by the system of voluntary repatriation operated by the French as soon as they arrived in the region. The precise number of voluntary repatriations can only be estimated, and allowance should be made for the departure of the German military at the end of the war. In 1910 there had been 22,228 military stationed in the Moselle. The death toll exacted by the war and the flight of some Germans before the French arrived must also be considered, but taking all these factors into consideration it is estimated that roughly 90,000 German residents opted for voluntary repatriation from the Moselle between 1918 and 1921.

AN UNDIGNIFIED DEPARTURE

The trains carrying the expellees and refugees from the Moselle region passed into Germany either through Strasbourg and across the Rhine to Kehl, or through Forbach and across the border to Saarbrücken.

Most departed from Metz, Thionville, or Sarregemines. At the stations there was a heavy military and police presence and vivid accounts survive of some of the departures. On April 2, 1919 a train awaited expellees at Metz station, guarded by soldiers and police to ensure that only those permitted to depart boarded the train. An officer was grouping the men and women separately when suddenly an incident occurred. A uniformed customs officer assisted a woman with her baggage, only to be reprimanded by Special Commissioner Wagner for "his hideous attitude under the circumstances and his lack of dignity in uniform in the presence of 400 expelled Germans." As the train eventually left under military guard a crowd estimated at a thousand stood behind fencing alongside the track to bid their silent farewells by waving their handkerchiefs.[35]

Conditions during the journey were reportedly poor[36] with trains sometimes taking thirty-six hours to arrive in Kehl. Children were reported to have contracted diarrhoea and other hygiene-related illnesses. There were further concerns regarding the treatment of women. A major in the German army was horrified to discover that his wife had been frisked at the checkpoint in Kehl before her expulsion to Baden. It was proposed that women might be substituted for the male soldiers or police officers carrying out the searches, deemed essential to prevent individuals from carrying extra currency of valuables, but the intimidatory nature of this process should not be overlooked. In fact, humiliation appears to have been the order of the day. On April 9, 1919 the director general of the Knüttingen (Knutange) Foundries was arrested and taken to Metz "chained to a vagrant." At Kehl jeering crowds gathered at the bridge across the Rhine and even resorted to violence. As one report observed: "Heartbreaking scenes occurred there, particularly when the populace, who appear to have been paid for this purpose, hurled stones."[37] Indeed, the humiliation and hopelessness of the situation sometimes had extreme consequences, with one German police superintendent committing suicide in January 1919 just days after his imprisonment. He left a wife and four children.[38]

It is not surprising, therefore, that people threatened with departure faced the prospect with dread and fear. Soon enough the indigenous population began to sense the shame in the *épuration* process and also began to fear the possible consequences of the humiliation visited on those expelled or repatriated, not all of whom were necessarily German. One letter to the Commissioner General in Metz urged moderation, predicting with alarming accuracy that: "Something terrible will happen which will result in war, for the humiliation you are inflicting on these people will leave them gripped by a secret, implacable and wrathful anger which will avenge itself in an indescribable manner."[39]

THE SIFTING PROCESS

Of all the aspects of the *épuration* process to come under heavy criticism, the *commissions de triage* appear to have been the most disturbing and disliked. They have been variously described as "a sort of high court of justice in patriotism,"[40] or as "lacking all the guarantees and procedures of orthodox justice."[41] Georg Wolf condemned them as "a blot on the transition period," indeed a shameful stain on the history of France.[42] So what were these tribunals, why were they set up, and for what purpose?

They were first proposed by the abbé Wetterlé during war-time discussions on the future of Alsace and Lorraine and then adopted by Clemenceau even before the armistice had been signed. Wetterlé insisted on the expulsion of all Germans who had emigrated to the region between 1870 and 1918, as well as their descendants. However, this initial idea, of weeding out "politically unreliable" Germans, was soon extended to the *Mosellan* and Alsatian populations, forcing them to prove their reliability to the incoming French authorities. Indeed Germans or Austro-Hungarians, normally condemned to removal from the outset, were only to go before the commissions in exceptional cases. In his book *Têtes de boches*, published in 1917, Wetterlé indicated that Alsace-Lorrainers who had "licked the feet of the Prussian masters" should join the defeated Germans on the other side of the Rhine.[43] This may have been completely at odds with French claims that Germanisation had had no impact on native *Elsaß-Lothringer*, but all *Mosellans* and Alsatians who had worked as civil servants, or had held political appointments under German rule came under immediate suspicion. Even some émigres, who had spent all or part of the war in France were not necessarily exempt from scrutiny.[44]

Cases were sifted through a *commission du premier degré*, comprising an army intelligence officer and two civilians.[45] After considering evidence produced by the Gendarmerie, witnesses and the accused themselves, these commissions, although lacking any legal expertise,[46] would either drop the case or pass it on to the *commission du deuxième degré* in Metz.[47] Little is known of the composition of this second, shadowy tribunal, but after 23 January 1919 the final say regarding an individual's fate lay with the Commissioner of the Republic in Metz. Three verdicts were possible: "not suspected," "suspected but not immediately dangerous," or "dangerous"; the commensurate outcomes normally being complete freedom, continued surveillance, and (for Germans) immediate expulsion on the next convoy to Germany.[48] Matters became more complicated for natives of the regions, however. "Dangerous" *Mosellans* and Alsatians were normally sent to camps in the French interior, and less often to Germany, whilst even those declared innocent, but who had worked as civil servants before 1918, were obliged to accept demotion, premature retirement, or transfers from their home towns.[49]

Adjustments to the tribunals system followed. In February new regulations demanded of the officer in charge of each tribunal an adequate command of German and the local *fränkisch* or *allemanisch* dialects.[50] On 7 May it was announced that civil servants would appear before special disciplinary tribunals and days later special commissions were established to deal with German and Austro-Hungarian nationals "whose presence in Alsace-Lorraine could prejudice public order."[51] From then on, therefore, the original *commissions de triage* dealt solely with the indigenous population. On 16 June Millerand, as High Commissioner of the Republic, suspended these notorious commissions, but they were only finally abolished in October 1919. The numbers expelled may have been limited, but the depth of bitterness engendered remained acute even a decade thereafter.[52]

Beyond the ruination of individual lives, the tribunals had caused untold damage to the reputation and perceived integrity of the new French regime. The expulsion of Germans was initially welcomed by many and following the regions' brush with revolution during November 1918 before the entry of French troops, it was easy for a jittery middle class to convince themselves that all Germans posed a "Bolshevik" threat. However, as time passed personal experience brought home the injustice of the tribunals system. Increasing numbers of native *Mosellans* and *Elsäßer*, rather than German immigrants, found themselves before the tribunals. Newspaper attacks against the tribunals followed and some ten years later Robert Redslob wrote in *Le Temps* that Alsace-Lorrainers were forced to defend actions and "attitudes they had shown towards a regime established constitutionally and based on a legitimate treaty."[53] Anticipating, as they had, a continuation of German rule, should *Mosellans* and Alsatians really have turned down opportunities to work in their own regional civil service?

Alsatian autonomists complained that the tribunals were manned by former émigres or die-hard anti-Germans who displayed little empathy for the region and its people; furthermore the composition and precedures of these tribunals showed scant regard for the normal judicial process.[54] As Lucien Minck complained in the *Depêche de Strasbourg* in 1930: "One has to admit that the tribunals used and abused this illegal situation, to the point where their verdicts were sometimes based on knowingly false dossiers and on non-existent documentation."[55] The secrecy surrounding these tribunals was such that it is hard to confirm or refute these claims, although Mirman's observation that "the commissioners" verdicts need not accord with regulations," hardly inspires confidence. Subsequent efforts to rescind the tribunals' decisions and win compensation for their victims attracted support from almost all deputies from Alsace and the Moselle, Robert Schuman included, but without success.[56]

The *mosellan* author, Mungenast, highlighted the tribunals' fundamental flaw, stating that "instead of looking to the future they only considered the past."[57] The fact that they survived a mere six months after integration testifies to their singular lack of appropriateness, but exactly who was responsible for the injustice served upon both the immigrant and indigenous populations is difficult to say. That said, the damage caused by these commissions would have been minimal were it not for the willing, even enthusiastic, flood of denunciations, the letters of accusation against neighbours, colleagues, and competitors, that flooded Mirman's office in the months following integration. Was the disgrace of the tribunals not theirs, just as much as the new administration's?

A WITCH-HUNT

The priest Louis Pinck was among the more prominent victims of the tribunals process. Although a card A holder, he had been involved with the German Catholic Centre Party and had allegedly preached loyalty to the Kaiser from the pulpit in his home town of Hambach. Severe restrictions were placed on his freedom of movement throughout 1919, before the local *sous-préfet* finally lifted these restrictions in December.[58] However, many victims were less well placed than this respected and articulate parish priest. Officials were flooded with letters of denunciation of ordinary citizens, including one from a resident of Metz who railed against twenty-seven of his neighbors. On the basis of overheard conversations he accused them of being anti-French revolutionaries, as "bad as boches," or alternatively as "upper class boches."[59] Whether or not this particular letter was taken seriously, all too many such denunciations evidently were, as the case of Louis Pinck illustrates.

Local officials encouraged the process. The mayor of Sarregemines, a M. Sigwald, announced in the local *Saargemünder Zeitung* that: "Persons who wish to communicate with the *Commission de triage* regarding the evacuation of undesirables are requested to do so in writing and duly signed to: The President of the *Commission de triage*, Town Hall, Sarregemines."[60] Regular advertisements in local newspapers informing Germans of repatriation procedures also served to intensify the highly charged atmosphere within the Moselle region. The pitiful sight of wagon-loads of Germans leaving the region brought a sense of satisfaction to many who felt that justice was being served.[61] Obviously, not all accusations were fabricated, but as each convoy made its way into "Bochie" so the denunciations multiplied until not just remaining Germans, but also *Mosellans* were threatened. Gradually, opportunism crept into the equation and business competitors, feuding neighbours, and disgruntled tenants were to be found among the denouncers. Even the normally Germanophobic newspaper, *Le Messin*, admitted that: "Some [denunciations] stem from commercial rivals, others seeking to buy a house cheaply from a German threatened by expulsion; some are inspired by crude vengeance."[62] Some mayors felt that by "advertising" voluntary repatriation, they could stem the flow of false denunciations.[63] In other words, instead of preventing false denunciations by punishing those who invented them, the authorities chose simply to speed up the departures, so that there would be fewer people to denounce.

Given the miserable atmosphere created in the post-war period by the expulsions, why was such a great effort needed to persuade "Germans" to make their way back to "Germany"? For one thing Germany in the post-war years presented a most unappealing destination for many Germans, being both impoverished and gripped by revolutionary upheaval. Furthermore, the western parts of Germany were under allied military occupation and in this regard barely more congenial than Alsace or Lorraine. That said, however, it would be inaccurate to say that all such people were "returning" to Germany. Many of them had been born in the regions and considered themselves Elsaß-Lothringer for whom it was almost impossible to consider a future anywhere else. It was inevitable that some would remain loyal to Germany and thus, if they remained, oppose the new regime, but this only partially excuses the enthusiasm to denounce. The viciousness and falsehood of so many accusations have cast a dark shadow over the inter-war history of the region. It is perhaps this, more than anything, which has produced such a stubborn reluctance to record the history of this period. Few have been willing to ask questions of those who lived through this, either as denouncers, or as denounced.

LIMITS TO ÉPURATION

The desire to tone down the *épuration* process was increasingly voiced from 1919 onwards. Whatever the private feelings of locals, if negative these could hardly be expressed openly during a period of censorship, postal controls, and ongoing expulsions. The imprisonment of Victor Demange, for example, founding editor of the *Metzer Freies Journal*, was due in part to his enunciation of the problems afflicting the region including the arbitrary nature of the *épuration* process.[64] However, the economic dislocation visited on Lorraine in particular by the flood of departures demanded a measure of restraint. It served little useful purpose if mines were forced to close or farmland was abandoned.[65] Even the francophile newspaper *Le Messin* recognised the population issue, although it advocated settlement by replacements from the French interior, rather than the retention of Germans.[66]

However, just as the new administration failed to understand the subtleties of language, religion, and education within the region, so it failed to recognize the overriding economic and social need for an avoidance of a dramatic and devastating demographic rupture, along the lines of that which had occurred in the 1870s. Instead of preaching caution, and assisting in creating a calm and reflective atmosphere, the new administration gave its blessing to the witch-hunt, encouraging vengeance. The example set during the period of political void between the armistice and the arrival of French troops, when the region's *Nationalrat* set about maintaining stability and security within the regions, was to have no impact on the incoming administration. Again, the long-term effects were only guessed at by a few, more perceptive, observers within the population.

NATURALIZATIONS

Article 79 of the Treaty of Versailles allowed Germans resident in Alsace Lorraine to apply for French citizenship through a process of naturalization. Despite considerable disquiet within France at the prospect of Germans acquiring French nationality and with it the right to vote,[67] and despite the anti-German policy of *épuration* between 1920 and 1921, an overwhelming number of 95,893 applications for naturalization (although not exclusively from Germans) were received by the French authorities.[68] Of these 77,064 were accepted,[69] many of these being married to *Mosellans* and Alsatians. Indeed the priest Louis Hackspill, editor of the *Lothringer Volkszeitung*, observed that not all applications were motivated by pro-French sentiments, with financial or family considerations often uppermost. This was unsurprising, Hackspill continued, and it was this generation's children who might eventually become true French men and women. None the less, politicians and political commentators worried away at this problem through the 1920s and 1930s, until the outbreak of the Second World War annulled all their efforts.

EPURATION: THE RESULTS

By 1921 the *épuration* process had largely achieved its principal objective with the removal of approximately 100,000 Germans and undesirable Lorrainers removed from the Moselle region. Only a fraction of these were literally expelled, yet the evidence suggests that the "voluntary" nature of repatriation is questionable. On the face of it there were very few differences between voluntary repatriation and expulsion. In the early stages, when most departures occurred, both methods placed exactly the same tight restrictions on the amount of luggage and money individuals could carry. Each dictated the time and place of departure. Each involved the segregation of men and women for the duration of the uncomfortable journey into Germany, which could take several days. And upon arrival in Germany both those expelled and those repatriated faced the same problems: refugee status, a lack of money, no accommodation, and the traumas of arriving in a country in disarray, even on the brink of collapse.

Why then opt for voluntary repatriation at all? In its favour repatriation avoided the traumas of denunciation, arrest, police enquiries and possible imprisonment. Other pressures also encouraged repatriation, for those who temporarily prolonged their residency in the Moselle found that everyday life contained numerous pitfalls and dangers. After 10 pm the use of German was forbidden in public places and many shops refused any longer to serve "boches." The poor currency exchange rates offered to holders of card D and the lack of employment also weighed on the German population. However, the greatest fear stemmed from the threat of physical violence and intimidation, for a small number of native *Mosellans* who now felt they had the upper hand indulged their desire for vengeance.[70] Voluntary repatriation, therefore, despite all its drawbacks, became the best option.

Epuration was in part a response to French public opinion and to the wishes of those in Alsace and Lorraine who sought vengeance for German heavy handedness during the war. It was also a policy pursued by the French military and civil authorities, who felt that the only way to secure the regions and to implement a policy of *francisation* was to racially cleanse the Moselle and Alsace. This was decisive, for apart from the free-lance local initiatives, *épuration* required authorization and instructions from above. How things were determined in Paris requires further research, but on the ground in the Moselle, without any reference to the Treaty of Versailles, civilian and military personnel combined orders from Paris with their hatred of Germans to make *épuration* of the population very effective indeed.

NOTES

1. Château de Vincennes, 16 N 1464, report of the commission de Contrôle Postal Civil de Metz; post read between Jan. 13–26, 1919, extract 7.
2. Alfred Wahl, "Changement et Souveraineté et Option et Nationalité," *Cahier du Cercle Jean Macé*, 27(3) (1988), pp. 1–10.
3. Ibid, p. 10.
4. Change was sometimes achieved by simply painting over the German signs. However, the paint did not always adhere properly, to the embarrassment of the French authorities. Archives départementales de la Moselle (ADM), 304 M 296.
5. Procès verbaux of 20 and 21 sessions in Centre d'accueil et de recherche des archives nationales (CARAN), AJ 30/95.

6. ADM, 304 M 325, "Instruction sur l'application de l'arrêté du 14 décembre de Général Gouverneur de Metz."
7. J Rossé et al, *Das Elsaß von 1870–1932*, 4 vols (Colmar, 1936–1938), p 528. See also: Georges Philippot, "Gendarmerie et identité nationale en Alsace et Lorraine de 1918 à 1926," *Revue historique des armées*, 4 (1998), pp. 61–78.
8. Grayson Kirk, "French Administrative Policy in Alsace-Lorraine, 1918–1929" (PhD, University of Wisconsin, 1930), p. 137.
9. Thus where a mother had a card B, but the father a card C, the child would follow the father's classification and also receive a card C. Cf. Rossé, *Das Elsaß*, p. 529.
10. Pierri Zind, *Elsaß-Lothringen, Alsace-Lorraine, une nation interdite, 1870–1940* (Paris, 1979), p. 111.
11. G. Suffert and J.-M. Pelt, *Marguerite Puhl-Demange. La Lorraine au quotidien* (Metz, 1986), p. 32.
12. Château de Vincennes, 16 N 1464. Report of Jan. 25, 1919.
13. Kirk, "French Administrative Policy," pp. 137–9.
14. ADM, 301 M 53.
15. Rossé, *Das Elsaß*, p. 518.
16. Kirk, "French Administrative Policy," p. 137.
17. ADM, 301 M 53. Weekly report from the *administrateur* in Sarregemines to the *commissaire de la République*, Apr. 21, 1919.
18. ADM, 802 P (provisional code). This was known as the *Affaire Kieffer*.
19. ADM, 6 T 3, *Le Lorrain*, Aug. 1, 1919.
20. Joseph Rohr, *La Lorraine mosellane, 1918–1946* (Sarregemines, 1975), p. 11.
21. These commissions are discussed below. See: *The sifting process*.
22. Cf. ADM, 26 Z 26. Letter to the administateur de Sarregemines, Feb. 25, 1919, part II.
23. ADM, 304 M 212. Undated, but with reference to a ministerial note of Jan. 23, 1919 and evidently composed before such responsibilities were transferred in March to the commissariat général in Strasbourg. See also: ADM, 10.PL.17, pp 1–23, Pierre Brasme, "Expulsions et rapatriements d'Allemands de Moselle au lendemain de la Première Guerre Mondiale (1918–1921)," *Bulletin de liaison de l'association nationale du souvenir de la bataille de Verdun et de la sauvegarde de ses hauts lieux*, 18 (1991), pp. 53–9.
24. ADM, 26 Z 26. Section VI of letter.
25. ADM, 301 M 53. Weekly report from the *administrateur* in Metz-Campagne, Mar. 7, 1919.
26. Brasme, "Expulsions," ADM copy, p. 13.
27. Ibid., p. 5.
28. ADM, 27 Z 6. These bilingual forms were habitually completed only in French by the military, few of whom understood German. At the point of departure only details completed in French were of concern to the military authorities.
29. ADM, 27 Z 6.
30. Exceptions were eventually made for civil servants, who were granted permission to retrieve their furniture from the provinces.
31. Cf. Brasme, "Expulsions," ADM copy, p. 5.

32. ADM, 304 M 220. This file is located in the *Répertoire numérique* under the section "Relations franco-allemandes." It is not possible to tell exactly how many among these expellees were native *Mosellans*, and how many were Germans.
33. ADM, 304 M 213.
34. *Annuaire Statistique, Office Régional de Statistique d'Alsace et de Lorraine*, vol. 1, 1919–1931.
35. ADM, 304 M 212. Sent to the *commissaire de la République* in Metz. It is unclear why men and women were separated in this way.
36. Thus: François Reitel and Lucien Arz, *Montigny-lès-Metz* (Metz, 1988), p. 341.
37. Château de Vincennes, 16 N 1464. Report from the *Contrôle postal* in Metz, extract 28.
38. ADM, 304 M 2. Letter of Apr. 22, 1921.
39. ADM, 304 M 212. Anonymous letter.
40. Robert Redslob, quoted in Zind, *Elsaß-Lothringen*, p. 117.
41. Lucien Minck, in the radical newspaper *Dépêche de Strasbourg*, Jan. 12, 1930, cited in Rohr, *La Lorraine*, p. 16.
42. Quoted in Rossé, *Das Elsaß*, p 531. Cf. Kirk, "French Administrative Policy," p. 46.
43. Rossé, *Das Elsaß*, p. 530.
44. Ibid.
45. ADM, 304 M 329, account regarding the setting up of the Metz *commission de triage*, written by General Violand, commandant of the Metz tribunal.
46. ADM, 304 M 329.
47. ADM, 304 M 214. This file contains hand-written reports by Gendarmes on information gathered about individuals.
48. ADM, 304 M 329. Note of Dec. 9, 1918.
49. Soldiers who had served in the German army were also heavily scrutinized at special military tribunals, which considerably delayed their return home at the end of the war. See Pierre Brasme, "Le rapatriement des prisonniers et des combattants alsaciens-lorrains" (1918–1920), *Bulletin de liaison de l'association du souvenir de la bataille de Verdun ...*, (1988), p. 142.
50. It appears there were not even translators present in the early stages of the tribunals.
51. ADM, 304 M 154, written by Millerand, the *commissaire général de la République*.
52. Kirk, "French Administrative Policy," p. 46.
53. Robert Redslob, published in *Le Temps*, Apr. 1929, quoted in Rohr, *La Lorraine*, pp. 16–17.
54. Public Record Office (PRO), FO 371/3750. Signed by The Executive Committee of the Free State Elsaß-Lothringen. This rather poor translation was published in Geneva.
55. Quoted in Rohr, *La Lorraine*, p. 16. The *Dépêche de Strasbourg* was a radical newspaper favored by autonomists.
56. Rossé, *Das Elsaß*, p. 535; Rohr, *La Lorraine*, p. 18.
57. Quoted in Laurent Commaille, "Ernst-Moritz Mungenast et la Lorraine," *Les Cahiers Lorrains*, 3–4 (Oct. 1992), pp. 545–55.
58. Henri and Charles Hiegel, "L'ouevre du folkloriste lorrain, Louis Pinck (1873–1940)," *Les Cahiers Lorrains*, (1981, 3rd trimester), pp. 199–218.
59. ADM, 304 M 212. Date on letter illegible.

60. Quoted in Rohr, *La Lorraine*, p. 15.
61. Château de Vincennes, 16 N 1464. Report of Mar. 16, 1919, section entitled "Opérations de contrôle et impressions générales."
62. *Le Messin*, May 2, 1919, quoted in Brasme, "Expulsions," ADM copy, p. 8.
63. Brasme, "Expulsions," ADM copy, p. 10.
64. See François Roth, *Le temps des journaux, presse et cultures nationales en Lorraine mosellane, 1860–1940* (Metz-Nancy, 1983), pp. 211–24.
65. ADM, 26 Z 26. Cf. ADM, 310 M 50.
66. Brasme, "Expulsions," ADM copy, p. 17.
67. Article sent to the British Foreign Office, May 11, 1919. PRO, FO 371/3748, "Problems of new administration."
68. CARAN, AJ/30/296.
69. PRO, FO 371/6990, report from Sir M Cheetham in Paris to Foreign Office London, "Political situation in Alsace Lorraine September, 1921," section 19.
70. See "K's" diary entry, Dec. 8, 1918. For details on this source, Carolyn Grohmann, "The Problems of Integrating Annexed Lorraine into France, 1918–1925" (PhD, University of Stirling, 1999), p. 207.

THE VERSAILLES SETTLEMENT AND IDENTITY IN FRENCH FLANDERS

Timothy Baycroft

The end of the First World War was greeted with both joy and relief throughout rural France. Families would finally be reunited with their sons, brothers and fathers, the carnage and destruction would cease, and all hoped for a speedy return to normal life. At the same time, the national government entered into peace negotiations which, the French public expected, would return France to the dominant position in Europe which was its own, and even more importantly would protect France from another such conflict. The expectations of the peace settlement were perhaps higher than average in French Flanders, given the region's proximity to the war zone, the personal experience of war among the civilian population, and the urgent need for the reconstruction of the damaged areas. The object of this study is twofold: firstly, to examine the local reactions to the Versailles negotiations and final settlement within a particular region along the north-eastern frontier of France, and secondly, to question how the settlement influenced longer-term trends in identity formation within the region, including the ways in which the peace objectives altered attitudes towards the border and neighbouring Belgian population. After a brief presentation of the characteristics of the region and the way in which the war had been experienced and commemorated, the paper will examine in turn the two major objectives for the peace settlement, reconstruction and future security, as well as the effects of population movement at the time of the negotiations with respect to the two questions of local opinion and identity.

REGIONAL BACKGROUND

French Flanders is difficult to define precisely, as political, cultural and historic boundaries continued to shift and did not often coincide. For the purposes of this study, French Flanders will be considered as synonymous with the region known in Flemish as the *Westhoek*, which comprises the area of the Département du Nord from the Lys river valley up to the North Sea coast around Dunkirk. It was this highly developed rural area which remained Flemish-speaking up until the Second World War, and was culturally distinct from the surrounding areas in France at the time of the Versailles settlement, when it still formed a part of the larger Flemish cultural region which spanned the Franco-Belgian border. Using a cultural definition of the region is particularly important for the second of the questions under study, as identity formation in the region can usefully be analysed alongside of cultural change. Such a definition excludes the Lille industrial basin, which neighbours, but is not in the Westhoek. Although large numbers of the French Flemish had already migrated from the Westhoek to the Lille area at the time under consideration, the overall urban population was drawn from all sides, and was not predominantly Flemish in culture.[1]

The rural area of the Westhoek had a high population density, a long tradition of intensive agriculture with a concentration of industrial crops such as sugar beets and flax, and a highly developed communications network of roads, railways and canals which linked it to the rest of France as well as to Belgium and beyond to the east. It served as a hinterland for Lille, as well as the mining areas of the Pas-de-Calais. Culturally, the French Flemish were highly practicing Catholic, and although moving towards bilingualism, Flemish was still the principal language of the population in 1919.[2] Politically conservative in a larger French region which was predominantly left leaning, the inhabitants maintained close social relations with the Belgian Flemish, and regular contact as well as cross-border marriages were still extremely common.[3]

Although not occupied territory during the war, the Westhoek had been cut off from many of its traditional trading areas, as well as from Lille, which was in German control for most of the war. The Western Front ran just south of the Westhoek, and many of those in the region who felt that it was too close for comfort had left the region as refugees to other areas of France for the duration of the hostilities. The area suffered a great deal of material damage from troop movements and aerial attacks, and was in need of much investment after the end of the war to rebuild and repair the damage.

While remaining culturally Flemish and perfectly conscious of their ties to the Belgian Flemish, the inhabitants of the Westhoek at the same time fully considered themselves French citizens, and for several decades before the war had seen no contradiction between simultaneous Flemish and French identities. With roots dating back to the mid-nineteenth century, a culturally-defined Flemish movement had been gathering momentum among the Belgian Flemish which would see a significant rise in the inter-war period, and which had affiliate voices in French Flanders.[4] Given the close contact with their Belgian neighbours across the border, the question of French Flemish participation in this wider Flemish movement in the years which followed the First World War was a serious one.

In the long run, the culturally-based Flemish identity present in 1919 did not grow in parallel with that of Belgium. By the end of the twentieth century very little of the original Flemish cultural identity remained on the French side of a border which had developed into a solid social and cultural division between the two communities, by which time the Westhoek had become well integrated into the greater Nord-Pas-de-Calais region.[5] The experience of war and local reactions to the Versailles settlement contributed in several important ways to this process. Although perceptions of the international situation at the same time reinforced solidarity and connection with the Belgian Flemish, pressing financial and security concerns forced them to think increasingly in terms of France, while also enhancing the "otherness" of the Belgian Flemish and the role of the border in defining identity in the French Westhoek.

MEMORIES OF THE WAR

The end of the war left the Westhoek scarred both with material damage to the local infrastructure and the experience of having lived with a permanent threat of invasion, in addition to the loss of men which was common throughout France. After the victory, however, French Flanders, like the rest of the country, sought primarily to remember the heroic sacrifice of the soldiers, in particular those who had died.[6] In immediate expressions of the memory of the war in the post-war public discourse, neither suffering, occupation nor privations were dwelt upon. The local press in the Westhoek devoted a large amount of space to the commemoration of the fallen, with editorials primarily expressing relief that the war was finally over.[7] When discussing damage and local rebuilding, the tone often suggested that it was simply part of the national sacrifice, without dwelling upon or indeed mentioning the grievances of the region at an emotional level, or suggesting that anything extra was their due because of what they had undergone. The concentration was upon the glory and dignity of victorious France, with pride and contentment that the damage was being repaired and that the "bells were ringing again" throughout the region.[8] Any recognition of differences of experience with the rest of France were not expressed at the local level, and the pattern of commemoration followed that for France as a whole. The local papers did inform their readers of how to get in touch with the various commissions dealing out money to help those individuals whose farms or buildings had been damaged, but as an experience the overall effects on the entire region were passed over in silence.[9]

As a group, the French Flemish were therefore among those who Annette Becker described as the "forgotten" of the First World War.[10] While war damage was discussed, variety of experience was not, leaving several groups outside of official memory. A significant effort was made to consider that the entire French nation was equal in the heroic sacrifices which had led to the victory, in such a way that those who had in fact suffered more greatly or in a different way gained no extra recognition for that fact. One could talk about relative levels of damage, but not relative levels of sacrifice or indebtedness. Hence the specific war experiences of refugees, civilian deportees, those in the various occupied territories, those whose homes were destroyed or "victims" in general were passed over with a conspicuous silence, in stark contrast to the widespread commemoration and attention which such groups would receive after the Second World War.[11] Furthermore, although specific memories of the war had in fact been shared by the French Flemish most closely with their near neighbours in both the north of France and in Belgium, rather than with the majority of their fellow countrymen, that memory found no expression within either the local or the national commemorative structure.

Far from complaining that their local sacrifices deserved more credit in the eyes of France as a whole, the French Flemish sought quite clearly to demonstrate their loyalty in the eyes of the rest of the French. The pejorative term "les Boches du Nord," which would come back to haunt the region much more strongly during and after the Second World War, was nevertheless coined during the First. Meaning roughly "the northern Hun," the underlying suggestion was that those speakers of a Germanic dialect (Flemish) were in some way affiliated with the enemy, and therefore less than fully French patriots.[12] Occasionally the suggestion even hovered around the term that those living in the occupied areas in and around Lille had at least collaborated, when not positively welcoming the German occupation. While at no time repudiating their Flemish cultural origins, such implied accusations of disloyalty or treason led to an increased desire to be seen as extra loyal by the rest of France, and contributed therefore further encouragement to downplay, or at least not to stress or attempt to profit from their potential status as "victims."

RECONSTRUCTION

Recognizing that when challenged, the position of the region was primarily defensive, seeking to prove that it had been just as loyal as the rest of France during the war, and that it was not asking to be accorded any privileged status or special treatment, the principal objectives for the peace settlement in French Flanders resembled those of the rest of France: a return to normal, and future guarantees of peace and security. The main preoccupation at the end of the war was to receive enough money to finance the rebuilding as quickly as possible. Numerous co-operative or international aid organizations, as well as church-run reconstruction societies participated in the work, but the main source of revenue to finance the rebuilding was to be French government funds, themselves derived from reparations payments from Germany. An entire network of special courts was set up to deal with war damages, to which individuals could make claims to have their property repaired or rebuilt.[13] Damages were classed by economic sector, and each commune drew up a form of redevelopment plan ("plan d'aménagement") for its territory in order to have an overall perspective on the extent of the damage in each area, as well as to be used as a norm against which to judge individual claims and to help the courts in their handling of individual claims.[14]

Given the extent of the damage, the work of identifying the needs and then rebuilding the region took several years, as well as generating a large amount of paperwork and regional anxiety about where they were going to get sufficient financial resources. Independent of the ultimate source of the money, be it taxes, government loans or reparation payments, the inhabitants of the Westhoek were well aware that if they wanted to obtain any funds it would be from the French government and the state institutions set up to hear the claims. While reparations from Germany were considered just, no matter what else happened internationally it was Paris which held the purse strings as far as the locals in French Flanders were concerned. The wider considerations of finance discussed and then incorporated into at the Versailles settlement, while not ignored, were nevertheless of decided secondary importance alongside the way in which the decisions affected the specific material needs of the region, and the conditions for distribution of whatever resources were forthcoming at the national or international level. Writing in the Dunkirk paper *Le Phare du Nord*, Jean Guiscard reported back to the region his impressions of the discussion of the Versailles Treaty in the French Chamber of Deputies which he had attended.[15] He was responding to local expressions of criticism that the negotiations had been taking too long, and although he defended the time taken, he expressed concern over the allied disagreements over the sum of reparations. In describing the differences between the British and French positions wanting more, opposed to the United States who wanted lower sums, his position was that the interests of the Westhoek and their neighbours would be better served by a fixed sum, even if it were quite a bit lower than the French government hoped, as long as specific guarantees for the north of France and Belgium were written into the treaty. In this way, he argued, even if the money was to be forthcoming only after several years, a solid commitment to obtain a fixed sum would at least allow them to borrow against it. The national position of holding out for more, but without a specific notion of the final amount, left the region unsure of where it stood, and unable to proceed with the immediate task of rebuilding as quickly as they would have liked. His fear of the region being left high and dry is further manifest in his call for the allies at least to give his region "the guarantees which the treaty does not give us," as a backup solution.[16]

The prevailing opinions and priorities of the region in the aftermath of the Versailles treaty, as well as their attitudes towards their neighbor across the Franco-Belgian border were further expressed by a diverse range of local leaders meeting under the auspices of the *Fédération Régionaliste du Nord et du Pas-de-Calais*. These meetings and regional congresses brought together a wide sample from among the regional elite representing different interests within the Nord-Pas-de-Calais, including industrialists, politicians and leaders of numerous cultural associations. One such meeting which received a great deal of publicity, and which focussed specifically upon the international situation was held on January 9, 1921. Sponsored by the Federation but aiming at a wider audience, the primary purpose of the meeting was to assert the rights of the regions which had been devastated by war to the "integral reparation of all of the damage" via the "strict" application of the April 17, 1919 law regarding the devastated regions, as well as the genuine execution of the Treaty of Versailles.[17] The 1919 law had been put in place to provide for the administration and to regulate the financing of the reconstruction, and the association membership was clear that it wanted "no alleviation" or toning down of the clauses which they counted upon as their only guarantees for full repairs, and which they felt by early 1921 were already in question.[18] They were also quite clear that the ultimate responsibility for the payments, as stipulated in the Versailles Treaty, was Germany's, and they wanted to put pressure upon the French government to take a harder line than before in reparations negotiations. The meeting was set a few days before a key allied meeting to discuss reparations in Brussels, and was preceded by a (peaceful and orderly) protest at the Chamber of Commerce, in order to further assert their views that Germany should be the ones to pay for the damage, and to encourage the government to insist upon the application of the relevant clauses of the Versailles Treaty.[19] The main

meeting was attended by regional senators, deputies, many leading figures in the region, and was chaired by M. Vancauwenberghe, the president of the Conseil Général du Nord.[20] In terms of its general policies, the
Fédération was not regionalist in the strict sense of the word, but aimed to
defend specifically regional interests within the national context, for
which this meeting was a good example.[21]

The contents of the local press and the speeches at such meetings confirm that the local feeling that Germany should be the one to pay for the
reconstruction was strong, but there was likewise the constant nagging
fear that it might not be able to pay, or that it simply might not be forced
to pay because of allied disagreements or lack of sufficient force of will to
insist on payment. Simple concern over the economic situation in Germany,
the state of its recovery, tax system, and potential exports was expressed
alongside of more traditional types of hostility towards Germany and German
behaviour such as had been commonly expressed during the war.[22] While
there is no doubt that they would have liked Germany to be forced to pay,
it is also clear that they would settle for payment originating with the
French government, or indeed any allied or other source provided that the
reconstruction took place and was appropriately financed. It was clear
from the outset that the pressure was aimed at the French government,
whom they hoped would insist on the payments from Germany, but failing that would come through with the promised finances themselves. As
the years went by, and it seemed less and less likely that the reparations
payments sought under the auspices of the Versailles treaty would be sufficiently forthcoming, they abandoned that strategy and turned to alternative suggestions, such as a special tax within France destined to finance
the reconstruction.[23]

Local attitudes in the Westhoek to the Versailles negotiations on reparations and their aftermath were thus solidly grounded in pragmatism with
respect to their immediate needs, and relatively void of any longer term
ideological content of pure animosity towards Germany such as could be
found elsewhere in France.[24] Their position was that the sooner a clear
agreement could be reached the better, even if that meant that the French
government needed to compromise much more strongly on their stance
regarding the final amount of reparations. The prime motivation in the
quest for reparations from Germany was not to make Germany suffer in
principle, out of a spirit of revenge, but primarily to ensure that local damage was repaired, and a feeling that it would be just for the money to
come from Germany rather than France or her allies.

The episode of negotiations in order to finance the reconstruction had
implications for the evolution of identity in the region as well. At several
meetings of the Regionalist Federation, questions of Flemish regional culture and links with the Belgian Flemish population and separatist activities

also appeared on the agenda. At their regional congress held on December 7, 1920, one of the principal speakers was Camille Looten, the president of the Comité Flamand de France (CFF), an association which had sought to promote Flemish culture in the region through meetings, sponsored activities and a variety of publications since its foundation in 1853. He wanted to encourage the re-instatement of Flemish in the schools of French Flanders in order to preserve its use, for "a people who changes its language, changes its soul."[25] He argued that the preservation of Flemish would furthermore be beneficial for the French State, providing a valuable resource in a group who could be used to ease communication not only with Belgium, but also with the Netherlands and Germany. In a further intervention, Monsieur Mabille de Poncheville put forward three propositions which were all accepted unanimously by the federation: that a Flemish literature course, as well as a course in regional History, be instigated at the University of Lille, that regional authors be studied and regional songs sung in the schools, and that the schools teach local and regional history.[26]

While such interventions in favour of a greater place for the Flemish culture in France did not make any headway with the French authorities and were unsuccessful in their aims, they demonstrate that in the years which immediately followed the First World War, the French Flemish still had an identity as a "people" distinct from the French. The experience of war with Germany, greater dependence upon France and temporary loss of contact with others among the cultural community had not destroyed the Flemish identity, cultural specificity or friendliness with the Belgian Flemish. Looten was quick to assert, however, that the 200,000 Flemish speakers of the Westhoek were nevertheless all loyal, patriotic French citizens, active combatants and heroic soldiers in the French army, but whose love of the "grande patrie" did not prevent them from at the same time loving their own language and culture.[27] The historian of French Flanders, Jules Dewachter, analysed the situation in a similar manner to Looten, considering that the French Flemish, while both conscious of and proud of the language, history and culture which they shared with the Belgian Flemish, were nevertheless "sincerely attached" to France, and posed no threat to the French State.[28] The French police, investigating the regionalist movement also concluded that Looten's attitude was "irreproachable" with respect to France, that his actions had never led to "the slightest negative comment from the national point of view" and that he and his movement were neither separatist nor in any way associated with the flamingant activists in Belgium.[29] From other sources it is clear that Looten and his association were in regular contact with cultural activists from the Belgian Flemish movement, that the French Flemish continued to identify themselves with wider Flemish culture and society, while at the same time cultural and political identities remained clearly separate and distinct in the Westhoek.[30]

Thus the clear distinction between political and cultural identities which has already been observed can at least in part be attributed to the obvious dependence of the region upon the French State to finance the post-war reconstruction, so necessary for the return to normal. As seen above, they had not been separatist before the war either, and the dual French-Flemish identity had existed without apparent contradiction in the Westhoek for several decades. Between the genuine pride from the victory, a desire to appear extra-loyal faced with potential criticism from the rest of France combined with the pragmatism of a claim on the French government and a general tendency to co-operate with authority, the immediate post-war period saw Flemish organisations put a great deal more effort into asserting their Frenchness than had been the case previously.

Forceful assertion of Frenchness, as it has been suggested, did not imply an end to Flemish cultural identity, or a decrease in either friendliness towards or sociability with their fellow Flemish in Belgium. On the contrary, expressions of solidarity with Belgians were not infrequent in the local press, and Mabille de Poncheville, who spoke at the regionalist Congress discussed above, was also the director of a series of publications expressing Franco-Belgian solidarity and friendship.[31] That being said, the two local populations lacked a "common cause," at least at the political or administrative level. Faced with the more immediate, concrete concerns to obtain funding for the reconstruction of their particular villages, buildings or farms, the two Flemish groups were each caught in up in their own national structures for obtaining resources. At the international level they were of course interested in obtaining as much for both groups from Germany as possible, and equally outraged at the damage on the other side of the border, although in some ways the nature of the international situation put them in competition with each other for resources. Thus while friendliness and fellow-feeling were as strong as ever with the Belgian Flemish, the national structures put in place to implement the post-war settlement encouraged a deepening of the dual identity of the region, accompanied by the increased pertinence and prominence of the French one, the corresponding downplaying of the regional cultural claims being advanced by the CFF and others like them, as well as the greater presence of the border as an element of that identity.

SECURITY

The second major concern of the population at the time of the Versailles settlement was for peace and security. The experience of the war was clearly not one which they wanted to repeat, and there was a vivid interest in finding the best possible guarantee of future security from a second military invasion of the region. The region's position at the frontier simply heightened such concerns since any future invasion would in all probability come through their region. At the level of simple defence, France was clearly the best guarantee for the locals of future security from such a future invasion. The Belgians were friends if not allies, and there was no fear of attack by them, but given their size and commitment to neutrality, they were not the obvious place to turn as a bulwark against invasion. It was therefore not towards the rest of Flanders that the Westhoek needed to turn for defence, but to the rest of France, and hopefully an alliance structure which the French government would be able to preserve. Thinking of future defence and security, even if the main desire was to establish a pacifist scenario to prevent war in the first place, the underlying means to achieve greater security was to be obtained through the support of the rest of France. As has been seen for the question of financial need, dependency upon the French State encouraged the French Flemish to turn further away from the border and to think of themselves increasingly in "French" terms.

As seen above, French-Flemish opinion was in favour of ensuring that Germany paid for the damages, but talk of keeping Germany down and talk of "revenge" was not prominent among the local discourses, which tended to defend a pacifist, or at least "pro-peace" position. Some disillusionment with the Versailles settlement on this score had already taken hold by the Autumn of 1919. Just a few short weeks after it had come into force, regional analysis of the world situation had already led some to the conclusion that, at least as far as bringing about an end to world conflict, the Versailles Treaty had manifestly failed.[32] While partly inevitable given the post-war environment, a strong current of feeling was that more pacifist governments were needed in order to make the peace work, and that this could only be brought about through a strongly expressed desire from the local populations around the country. Likewise regarding the League of Nations, which after its creation was warmly welcomed in the region, but which also prompted local reactions suggesting that it was far more important to begin at a smaller scale, and work on building peace within their own society first, before trying to extend it to the rest of the world.[33] Here again the focus for the expression and manifestation of such ideas was through local representation within the French national political system. It is clear that the position of the Westhoek on the border also heightened the desire for pacifism to take hold, since so much more was at stake for them than for those in the rest of France. Any attack would come through them, and even if eventually repelled, it was clearly preferable for those living in the potential battle zone to prefer that a war not start at all.

A final implication of the post-war settlement which influenced identity formation in the Westhoek was population movement and immigration. The great damage combined with the loss of young men created a high demand for workers in the region. The result was a huge influx of foreign workers with diverse origins. By far the largest group was the Belgian Flemish, who had long been in the habit of coming into the Westhoek and other areas of northern France seeking work. For many decades they had followed a pattern of seasonal migration for a period of work to both the rural and urban centres, and as transportation networks had increased, many also chose to commute weekly or daily across the border.[34] By the early post-war years, their presence was therefore familiar in the Westhoek, reminding them of the years before the war, and unthreatening to the French Flemish population. Immigrants from further abroad, primarily Italians, north Africans and Poles had been present in smaller numbers before the war, but mostly in the coal mining areas neighbouring the Westhoek rather than in the countryside, the smaller centres of French Flanders or the Lille industrial basin. Because of the extra demand and the difficult and dangerous nature of the cleanup work, such groups became more numerous in the immediate post-war years, and many of the teams of rural workers coming into the Westhoek were drawn from China. The presence of such workers increased ethnic awareness among the French Flemish, and led to critical public comments regarding the presence of these "foreigners."[35] It also reinforced the solidarity with the Belgian Flemish, who were not referred to as "foreigners" but simply "Belgians," conferring upon them a special status, familiar but not the same, not foreign but not quite "self" either.[36] Within this environment, regional identity was therefore defined against a hierarchy of otherness; while the border was present as a real limit, cultural and historical cross-border affinities were at the same time reinforced given the presence of other groups who were even more foreign.[37] In this scenario, although they made up a single cultural zone, the two distinct political identities had increased resonance.

CONCLUSION

The local reactions to the Versailles Settlement in the Westhoek were closely associated to local conditions and the immediate needs of the French Flemish within the post-war climate. Although by and large consistent with the general reaction of the French population as a whole, the French-Flemish attitude towards the peace objectives nevertheless demonstrated several specifically local characteristics. The material damage to the region confronted them with the problem of rebuilding as their immediate priority, rendering their position with respect to reparations payments much more pragmatic compared with the rest of France, and less based on an ideology of revenge against the Germans. While thinking it just that Germany be required to pay, they were more interested in the underlying guarantees of payment, and less concerned about where the funds actually came from. Similarly, holding out indefinitely for total reparations payments as high as the national negotiating team was aiming for was not considered worth the expense of uncertainty about the final figures. As a border region which was among the most at risk should another war break out, their dependence upon France for future security was also keenly felt. Their vulnerability also meant that the region was more pacifist than the average, given that they had more to lose in the event of a new invasion.

The Versailles settlement and the post-war climate also had an impact upon the evolution of local identity in the Westhoek, in which a Flemish cultural identity and a French national political identity had coexisted for some time without contradiction. In spite of four years of war, their Flemish cultural identity which was shared with those across the border in the province of West Flanders in Belgium remained in place, and the social interaction between the two populations continued as before the war. Commemoration of the war and dependency upon the French State both for security as well as to administer and to finance the reconstruction of the region had the effect of enhancing their national political identity, and the national border as a symbol of who they were and where they stood. While not affecting the reality of their cultural connections across the border, active concern for the peace process rendered the French Flemish much more aware of their place within France. Not just the war itself, but also the stakes at the Versailles discussions increased local awareness of world affairs, and the fact that it was connection to France which was the best way to promote local and regional interests. The ideology behind a Europe of nation-states enshrined in the Treaty at Versailles was in the process of becoming more true on the ground, as national political affinities had a greater impact than ever upon daily life and hence upon consciousness.

NOTES

1. Jules Dewachter, "Sur le Front des Langues," in N. Bourgeois et al (eds.), *Flandre Notre Mère: La Flandre Française en douze tableaux* (Steenvoorde, 1994), p. 101. (Originally published in Bailleul, 1931).
2. Jules Dewachter, "Le recul du Flamand dans le Nord de la France depuis 1806," *1er Congrès International de Géographie Historique. Tome II Mémoires* (Brussels, 1931), pp. 89–98.
3. Frank Logie, "Grens en sociale relaties: huwelijkskringen als voorbeeld van de sociale invloed van staats grenzen," *De Fraanse Nederlanden/Les Pays-Bas Français* 11 (1986), pp. 46–58.

4. On the Belgian Flemish movement see John Fitzmaurice, *The Politics of Belgium: A Unique Federalism* (London, 1996), and Cyriel Verschaeve, "The Flemish nationalist's catechism (1918)," in Theo Hermans, Louis Vos and Lode Wils (eds.), *The Flemish Movement: A Documentary History 1780–1990* (London, 1992), pp. 240–53.

5. For a full discussion of the evolution of identity in French Flanders, see Timothy Baycroft, *Culture, Identity and Nationalism: French Flanders in the Nineteenth and Twentieth Centuries* (London, 2004).

6. See Antoine Prost, *Republican Identities in War and Peace: Representations of France in the Nineteenth and Twentieth Centuries* (Oxford, 2002), pp. 11–44, 93–106.

7. See for example the *Journal de Bergues*, 4220 (Feb. 25, 1919), pp. 1–3. This was the first issue after the end of the war.

8. See "Comment Bergue passa de la guerre à la paix," ibid, p. 2.

9. See for example *Le Patriote de Flandres*, 432 (July 6, 1919), p. 1 (from Steenvoorde), or *Le Phare du Nord*, (Aug. 21, 1919), p. 2 (from Dunkirk).

10. Annette Becker, *Oubliés de la Grande Guerre: humanitaire et culture de guerre 1914–1918, populations occupies, déportés civils, prisonniers de guerre* (Paris, 998).

11. Ibid. pp. 359–76.

12. Ibid. pp. 49, 66.

13. See Archives Départementals du Nord (ADN) 10R 1129–1398.

14. For details by commune, see ADN 10 Ra 59–1490.

15. Jean Guiscard, "Dunkerque: Serons-nous payées?" *Le Phare du Nord*, 5897 (Sep. 13, 1919), p. 2.

16. Ibid.

17. Central Police Commissioner to the Prefect of the Département du Nord, Jan. 10, 1921. ADN M 154 318.

18. Ibid.

19. "Sinistés garde à vous," promotional poster, police files, ADN M 154 318.

20. Police Commissioner to the Prefect, Jan. 10, 1921. ADN M 154 318. The Conseil Général is the French equivalent of an English county council.

21. See *Le Nord Fédéral. Organe de Défence des Droits de la Région du Nord*, (Mar. 18, 1929). For more on the regionalist movements in France see Maurice Agulhon, "Conscience nationale et conscience régionale en France de 1815 à nos jours," in J. C. Boogman and G. N. van der Plaat (eds.), *Federalism: History and current significance of a form of government* (The Hague, 1980), pp. 259–60.

22. See for example "L'Allemagne compte payer ses dettes, " *Journal de Bergues* 4244 (Aug. 1, 1919), p. 3, or "Par la faute de nos allies," *Le Patriote des Flandres* 444 (Sep. 1919), p. 1.

23. The Prefect of the Département du Nord to the Minister of the Interior, Trade and Liberated Regions, Dec. 14, 1925 and Aug. 28, 1926. ADN M 154 318, and "Le Nord au Service de la France, " *Le Télégramme du Nord*, 347 (Dec. 14, 1925), p. 1.

24. J. F. V. Keiger, *France and the World since* 1870 (London, 2001), p. 121.

25. Quoted in the Prefect to the Minister of the Interior, Jan. 5, 1921. ADN 154 318.

26. Special Police Commissioner to the Prefect, Dec. 31, 1920. ADN 154 318.

27. Quoted in the Prefect to the Minister of the Interior, Jan. 5, 1921. ADN 154 318.

28. See J. Dewachter, "La situation du français et du flamand dans le Nord de la France après la guerre mondiale," *RFB* 8e année, Nouvelle série No. 1 (Jan. 1928), pp. 31–2.

29. The Prefect to the Minister of the Interior, Jan. 5, 1921. ADN 154 318.

30. For more on the complimentarily of these identities see Timothy Baycroft, "Changing identities in the Franco-Belgian Borderland in the nineteenth and twentieth centuries," *French History* 13(4) (1999), pp. 417–38.

31. See for example the *Journal de Bergues* 4220 (Feb. 25, 1919), p. 2; 4245 (Aug. 5, 1919), p. 3. The Prefect to the Minister of the Interior, Jan. 5, 1921, the Prefect to the Sub-Prefect of Cambrai, May 9, 1921, ADN 154 318, and A Lorbert, *La France au travail: La région du Nord* (Paris, 1927).

32. See Paul Roume, "Est-ce la Paix? " *Le Phare du Nord*, 5931 (Oct. 18, 1919), p. 1.

33. See for example P. Chanturge, "La "Société des Français,"" *Le Phare du Nord*, 5935 (Oct. 22, 1919), p. 1.

34. F. Lentacker, "Les frontaliers belges travaillant en France: Caractères et fluctuations d'un courant de main d'oeuvre," *Revue du Nord* XXXII (1950), pp. 130–44, and J. Theys, "De evolutie van de grensarbeid tussen West Vlaanderen en Noord-Frankrijk in de 20ste eeuw," *De Fraanse Nederlanden/Les Pays-Bas Français*, 13 (1988), pp. 89–104.

35. "Les Crimes des Chinois dans le Nord de la France—Les Etrangers chez nous," *Journal de Bergues* 4248 (Aug. 19, 1919), p. 2.

36. Yola Verhasselt, Frank Logie and Bernadette Mergaerts, "Espace géographique et formes de sociabilité: quatre exemples de régions frontalières," *Revue du Nord*, LXIV (Apr.–Jun. 1982), p. 593.

37. See Paul Lawrence, Timothy Baycroft and Carolyn Grohmann, ""Degrees of Foreignness" and the Construction of Identity in French Border Regions during the Interwar Period," *Contemporary European History* 10(1) (2001), pp. 51–71.

"THE SORE THAT WOULD NEVER HEAL": THE GENESIS OF THE POLISH CORRIDOR

Roger Moorhouse

Like the Schleswig Holstein Question or the Macedonian Maze, the Polish Corridor was an issue that perplexed a generation. A vexed international problem, with its oppressed minorities, insensitive governments, and meddling Great Powers, it spawned a flood of pamphlets and polemics. Few inter-war intellectuals would have been ignorant of its minutest details. Few would have been unable to offer an opinion on the matter.

The "Corridor" itself was a strip of land of around 10,000 km^2 consisting of the former German Imperial districts of Kulmerland and Pomerellen. Between 20–70 miles wide, and containing a population of around 1.5 million souls, it divided the post-war German provinces of Pomerania and East Prussia, separating the latter from the main body of Germany. It was established in the aftermath of World War One in accordance with the thirteenth of President Wilson's "14 Points," which called for the creation of an "independent Polish state," which was to be assured "free and secure access to the sea." The problem at its heart, however, was that one Wilsonian principle; that of reconstituting a viable Poland, appeared to be incompatible with another; that of the self-determination of peoples.

This "strip of land" was to become infamous. For many later observers, it appeared to contain the seeds of World War Two. Indeed, this was a point that a brave few even dared to suggest at the time. The later South African Prime Minister Jan Smuts was one. He railed against the cessions of German land at Versailles demanding "Are we in our sober senses, or are we suffering from shell shock? What has become of Wilson's Fourteen

Points?"[1] British Prime Minister, David Lloyd George, was another. In his famous Fontainebleau Memorandum of 1919, he made what later appeared to be a visionary statement when he claimed that "the proposal . . . , that we should place 2 million Germans under the control of a people, which . . . has never proved its capacity for stable self-government . . . must . . . lead sooner or later to a war in the east of Europe."[2] Retrospective confirmation of this grim prediction was given at Nuremberg in 1946. General von Blomberg, formerly German War Minister and Commander-in-Chief of the German Armed Forces, stated that "I myself, as well as the whole group of German staff officers, believed that the Polish Question was to be solved by force of arms. . . . A war to wipe out the desecration involved in the creation of the Polish Corridor . . . was regarded as a sacred duty. . . ."[3]

A brief historical outline is perhaps desirable. The region of the later corridor straddled one of the linguistic and ethnographic fault lines of central Europe. Traditionally Polish, it had fallen to the Teutonic knights in the early fourteenth century, but unlike nearby East Prussia and Pomerania, had not been the scene of widespread Germanic settlement. It had then reverted to the Polish crown in the sixteenth century, before falling to the Kingdom of Prussia in the First Partition of Poland in 1772. Yet, despite, or perhaps because of these peregrinations, the region never developed either a German or Polish majority.

Indeed, by the early twentieth century, the ethnography of the Corridor was bewilderingly complex. Firstly, as in many regions of mixed settlement, clear boundaries between populations were almost impossible to divine. Rather than dividing along a neat demarcation line, ethnic groups tended to form islands of settlement. For instance, as was the norm in central Europe, immigrant Germans and Jews tended to make up the urbanised middle and lower-middle classes, whilst indigenous peoples (whether Poles, Czechs or Hungarians) were usually predominant in rural areas. Secondly, it is an open question how far even some of the inhabitants of the region were sure of who they were. What factors defined their identity, religion or language? Did they, indeed, have any developed sense of a wider "imagined community," beyond the more immediate allegiance to their hometown, their region or their province? Any attempt to disentangle the rival populations by the simple redrawing of frontiers, therefore, using the blunt instrument of nationality as a guide, was bound to be fraught with difficulties.

In the case of the Polish Corridor, there was a further complication. As well as Germans and Poles, the region was also populated by Kashubs; a west-Slavonic people numbering about 200,000 and speaking a Slavic dialect. The Kashubs, predictably, were in turn divided into two groups— a northern one (largely Protestant and Germanised) and a southern one (largely Catholic and Polonized). The exact demographics of the region are therefore notoriously difficult to pin down, but suffice it to say, they were extremely mixed. Two sets of statistics can give a flavour of the problem. The German census of 1905[4] gave figures for the relevant provinces of West Prussia and the Netze district, which at first sight appeared to give the Germans a clear majority of 65.5% to 34.5% over the indigenous Poles. However, count the Kashubs in with the Poles, and one is left with only a paper-thin majority of 50.2%/49.8% in favour of the Germans. Furthermore, according to the more detailed breakdown in the German census of 1900; one of the five administrative districts (or *Kreise*) of the region had a Polish majority, whilst two had a Kashub majority. In the remaining two *Kreise* the slim German majority was outweighed by the combination of Polish and Kashub elements.

It should perhaps be added at this point that the British delegation in Paris considered the German statistics gleaned from these censuses to be fraudulent and produced rival figures of their own, but they neglected to give their provenance. It is highly likely that they had come from the Polish lobby and were, in fact, equally questionable. One is tempted to complain of "Lies, damned lies and statistics." However, working on the German census figures, (which are the most apparently comprehensive) it would seem that the Polish Corridor was thoroughly mixed ethnically and could in no way be described as having an overall majority of any sort.

The creation of the Polish Corridor was initially suggested, not surprisingly, by the Poles, who arrived in Paris with historic, ethnographic, strategic, and economic justifications for their shopping list of real and imagined irredenta.[5] The Polish National Cammittee had, by this point, executed a near-perfect propaganda campaign. Formed in Switzerland in 1917 by the nationalist politician Roman Dmowski, it had toured Allied capitals persuading, charming and cajoling until Polish matters crept up the political agenda. The French were more than willing to listen to Polish requests. They saw a strengthened Poland as an essential counterweight to Germany, whilst Russia was mired in revolution. To this end, they sought to make Poland a Baltic power once again, and this, they considered, required that she be given a functioning port (Danzig) along with approximately 100 miles of neighbouring coastline (the Corridor). In Washington and London, meanwhile, the idea of the Corridor was considered to be wholly impractical. Former Deputy Foreign Minister Lord Cecil described it as "an impossible policy" and one which "will only create a sore which will never heal."[6] President Wilson's advisors considered the idea to be beyond the bounds of practical politics.

Nonetheless, the proposal was first aired in Paris early in 1919. The Anglo-American Howard-Lord agreement, reached in the absence of both Lloyd George and Wilson, foresaw both Danzig and the Corridor falling to Poland as the logical corollary to Wilson's thirteenth Point. This was then agreed by the Commission on Polish Affairs and approved by the Territorial Committee. However, it was then repudiated by the Foreign Office in London, as it went against British guidelines for the peace conference, which foresaw only the northern tip of the territory passing to Poland and a southern strip connecting Pomerania with Danzig remaining in German hands (a corridor through the Corridor, if you will).[7] As a result of the confusion, the co-author of the agreement, Esmé Howard, was rebuked by Whitehall and told not to commit himself to anything in future.

Lloyd George, meanwhile, was minded to resist Franco-Polish demands for the creation of a strong Poland at the expense of Germany, complaining that Berlin had to be able to swallow the terms of any treaty to make it viable and, in effect, self-enforcing. His stand was strengthened by the Prothero memorandum of February 21, 1919, which asserted the superiority of German over Polish "civilization" and concluded that the cession of the Corridor to Poland "would create a sense of gross injustice in the mind of Germany," which would be "fatal to the peace of the world."[8] Despite its obvious bias, the Prothero memorandum was warmly welcomed by some of the British delegation. Importantly, it also floated the prospect of establishing Danzig as a free state under the auspices of the League of Nations.

A response duly came in the Paton memorandum of February 27. Hamish Paton, an Admiralty intelligence official, declared that the interests and security of 20 million Poles should override those of a few hundred thousand Germans. Issues of culture or civilisation, he argued, were irrelevant. Poland's historical claim to the region was as strong as Germany's. In granting the corridor to Poland, he stated, Germany would suffer no "appreciable loss, other than sentimental."[9] Poland, however, if denied the corridor, would be reduced to the status of a German vassal. The safest way of achieving peace, he concluded, was to do the smallest amount of wrong.

Paton's memorandum carried the day, temporarily at least. The Commission on Polish Affairs and the Territorial Committee of the conference again approved the cession of both Danzig and the corridor to Poland. Lloyd George, meanwhile, was becoming increasingly concerned about the vindictive nature of the peace proposals. On March 7, 1919, he made it clear that Britain would not accept the suggested Polish frontier. Two weeks later, he formally proposed the creation of the free city of Danzig and a plebiscite for the Marienwerder district of East Prussia. His broader thinking then crystallised in the famous Fontainebleau Memorandum of March 25.

At Fontainebleau, Lloyd George and his advisors engaged in an intense session of discussions and presentations. They even acted out role-plays, in which each member of the team would be assigned a role; German officer, French woman, and so on, so that each proposal could viewed from all angles. The result was a call for a moderate peace, motivated by thoughts of "justice, not vengeance," which would leave a stable Germany at Europe's heart. With Russia consumed by revolution, it was thought sensible to attempt to win back those attracted by the radical appeal of Communism. "If we are wise," Lloyd George wrote, "we will offer Germany a peace, which, whilst it is just, will also serve to win all reasonable people away from the alternative of Bolshevism. . . . We must do everything possible to help the German people back on to their feet . . . Arrogance displayed in the moment of triumph," he warned, "will never be forgiven." On the Corridor issue, he advocated granting Poland only a corridor *to Danzig*, and leaving as few Germans as possible within the new Polish frontier.[10]

Yet, beyond annoying the French and frustrating the Americans, the memorandum achieved little. Despite his misgivings, Lloyd George ultimately dropped his protests. He accepted the principle of the Corridor, but with the rider that its border be drawn "irrespective of strategic or transportation considerations, so as to embrace the smallest possible number of Germans."[11]

Much has been made of Lloyd George's motives in "appeasing" Germany in Paris. Some have proposed that British trade interests were paramount. Others considered that he used Danzig as a stick to beat down excessive French ambitions. It has even been suggested that Lloyd George was vehemently anti-Polish. This last peculiar idea springs from the fact that he was the source of a series of derogatory comments regarding the Poles. Of Upper Silesia, he was said to have stated that he would "sooner give a clock to a monkey"[12] than hand the region to the control of Warsaw. The Polish president, he complained, was a pianist; the prime-minister—an idealist. And, the Poles themselves were a people who, he considered, had never proved their capacity for stable self-government. In much of this, Lloyd George was undoubtedly influenced by the trenchant opinions of his emissary to Poland; Sir Maurice Hankey, who shrank from no criticism.[13] Yet, though Lloyd George did spend a season as Poland's "public enemy number one," the idea of his anti-Polonism has since been convincingly refuted.[14] It is much more plausible that such utterances betrayed more about Lloyd George than about his attitude to the Poles.

Lloyd George liked to portray himself as one rising above wartime emotions to secure a lasting peace in Europe by reconciling the new German Republic to the otherwise harsh terms of the peace. This may, in part, be fair. But, undiluted altruism is a rare quality. Lloyd George had indeed wanted to give Berlin some crumb of comfort to sweeten the bitter pill of defeat, war guilt and territorial truncation. Yet, his motive in doing so, perhaps, was a little more selfish. It would appear that he was seeking to facilitate a safe British withdrawal from continental affairs by re-establishing a healthy Franco-German rivalry. A democratic, reconciled Germany, at ease with itself and inured to revolutionary infection was the best guarantee for British security. A prostrate Germany, prone to revolution and lorded over and truncated by a victorious France, he thought, would serve nobody's long-term interest.

But, rather than make a stand on the Corridor, he chose the stronger issue of Danzig as his battleground and successfully campaigned against Franco-Polish plans for outright annexation of the city in favour of the "free state" option, which in any case, he considered merely to be a temporary expedient.[15] The Corridor, meanwhile, became a reality and was duly enshrined in the Treaty of Versailles. The Poles were not consulted.

So, in the absence of a clear-cut demographic argument, the political, and strategic considerations became paramount. Poland's need for a "free and secure" access to the sea would override the fraught issue of self-determination of peoples. But what chance was there that another settlement to the issue of the Corridor might have been achieved? It is certainly clear that there was a surprising degree of latitude in the negotiation and planning on the matter. The French, so often seen as the villains of the piece, were adamant that Berlin should not have the region, and their preferred solution was that it should pass to Poland, but, beyond that, they were quite open to suggestion. Indeed, Paris had even aired the possibility of "internationlizing" Danzig and the Corridor in the event of British and American objection to the region's cession to Poland.[16]

The ultimate fate of the Corridor was not set in stone, therefore, and could conceivably have produced a very different outcome. One alternative that was suggested is perhaps surprising. The British, Americans and the French, for example, all examined the possibility of extending the League-controlled area of Danzig to include much or all of the Corridor. In a British memorandum[17] a similar suggestion was reported which foresaw a neutral, multi-national buffer state, under League of Nations control, separating Germany from Bolshevik Russia. The proposed new polity would meet all the targets demanded by Wilsonian idealism: granting access to the Baltic whilst not infringing the national rights and desires of the mixed native population.

Wilson's policy advisors had also come up with a similar suggestion. On March 27, 1919, the United States president suggested the creation of the free city of Danzig in a meeting with Lloyd George, Clemenceau and Orlando. Interestingly, his conception of the future free state encompassed, "not only Danzig itself but a large stretch of the surrounding countryside . . . that is the Polish Corridor."[18] A later discussion on the western border of the putative free state concluded with Wilson stating that the line should be drawn "so far west as is necessary to include any German minority."[19]

In August 1920, Danzig itself arrived at a similar conclusion. With the Red Army bearing down on the Polish capital, and with the ink still not really dry on the Treaty of Versailles, politically speaking, a revision briefly appeared possible. That autumn, the president of the Danzig senate, Heinrich Sahm, approached the British plenipotentiary in the city, with a plan for a "rectification" of Danzig's frontiers.[20] Concerns had often been raised about the viability of the Free State, which consisted of little more than the port and its immediate hinterland, and Sahm suggested that an extension of Danzig's territory would make the state self supporting and solve what he called the "corridor" question. He helpfully suggested a new border for the Free State, running from the Baltic coast south through Lauenberg, Konitz and Schneidemühl, turning east to Bromberg and Gilgenburg and then north again to the Vistula. If realised, this would have meant a tenfold expansion of the Free State's territory. The Polish Corridor would have ceased to exist. The new *"Freistaat Danzig"* would have been of a similar size to the province of East Prussia.

Lloyd George later stated that he considered the enlarged *Freistaat* to have been a reasonable solution, which would have solved the thorny matter of the corridor and might have reconciled Germany to the Versailles treaty as a whole.[21] But the British reaction at the time was predictably cool. They had rejected a similar proposal the year before as they were unwilling to create a Germano-Polish free state, which, it was thought, would prove wholly ungovernable. Moreover, in August 1920 the world as waiting with baited breath to see if Trotsky's Red Army would sweep across Poland, and, as Moscow predicted, unleash "world-wide conflagration." In such a scenario, a global revision of the terms of Versailles would very possibly have been on the cards, either at Lenin's insistence or as a result of a victorious Allied campaign against Soviet Russia. So, Sahm's pre-emptive tinkering with Danzig's borders smacked somewhat of fiddling while Rome burned. And, in addition, the Polish crisis of 1920 demonstrated most clearly that Poland was in desperate need of a free port. The strikes that had paralysed the passage of Polish supplies through Danzig had almost fatally hampered Warsaw's defence against the Soviets. Once Warsaw had held, therefore, Danzig's fate, and that of the Corridor, was effectively sealed. In the event, the 1920 crisis would strengthen the argument of the Poles and weaken that of Germans.

So, what other forces militated against a more equitable solution to the question of the Corridor? A number of factors appear to have influenced the decision-making process. Firstly, the tone of those deliberations could not but be affected by the preceding years of warfare. This was most obviously true of the French, whose anti-German prejudices were barely disguised at Versailles, much to the disgust of many British observers.[22] The feeling was nonetheless also in evidence amongst some members of the British delegation, where a fundamentally anti-German tone prevailed. Some, such as the advisors on Polish affairs Hamish Paton and Esmé Howard, were self-confessed germanophobes. They consistently argued against any concession to Germany. They used language that was often critical of Berlin, dismissive of its concerns, mocking of its wishes. The tone had been set by Lloyd George's victory in the 1918 election on the so-called "Hang the Kaiser" ticket.

Thus, it took a great deal of personal integrity and indeed bravery to advocate any sort of conciliatory line towards Germany in 1919. James Headlam-Morley, historical advisor to the Foreign Office, was one of those who were able to take that line. He believed passionately that Germany had to be granted some concession to ensure her acceptance of the broader terms of the peace. But he was in a minority. This shortcoming was exacerbated by the fact that the issue of Poland's border with Germany was treated, as Headlam-Morley complained, as if it were a Polish and not a German problem. Jan Smuts agreed, ruing the fact that there was no one appointed to consider the matter from the German point of view. This coincidence of factors meant that the British, though potentially the most sympathetic to German feelings, were unlikely to sponsor a favourable revision of Germany's eastern border.

Secondly, the tensions manifested between the allies during the conference so strained relations that negotiations were generally conducted though gritted teeth. These tensions were primarily the result of the differing attitudes and agendas represented by the British and the French. The primary concern for the French, for example, was to use the Versailles settlement as the opportunity to reverse two generations of history and reduce Germany to a secondary rank in Europe. The British, meanwhile, were more concerned about defending against the westward spread of communism.[23] As a result, tantrums and the trading of insults were often barely concealed beneath the veneer of diplomatic niceties. In addition, President Wilson, visibly ailing, was unable to bring to force of his fading vision to bear. The result, all too often, was a squabble between the British and French, which rapidly descended into acrimony.

Thirdly, with the notable exception of the League of Nations, the Wilsonian new world order of 1919 had little time for the sort of supranational solutions that might have solved the conundrum of the corridor. United States' planning was wedded to idea of national states in central Europe, despite the complex and untidy realities on the ground, and was not in the business of creating new multi-national states out of the old multi-national states that had just plunged the continent into war. In sharp contrast, Headlam-Morley had waxed eloquent in defence of the free city solution for Danzig. He stated that "we want to shake ourselves free of the obsessions of the unified and centralised national state. . . . It is the exaggeration of this which is the cause not only of the war, but of the difficulties of the peace."[24] He was right, of course, but he was hopelessly before his time. It would take another world war to make the majority of Europeans see the wisdom of his words.

Lastly, it must be borne in mind that the statesmen in Paris were not operating in a vacuum. Across Europe, they were forced to adapt their deliberations to realities on the ground. Central Europe was especially difficult. The collapse of the old empires had created a wealth of possibilities. As Lenin said of Petrograd in 1917, power was lying in the street, and all one had to do was stoop to pick it up. In the region of the Corridor, ethnic cleaning against the German population was on the rise. In the south, along the Netze river, a nasty border war spluttered throughout 1919, with one town after another penning agonised telegrams to Berlin and even London, before falling to Polish forces. In the north, the process was a little more gentle, with only the threat of force usually sufficing to send many German civilians westwards as refugees. But mass migration was the inevitable result. And against the background of such events, the deliberations in the smoke-filled rooms of Paris appeared more than a little surreal, even perverse.

So, the Corridor stood and only the issue of Danzig was the subject of any meaningful compromise at the conference. Unsurprisingly, no-one was satisfied. The Germans, as Lloyd George had predicted, felt humiliated and emasculated and the issue became a running sore in German-Polish relations and a primary complaint for those who advocated the revision of the peace treaty. The Poles too, were unhappy. Though they had gained the corridor, part of Upper Silesia and Poznan, they had not been granted Danzig, parts of West Prussia and had been forced to submit to unsuccessful referenda in other areas. In all, their wish list of irredenta had been cut by over a half. Little wonder, then, that they were happy to settle their eastern border by force of arms.

The British, content to have saved Danzig for *Deutschtum*, washed their hands of the Corridor, whilst the conviction grew at home that the treaty as a whole was too harsh and would prove unenforceable. The Americans, tired of the squabbles of "old Europe," retired to a generation of isolationism. The French, along with their weakened Polish ally, seethed at Lloyd George's deceptions and his slippery, enigmatic nature. The Polish Corridor, it appeared, had caused the maximum inconvenience to everyone.

What, then, of the theory that French *revanchism* was the main motivation behind the creation of the Corridor? Well, it is hard to see any motivation at all, apart from Lloyd George, who, as we have seen, was pushing in the opposite direction. Indeed, it appears that, compared to the thorny issue of Danzig, the question of the Corridor was treated as a secondary concern and barely given the necessary scrutiny. Whilst the commission on the future Polish borders held more meetings in the run up to the final treaty than any other issue,[25] and though a great deal of attention appears to have been devoted to the fate of Danzig, one searches almost in vain for references to the creation of the Polish Corridor. Only 3 or 4 memoranda, each of only a couple of pages, were devoted to the issue. It appears to have been passed by the peace conference virtually on the nod.

It also becomes clear that the creation of the Polish Corridor was not a foregone conclusion. Despite French strategic concerns, there was a considerable degree of latitude available to Allied planners. But, given the enormous scope of the Versailles Treaty, it is perhaps unsurprising that the relatively small and notoriously thorny issue of the Corridor was not afforded more attention and, crucially, more imagination.

The Soviet Foreign Minister, Vyacheslav Molotov once described inter-war Poland in his own inimitable style as "the monstrous bastard of Versailles."[26] There were many in inter-war Germany who would have agreed with him. There were many more who would have gladly applied that epithet to the Polish Corridor. But that would not be fair. Either as a sin of French commission, which it was not, or a sin of inter-Allied omission, which, I would argue, it was—the Corridor cannot really be fairly described as the "monstrous bastard" of the peace. Rather, to stretch the analogy somewhat, it might be seen as Versailles' neglected orphan: ill-conceived, unwanted and unloved by all sides.

NOTES

1. Anthony Lentin, *Lloyd George and the Lost Peace—from Versailles to Hitler, 1919–1940* (Basingstoke, 2001), p. 79.
2. Fontainebleau Memorandum quoted in PRO, FO 417/18, Headlam-Morley, *The Eastern Frontiers of Germany*, p. 86.
3. Cross-examination of General Werner von Blomberg, Jan. 4, 1946, in *Trial of the Major War Criminals before the International Military Tribunal* (Nuremberg, 1947–9), vol. 3, pp. 319–20.
4. *Encylopedia Britannica*, 1911 Edition, vol. 28, p. 559.
5. See Roland Gehrke, *Der polnische Westgedanke bis zur Wiedererrichtung des polnischen Staates nach Ende des Ersten Weltkrieges* (Marburg, 2001).
6. Lord Cecil, FO371/4354, Nov. 1918.
7. Anna Cieciala, "The Battle of Danzig and the Polish Corridor at the Paris Peace Conference of 1919" In P. Latawski (ed.) *The Reconstruction of Poland, 1914–23* (London, 1992), p. 72. See also Headlam-Morley, *Eastern Frontiers*, p. 80.
8. Headlam-Morley, *Eastern Frontiers*, p. 81.

9. Ibid., p. 80.
10. Ibid., pp. 85–88.
11. Headlam-Morley, *Eastern Frontiers*, Ibid, p. 86.
12. Quoted in: Norman Davies, *God's Playground*, vol. II. (Oxford, 1981), p. 393.
13. Norman Davies, "Sir Maurice Hankey and the Inter-Allied Mission to Poland, July–August 1920" in *The Historical Journal*, XV, 3 (1972), pp. 553–61.
14. On this issue see Norman Davies, "Lloyd George and Poland, 1919–20" in *Journal of Contemporary History*, VI, (1974).
15. Cienciala, "Battle of Danzig," p. 78.
16. Ibid., p. 73.
17. *Documents on British Foreign Policy*, Series I, Vol. VI, No. 199, Rumbold to Curzon, Oct. 5, 1919.
18. Headlam-Morley, *Eastern Frontiers*, p. 86.
19. PRO, FO608/66/20216, Headlam-Morley memorandum of interview with President Wilson, 2 Apr. 1919 in "Papers and Correspondence dealing with the establishment of Danzig as a Free City," p. 27.
20. PRO, FO 317/3934/210926 & *DBFP* Series I, Vol. XI, No. 401, p. 447, Tower to Earl Curzon, Aug. 8, 1920.
21. Cienciala, "Battle of Danzig," p. 78.
22. Lentin, *Lloyd George*, p. 83.
23. John Hiden, "Versailles, Germany's Eastern Border and Rapallo" in *Großbritannien und Deutschland seit 1918* (Munich, 1992), p. 29.
24. Sir James Headlam-Morley, *A Memoir of the Paris Peace Conference 1919* (London, 1972), p. 40.
25. Margaret Macmillan, *Peacemakers* (London, 2001), p. 217.
26. Quoted in Davies, *God's Playground*, p. 393.

CONCLUSION

Criticisms of the Treaty of Versailles which suggest that its terms mark the start of the road to the Second World War are still remarkably common,[1] but are greatly overdone and pay scant attention either to the continuation of pre-1914 problems or to the complexities, and genuine opportunities, of inter-war European history.[2] Nonetheless, both the negotiation of the treaty and its subsequent execution were as much about resolving inter-Allied quarrels as about dealing with Germany itself. Although the principal Allies, often with huge difficulty, eventually managed to compromise on the text of the peace treaty, there was still no clear consensus regarding its ultimate ends. This left its subsequent enactment problematic in the extreme, and the response of the German authorities was no less ambivalent. Confronted by a treaty whose terms they regarded as impossibly harsh and distracted by recurrent domestic crises, they swithered between reluctant compliance and dogged obstruction. British policymakers generally came to sympathise with Germany's predicament, but French leaders usually interpreted Berlin's behaviour as little more than a token of bad faith, thus reinforcing their deep-seated fears of latent German power.

It was against this backdrop that events took their course, sometimes steered by Europe's political leaders, but at others assuming a dynamic of their own. Germany's Rhineland was occupied by Allied forces shortly after the November 1918 Armistice and remained so under the terms of the Treaty. The occupation itself was a relatively benign affair and if rela-

---

1   See, for example, Jay Winter's comment 'The Peace Conference which ended the Great War was more about punishment than about peace. Perhaps inevitably, anger and retribution followed four years of bloodshed, ensuring the instability and ultimate collapse of the accords signed in the Hall of Mirrors at Versailles on 28 June 1919. The road to World War II started here.' Jay Winter and Blaine Baggett *1914–1918: The Great War and the Shaping of the Twentieth Century*(BBC Books, London, 1996) p.338
2   See Zara Steiner *The Lights That Failed. European International History, 1919–1933* (Oxford University Press, Oxford, 2005 and Sally Marks *The Ebbing of European Ascendancy: An International History of the World, 1914–1945* (Arnold, London, 2002)

tions between the Allies and Germans were seldom warm, a mood of live and let live generally prevailed. The unilateral Franco-Belgian occupation of the Ruhr District, which began in January 1923, proved the notable exception. Beyond this, however, rival Franco-British ambitions were played out along the Rhine as the men on the spot struggled to transform international agreements, but also their own governments' distinctive objectives, into concrete reality. France ultimately sought the detachment of the Rhineland from Germany in defiance of the Treaty, whereas Britain always planned to return Cologne to full German control once its occupation mandate had expired. In the event Britain's presence in the city did a great deal to frustrate French ambitions, beyond simply fulfilling London's obligations as an occupying power.

The post-war reparations agreements were particularly controversial at the time and have engaged historians to this day. It is instructive that during and after the Second World War Allied policymakers came to regard the post-Versailles reparations regime as deeply flawed, whether through Allied failure to enforce the terms, German refusal to comply with them, or a doomed attempt to prioritise German sovereign (reparations) debt over private, commercial obligations. The social and political price of total compliance upon post-1918 German governments would, it appears, have been far too high. As it was, German officials struggled to cope satisfactorily with the aftermath of a ruinous lost war as urban children literally starved and thus the ongoing payment of reparations on any terms could appear obscene, even to committed supporters of the Weimar Republic.

Was post-war disarmament to be universal, or simply imposed on the defeated powers? Sustained efforts were made by the League of Nations to establish international norms for arms control and most countries accepted that these efforts were legitimate in principle, whatever they did in practice. When it came to the particular case of Germany, however, immediate disarmament formed part of the peace settlement and here discrepancies between principle and practice seriously strained German-Allied relations. It would have been complex enough transforming armaments manufacturers, such as the mighty Krupp combine, into manufacturers of civilian products, but Krupp dissembled and, with governmental connivance, disguised rather than dismantled much of its military-industrial potential. Small wonder, then, that France in particular remained reluctant to scale down its own military establishment.

If disarmament proved controversial and difficult to achieve, whether by negotiation or enforcement, territorial change could always be imposed through the ultimate sanction of military force. Woodrow Wilson's civic concept of national self-determination proved difficult to apply in Eastern and Central Europe, partly because there were too many intermingled national groupings, partly because the concept of self-determination was not accepted by the inhabitants, who perceived nationality to be ethnically determined. There were simply too many Germans in Europe for such a principle to apply even-handedly. Germans in the former Austro-Hungarian Empire were barred from joining the new German Republic, whilst several millions of the Republic's citizens were transferred willingly or unwillingly to France and Poland. Where plebiscites were held Germany tended to do well, but in the Polish Corridor (apart from Marienwerder which voted for Germany) and in Alsace-Lorraine plebiscites were not held and campaigns of ethnic cleansing saw hundreds of thousands of refugees driven across the new German frontiers as the authorities in Paris and Warsaw hastened to alter the ethnography of these annexed regions in their favour. The war also changed national/cultural loyalties and perspectives in regions such as French Flanders, far removed from any contentious new border, but in a voluntary and evolutionary way.

The greatest contrast between the post-1918 and post-1945 settlements, at least as far as the western powers were concerned, lay in their vision of Germany's future role in the world, not least because of the more immediate menace of the USSR in 1945. Whereas bolshevism had been perceived as a rather inchoate and ill-defined, though disturbing threat in 1918, by 1945 Soviet communism was both a plausible alternative to western liberal capitalism and enjoyed the substantial occupying presence of the Red Army throughout Eastern Europe. In 1918 the Allies had to decide whether the defeated enemy was simply to be punished and contained for the foreseeable future, or was it to be rehabilitated as a major participant in a new global order? Woodrow Wilson's Fourteen Points and his other 1918 speeches had suggested the latter and the Germans did secure an undertaking from the Allies, conveyed to them on 5 November by the American Secretary of State, Robert Lansing, that the eventual Treaty would be based on the President's principles enunciated in those speeches. While the British authorities might have gone along with this in time, France's leaders perceived any German recovery as the stuff of nightmares. They were old men, some of whom had tasted defeat at the hands of Prussia in 1871 and had never forgiven or forgotten that earlier humiliation. The German onslaught against France in 1914 had simply served to confirm their pre-existing prejudices. Much of what went wrong after Versailles followed on from this clash of aims. There was no single Allied voice and no simple German response to the ambivalent nature of the peace settlement, not least because of the political withdrawal of the United States. After 1945 the United States' dominance ensured a more coherent Western response that focused on rehabilitation, almost entirely on the Allies' terms, hastened by the context of the Cold War. In the aftermath of Nazism there was to be no dissembling or prevarication on Germany's part.

However, for all its problems, the Versailles Settlement was successfully revised, firstly through the 1924 London Reparations Agreement (the

Dawes Plan), significantly with the substantial financial backing of the United States, and then the 1925 Locarno Agreements, significantly without a corresponding American political commitment.[3] Many believed that these readjustments, willingly endorsed by Germany and providing for its entry into the League of Nations as a permanent member of the Council, marked the real transition from war to peace. By 1929 Berlin's international prospects did not differ greatly from its objectives of a decade earlier, and Allied confidence in a peaceful future had grown considerably. Recovery remained fragile, however, and unable to withstand the ravages of the Great Depression and the accompanying Wall Street crash of October 1929. The untimely death at this critical juncture of Weimar Germany's great Foreign Minister, Gustav Stresemann, did nothing to help. Versailles, whatever its deficiencies, might have marked the first stage in the road to an enduring peace, but after the ravages of the Great War the peacemakers needed time, and their fair quota of luck. They were deprived of the first and arguably were short-changed on the second.

Conan Fischer
Alan Sharp

---

3 See Patrick O. Cohrs *the Unfinished Peace after World War I: America, Britain and the Stabislisation of Europe, 1919–1932* (Cambridge University Press, Cambridge, 2006

INDEX

AB Bofors 127
Abs, H.J. 77–8
Acts of Parliament 7
Adenauer, K. 64
Afghanistan 106
Africa 138–9
Africans 181
agriculture 82–3, 121, 172
aid organizations 175
alcohol 39–40
Algrange (Algringen) 156
Alliance Treaty 23
Allied Control Mission 122
Allies 2, 12–13, 15–16, 22–8, 30, 34, 61
  arms control 113, 120–2, 124
  Associated Powers 5
  BAOR 37–9, 43, 45
  criticisms 197–200
  disarmament 114
  Flemish identity 176–7
  Polish Corridor 187, 191–2, 194
  reparations 70, 73, 76, 81–5, 88, 90, 92, 98, 101–6
  sanctions 63
Alsace 153–6, 161–6, 199
Alsatians 157, 161
Altkirch 154
American Money and the Weimar Republic 73
Americans 6, 11–14, 22–3, 38
  arms control 138, 144
  buffer-states 59
  credits 71–2
  criticisms 199–200
  occupation 41, 58
  Polish Corridor 189–90, 193
  reparations 76, 78, 98–107
  Rhineland 57, 62

Amsterdam 126
animal feed 84
Annen 124
Anordnungen 39
appeasement 76, 189
Arbeiterstamm 120
Armaments Year-Book 142, 145
armistice 7–8, 22–3, 42, 113
  criticisms 197
  disarmament 115, 118–22, 126
  repatriation 153, 155, 157–8, 161, 165
  Rhineland 42, 51
arms traffic 113, 134, 136, 138–40, 142, 144–6
Armstrong 116, 125
army wives 49
Augusta, Kaiserin 40
Australia 143
Australians 38
Austria 155
Austrians 159, 161–2
Austro-German customs union 73
Austro-Hungarian empire 1, 199
autarky 73, 76
autonomists 62–5, 162

Bachmann, U. 72
bacteriological warfare 143–4
bad faith 81, 197
Baden 155, 160
Baden-Powell, R.S. 84
balance of payments 70, 72, 86
balance sheets 116
Balderston, T. 72
Baldwin, S. 33
Balfour, A. 6, 8
Baltic 7, 187, 190–1
Bank of England 66

Bank for International Settlements 72
banking 64, 74, 103, 119
Bardoux, J. 59
Bariéty, J. 57
Barrès, M. 59
Barthou, L. 59
Bauer, G. 24
Bavaria 15, 60–1, 63, 156
Baycroft, T. 171–84
Becker, A. 174
Beddington, E. 47
Belgians 12, 14, 31, 33, 38
    criticisms 198
    disarmament 115
    Flemish identity 171, 173, 177–81
    reparations 75, 88
    Rhineland 57–8, 62, 64
Belgium 11, 21, 34, 66, 81
    arms control 137
    disarmament 119
    Flemish identity 172, 174, 176, 178–9,
        182
    occupation 47
    reparations 87
Benes, E. 140
Berlin 24, 26, 28, 33, 49–50
    criticisms 197, 200
    disarmament 118, 122–4, 126–7
    Polish Corridor 188–90, 192–3
    reparations 74, 82–4, 87–8
    Rhineland 63
Beuel 33
Big Bertha 123
big business 113–31
billeting 38–9, 41–2, 90
Bismarck, O. von 61
Black February 45
black market 156–7
Black and Tans 46
Black Watch 46
Blomberg, - von 186
Blondel, G. 59
blueprints 122, 124, 126
Boches 155, 157–8, 163, 166
Boches du Nord 174
Bochum 25, 88
Bolivia 137
Bolshevism 1, 6, 45, 158, 162, 189–90,
    199
Bonar Law, A. 8, 26–7
Bonn 33, 41, 78
Borah, W. 146

Borbeck 121
Borchardt, K. 71–2
Bosch 114
Bourgeois, L. 134–5
Bradbury, J. 11
Brahms, J. 47
Braun, O. 83
bread 82–3, 86, 91
Briand, A. 11, 62–4
Britain 6–8, 10–11, 14, 16
    arms control 125, 135–8, 140, 142,
        144–6
    coal 86
    currency 66
    debt 74, 76
    occupation 66
    Polish Corridor 186, 188
    reparations 78, 97–8, 102
    sanctions 64
    venereal disease 43
British 1–3, 5–7, 9–10, 12–15
    arms control 123, 137
    buffer-states 59
    criticisms 197, 199
    disarmament 133
    enforcement 17
    fiscal arrangements 72
    Flemish identity 176
    occupation 57, 62
    Polish Corridor 187–93
    reparations 87, 98
    Rhineland occupation 21–55
British Academy 3
British Army of the Rhine (BAOR) 32,
    37, 39, 42–3, 49, 51–2
British Empire 37
The British in Germany 37
British Women Police 44
Bromberg 191
brothels 43
Brüning, - 72–6
Brussels 176
Buchheim, C. 77
Buer 89
Bulgaria 155
Burton, T. 144

Café Germania 47
Cambon, J. 9
Cambon, P. 9, 14, 26–7
Cameron Highlanders 44, 49–50
Canadians 38, 46

capitalism 78, 199
casino diplomacy 10
Catholics 60–1, 163, 172, 187
Cecil, R. 9, 135–6, 140, 143, 145, 187
censorship 164
Center for German and European
    Studies 69
Central America 144
Central Banks 72
Chamber of Commerce 176
Chamber of Deputies 175
chemical weapons 142–4
children 83–4, 88–91, 198
China 137, 181
chocolate 41–2, 84, 88
Christmas 39–40, 49
Churchill, W. 8, 46
citizenship 2, 154–5, 165
civil servants 61, 64–5, 72, 83
    disarmament 122
    reparations 85, 88, 92
    repatriation 154, 157–8, 161–2
civil war 6
Clark, N. 41
Clavin, P. 97–112
Clemenceau, G. 2, 6–8, 14, 23, 59, 62, 65,
    161, 190
clothing 89–90, 119
coal 65, 81–2, 84, 86, 88, 121, 181
Codyre, - 51
Cold War 77, 100, 106, 143, 199
Cologne 22, 25, 38, 42–7, 49, 51
Cologne Cathedral 42
Cologne Post 42
colonies 37, 41, 46, 134, 145
Comité Flamand de France (CFF) 178–9
commission de triage 157, 161–3
commission du deuxième degré 161
commission du premier degré 161
Commission on Polish Affairs 188
Committee on Intellectual Cooperation
    143
Committee of the Left Bank of the
    Rhine 59
Committee for the Regulation of the
    Trade in Arms 145
Communism 8, 15, 25–7 33, 83, 189, 192,
    199
company records 114–15
compliance 1–4, 13
Conference of Ambassadors 7–9, 25
Conference for the Supervision of the

International Trade in Arms and
    Ammunition and in Implements of
    War 139–40
conscription 119
Conseil Général du Nord 177
constitutions 33, 60–1
Contagious Diseases Act 43
Convention for the Control of the Trade
    in Arms and Ammunition 138
Convocation of Canterbury 43
Corbett Ashby, M. 44
Corfu 10
Costigliola, F. 101
Coulson, R. 43, 45, 49
Council of Four 7
Council of Ministers and Ambassadors 9
1/2nd County of London Yeomanry 47
Creek, P. 38, 41, 47
Crowe, E. 14, 33, 136
curfews 39
currency 126, 166
curriculum 121
Curtius, - 73
Curzon, G. 8–11, 14–15, 25, 29, 34
Czechoslovakia 137, 140
Czechs 186

D'Abernon, - 28, 30
Daimler 114
Danzig 9, 187–91, 193–4
Dard, - 62–3
Darmstadt 9, 26
Daudet, L. 59
Dawes Plan 57, 66, 71–2, 77, 103, 199
debt restructuring 78
Decisions 77
deflation 70–1, 73, 75–6
Degoutte, J-M. 58–9, 61–2 65, 87
Demange, V. 164
demilitarization 59
demobilization 1, 45–6, 114–15, 119
demography 165, 187, 190
Dendramis, V. 139
Denmark 135, 137
Départment du Nord 172
depression 69–70, 72–3, 76, 99, 101, 200
Derby, - 25
Deutsche Gesellschaftsgeschichte 114
Dewachter, J. 178
Dieburg 9, 26
diplomacy 2, 10–11, 16, 60
    disarmament 113–14, 146

Polish Corridor 192
reparations 99, 101
Rhineland 63–4
disarmament 2–3, 7, 10–11, 15–16,
    113–31, 133–51, 198
Dmowski, R. 187
Dominions 7, 38
Dortmund 25, 89
double-think 100
Doumer, J. 11
10 Downing Street 8, 14
Du Cane, J. 49–50
Dudley Ward, C.H. 38–40
Duisburg 12, 21, 28, 33, 64, 120
Duke of Cornwall's Light Infantry
    (DCLI) 51
Dulles, J.F. 12
dumping 70
Dunkirk 172, 175
Düren 33
Düsseldorf 12, 21–2, 28, 64, 127
Dutasta, P. 7

East Prussia 185–6, 191
Eastern and Central Europe 1, 9, 69, 85,
    139, 186, 192–3, 198–9
econometrics 71
Economic and Financial Organization
    104
Economic, Financial and Transit
    Department 105
economics 3, 12, 16, 23, 28–30
    disarmament 117, 136–7
    Flemish identity 175, 177
    Lorraine policy 158, 164–5
    Polish Corridor 187
    reparations 70–6, 78, 82, 86, 88, 90, 92,
        98–106
    Rhineland 32, 58–62, 64–5
The Economist 87
Edmonds, J. 37–8 43
Education Ministry 83–4
eggs 88
Einwohnerwehren 63
El Salvador 139
elastic formula 98
Elberfeld 25
Elliot, W. 43
émigres 161–2
Ems 33
English language 38, 49–50
Entente 14

épuration 154, 157, 160–1, 164–6
Essen 26, 82, 113, 115, 119–26, 128
ethics 92, 121
Ethiopia 146
ethnic cleansing 154, 193, 199
ethnicity 155–6, 181, 186–7, 198
ethnography 186–7, 199
Europe 1–3, 11, 14, 21–2, 28
    arms control 140
    criticisms 197–9
    disarmament 114, 116, 127, 133,
        137–8, 143
    Flemish identity 171, 182
    Polish Corridor 186, 189, 192–3
    reparations 73, 88, 99–101, 104
    Rhineland 34, 42, 62–3, 67
Everett, - 124
exchange rates 47, 156, 166
Executive Committee on Economic
    Foreign Policy 100–1
expulsion 153–66

famine 88, 92
Far East 76
fats 82–3
Federal Reserve 100
federalism 60–3
*Fédération Régionaliste du Nord et du
    Pas-de-Calais* 176–7
Feldman, G.D. 69–80, 82, 97
feminists 43–4
Ferguson, N. 70
Field Punishment Number One 41
final solution 74
financial institutions 92
Finland 137
First World War 1, 3, 21, 66
    identity 171, 173–4, 178
    reparations 76–8, 97, 99–100, 102, 104,
        106
Fischer, C. 1–4, 81–97, 197–200
fish 83–4
Fisher, H.A.L. 135
Flanders 171–82
Flemish language 172, 178
Flying Dutchman 37, 47
Foch, F. 7, 9, 15, 22–3, 25, 38, 65, 115,
    121
Fontainebleau Memorandum 186, 188
food 24, 45, 81–5, 88–9, 91–2, 118–19
footwear 89
Forbach 159

Foreign Economic Administration (FEA) 100
Fourteen Points 101, 185–6, 188, 199
Fourth Army 46
France 2, 5–8, 10–11, 14, 16
  arms control 118, 134–8, 140, 142–6
  criticisms 198–9
  debts 74
  Flemish identity 171–82
  Lorraine policy 153–5, 157, 161
  occupation 38, 45, 47
  Polish Corridor 188, 190
  politics 74
  reparations 76, 81, 87–8, 91, 102
  Rhineland 21, 27–8, 30, 32, 34, 54–68
Frankfurt 7, 9, 21–2, 26
Frankfurt Treaty 155
fraternization 41, 46–7, 49
Freistaat Danzig 191
French 1–3, 6–7, 9–14, 17
  arms control 115, 123–4, 126, 136–7, 140–1, 143
  criticisms 197–8
  Flanders 171–82, 199
  identity 171, 173–82
  language 154, 156
  Lorraine policy 153–9, 161–6
  occupation 38–9, 46, 49
  Polish Corridor 187, 189–90, 192–4
  reparations 74, 76, 81, 87, 90–1, 101
  Rhineland 22–33, 54–68
French Revolution 58–9
Fuchs, L. 50

gage productif theory 65
Gaiffier, E. de 14
Gelsenkirchen 88
Gendarmerie 161
General-Officer Commanding (GOC) 42–4, 47, 49–50
Geneva Protocol for the Pacific Settlement of International Disputes 144
George V 7
German Armed Forces 186
The German Business Cycle 71
German Federal Republic 77
German Historical Institute 69
German History Society 3
German Revolution 86
Germaniawerft 115
Germanisation 154, 161, 186

Germans 2–3, 5, 8–10, 12, 15, 17
  BAOR 38, 40–4, 47, 49–51
  big business 113–28
  criticisms 197–9
  enforcement 17
  Flemish identity 172, 174, 177
  language 50, 155, 157, 162, 166
  Lorraine policy 153–8, 160–6
  Polish Corridor 186–93
  reparations 70, 77, 81–94, 97–107
  Rhineland occupation 30, 32
  women police 44
Germany 1, 3, 5–16, 21, 23–8
  BAOR 37–52
  big business 113–28
  criticisms 197–200
  disarmament 133–46
  Flemish identity 175–80, 182
  Lorraine policy 153, 155, 158–9, 161, 164, 166
  Polish Corridor 185, 187–92, 194
  reparations 69–94, 97–107
  Rhineland occupation 30–4
Gilbert, P. 71
Gilgenburg 191
Godesberg 33
Godley, A. 32, 47
Goethling, - 51
Gogarty, O. St John 46
gold 85, 159
Goldstein, E. 3
governments 1–3, 6–9, 11–13
  arms control 140
  criticisms 198
  disarmament 115, 122, 125, 127, 134–9, 141
  enforcement 15–16
  Flemish identity 171, 175–7, 179–80
  Lorraine policy 155
  Polish Corridor 185–6, 189
  reparations 81, 83–6, 88, 90–2, 97, 99, 105
  Rhineland 25–6, 29–31, 33
Grahame, - 26
Grand Alliance 106
Gravenbroich-Düren line 32
Great Depression 76, 99, 101, 200
Great Powers 3, 185
Great War 1, 37, 113–15, 125, 142, 200
Greece 137
Greeks 139
Grey, E. 133

Grohmann, C. 153–69
Gross National Product 118
Grusonwerk 115
Guatemala 137
Guben 90
Guerrero, J.G. 139
Guiscard, J. 175
Gulf Wars 146

Haas, - 50
Hackspill, L. 165
Half, H. 51
Hall of Mirrors 5
Halliday, G. 49–50
Hambach 163
Hamborn 89
Hanau 9, 26
Hankey, M. 10, 189
Hansen, E-W. 114
Harding, H. 47
harvests 82–3
Headlam-Morley, J. 5, 8, 192–3
Heads of Delegation 7
Hermes, A. 85
Hessen 64
Hewart, G. 13
Heyde, P. 77
High Command 23
High Commission/High Commissioners 23–4, 29–31, 58, 61, 65, 162
High Seas Fleet 7
Hindenburg, P. von 7, 75, 118–20, 122
Hirsch, - 85
historians 1, 71, 97–8, 100–1, 103–4, 153
historiography 77, 97, 100
Hitler, A. 63, 75, 128
Hitler *Putsch* 63, 66
hoarding 82
Holland 1, 7
Hollweg, B. 7
Holtferich, C-L. 70
Homburg 9, 26
Hoover Moratorium 74
House, Colonel 22
Howard, E. 187–8 192
Howard, T.H. 38, 42
Howard-Lord Agreement 187
Hughes, C.E. 138
Hungarians 159, 161–2, 186
Hungary 155
Hut ab 37, 39
hyperinflation 45, 47, 70, 92

identity cards 39, 154, 156–7
identity formation 1–4, 7, 171–82, 186
Imperial General Staff 46
implementation 133–46
industrialists 60, 87, 118, 124, 158, 176
inflation 69–71, 85, 120–1, 126
intellectual property 124
Inter-Allied Military Control Commission (IMCC) 10–11, 115–16, 123–7
Inter-Allied Military Food Committee 23
Inter-Allied Rhineland Commission 7, 11, 23–4, 31, 38, 58
interest 75, 78
International Financial Conference 137
investment 71, 117, 121, 126–7, 173
Iran-Iraq War 146
Iraq 16, 113
Ireland 46, 106
Irish 44, 46
Israel 78
Italians 14, 141, 146, 181
Italy 7, 11, 137, 145–6

James, H. 71
Japan 7, 106, 126, 137, 145–6
Japanese 14
Jeannesson, S. 57–68, 101
Jeffrey, K. 3, 37–55
Jews 92, 186
journalism 59
Jouvenel, H. de 137

Kapp *Putsch* 6, 8, 10–11, 13–15, 21, 24–7, 47, 115
Kapp, W. 8, 15, 24
Kashubs 186–7
Kehl 159–60
Kent, - 101
Kerr, P. 8
Keynes, J.M. 87, 99, 101, 105
Keynesians 105
Kiel 113, 115, 120, 123
Kilmarnock, - 26, 31–3
King, - 43
Kladderadatsch 50
Knüttingen (Knitange) Foundries 160
Koblenz 23, 25–6, 57–8, 62
Koch & Kienzle 127
Königswinter 33
Konitz 191

Konstruktionsbüros 122
Kreise 58, 187
Krosigk, S. von 74
Krueger Plan 77
Krupp 113–31 198
Krupp, A. 124
Krupp von Bohlen und Halbach, G. 118, 122, 126
Kulmerland 185
Kulturkampf 58

Lancaster House 77
Lange, C. 137
Lansing, R. 199
Lasteyrie, C. de 65
Latin America 138
Lauenberg 191
Lausanne Conference 74–7
Laying, I. 47
League Council 134–5, 137–8, 140–3
League of Nations 9–10, 104–5
    covenant 133–46
    criticisms 198, 200
    identity 180
    Polish Corridor 188, 190, 192
Lee-Higginson Credit 77
Leffler, - 101
Lenin, V.I. 191, 193
Liberia 137
Liège 123
Lille 172, 174, 178, 181
Lincoln, Dean of 43
liquor traffic 134
Lloyd George, D. 6, 8, 10–15, 22–3, 25, 28–9, 58–9, 115, 186, 188–9, 191–4
Lloyd-George, D. 187
Locarno Agreement 200
London Debt Agreement 77–8, 85
London Reparations Agreement 199
London Schedule of Payments 21, 30
Long Gustav 123
Longhorne, - 123
Looten, C. 178
Lorenz-Mayer, M. 106
Lorrain 156
Lorraine 2, 153–66, 199
Lorrainers 153, 155–6, 165
Lothringen 153–66
Loveday, A. 105
Ludendorff, E.F.W. von 118
Luxembourg Commission 23
luxury goods 84

Lyautey, - 58
Lys river 172

MacDougall, W. 57
Macedonia 185
McNeil, W. 73
Madariaga, S. de 134
Magdeburg 113, 115, 120, 126
Main 34
Mainz 57–8
Malkin, H.W. 12
Manchester Regiment 50
Manchester, W. 128
manganese 117
Mangin, - 59
manufacturing 1
maps 2
Marienwerder 188, 199
Marin, L. 59
Marks, S. 16, 70
Marshall Plan 77–8 99
martial law 58
Marx, W. 66
media 59
Melchior, C. 74–5
Meppen 123–4
Metz 158–61, 163
Middle East 138–9
Middlesex Regiment 46
Military Police 41–2
military-industrial complex 87
milk 82–4, 88
Millerand, A. 9, 14, 25–6, 59, 62–3, 162
Minck, L. 162
Mirman, L. 158, 162–3
mobilization 1, 116, 141
Molotov, V. 194
money 42–3, 82, 104, 158–9, 165–6, 174–7
monopolies 115
Montgomery-Massingberd, A. 45
Moorhouse, R. 185–95
Morgenthau, H. Jr 102
Morgenthau Plan 100
Morland, T. 43
Morocco 58
Moscow Conference 98
Mosellans 157–8, 161–3, 166
Moselle 153–5, 157, 159, 163, 165–6
Muhr, W. 50
Mungenast, E-M. 163
Munich 62

Münster 123
mutinies 45
Mutual Assistance Treaty 144
mutually assured destruction 143

Napoleon 14, 113
Napoleonic Wars 3, 76
National Anthems 39
National Council of Women of Great
    Britain and Ireland 44
National Grain Bureau 85
National Socialists *see* Nazis
nationalism 63, 76, 158, 187
naturalizations 165
Nazis 63, 75–7, 92, 103, 106, 199
Near East 1
Netherlands 78, 98, 126–7, 137, 178
Netze 187, 193
New Zealanders 38, 49
Newfoundlanders 38
Nicolson, H. 2
North America 143
North Sea 172
Northern Ireland 16
Norway 78, 135
Norwegians 137
Noyes, - 23
nuclear weapons 143
Nurembourg 186

Oberammergau Passion play 47
Occupied Germany 38
Offenburg 156
Office of Strategic Services (OSS) 98, 100
oil 117
opera 47, 49
O'Riordan, E. 21–36
Orlando, - 190
Ottoman empire 1
over-employment 120

pacifism 180, 182
Palatinate 64, 156
Panzerplatten 115
Paribas 66
Paris Peace Conference 1–3 6
    criticisms 199
    enforcement 8–9, 13
    identity 175
    Polish Corridor 187, 189, 193
    reparations 102–3, 105
    repatriation 166

Rhineland 21–4, 59, 65
Parisians 155
Pas-de-Calais 172–3, 176
Paton, H. 188, 192
Paton Memorandum 188
patriotism 49, 63, 156, 161, 174, 178
Permanent Armaments Commission
    (PAC) 134–6, 141–2, 144–5
Pfalzburg (Phalsbourg) 153
photography 39, 88
Pinck, L. 163
Pinon, R. 59
plan d'aménagement 175
plebiscites 6, 10, 154, 188, 199
Plumer, H. 39, 42, 46–7
Poincaré, R. 7, 11, 22, 59, 62, 65–6,
    87
poison gas 142–4, 146
Poland 9, 137, 139, 144, 185–94, 199
Poles 181, 186–90, 193
police 44–5, 160, 166, 178
Polish Corridor 2, 185–95, 199
Polish Nationalist committee 187
politics 2–3, 6, 11, 16, 21–3
    criticisms 197, 200
    disarmament 114, 117, 128, 136, 140–1
    Flemish identity 172, 176, 179–82
    Lorraine policy 158, 161, 165
    Polish Corridor 187, 190–1
    reparations 70, 73–4, 76, 78, 82–3, 88,
        92, 99–101, 103–4, 106
    Rhineland 28, 32, 51, 58–9, 61, 64–5
Pomerania 83, 185–6, 188
Pomerellen 185
Poncheville, M. de 178–9
population of Lorraine 154–7
Portugal 106
potatoes 83–4, 88
poverty 44, 91, 158
Poznan 193
Preparatory Commission for a World
    Disarmament Conference 144
Princeton Mission 105
procuring 45
profit 66, 74, 82, 86, 116–17, 121, 174
prohibition law 41–2
propaganda 63, 101, 107, 140, 187
prostitutes 42–3, 45, 49
protectionism 105
Protestants 60–1, 186
Prothero Memorandum 188
Protocol for the Prohibition of the Use in

War of Asphyxiating Poisonous or Other Gases 144
Prussia 22, 58, 60–1, 63–4
  criticisms 199
  disarmament 113, 116
  Polish Corridor 185–7, 191, 193
  repatriation 156
Prussians 161

Quai d'Orsay 59, 61, 63, 66
Quakers 84
Queen Alexandra's Imperial Nursing Service Reserve 47

racketeering 83, 85
railways 31–2, 64, 74, 83
  Flanders 172
  Krupp 116, 118, 121
  Lorraine 159
rationing 82, 159
Rawlinson, H. 46
Recklinghausen 89–90
Recouly, R. 59
Red Army 126, 191, 199
Red Cross 89
Redslob, R. 162
Rees District 89
refugees 154, 158–9, 166, 172, 174, 193, 199
Reichsbank 71
Reichswehr 15, 25
reparations 3, 10–12, 16, 23
  crisis 27–30
  criticisms 198
  debate 69–80
  disarmament 137
  Flemish identity 175–7, 181–2
  human price 81–96
  long run 97–112
  Rhineland 30–1, 62, 64–6
Reparations Commission 7, 10–11, 30
Reparations Subcommittee 103, 106
repatriation 153–66
Réquin, E. 136, 143
requisitioning 81
restaurants 47, 88
revanchism 87, 193
Rheinhausen 121, 124
Rheinmetall 127–8
Rhenish State 61
Rhine 22–4, 30, 34, 38, 40
  disarmament 120

occupation 44, 46–7, 59, 65
repatriation 159–61
Rhine Command 37, 47
Rhineland 2, 7, 12–14, 42–4
  British soldiers 37–55
  criticisms 197
  disarmament 126
  French policy 54–67
  occupation 7, 21–36, 46, 115
  reparations 72
Rhineland Agreement 57–8
Rhineland Commission 17
Rhinelanders 38, 45, 60
Richelieu, A.J. 58–9
riots 88
Ritschl, A. 71–3, 76
Robertson, A. 17, 29–31, 34
Robertson, W. 42–3, 45–7, 49
Romania 139
Roosevelt, F.D. 99
Root, E. 143
Royal Army Medical Corps 50
Royal Institute of International Affairs 105
royalties 116
rubber 117
Ruhr 7–9, 12–13, 15, 30
  catastrophe 71
  coal 86
  criticisms 198
  evacuation 57, 66
  invasion 87–90, 92, 101, 115, 126–7
  occupation 21–2, 24–7, 30–4, 47, 61, 64–5
Ruhrort 12, 64
Rupprecht, Prince 7
Rural Visits Scheme 89
Russia 1, 6, 63, 101, 187, 189–90
Russians 98

Saar 9, 23
Saarbrücken 159
Saarburg 33
Saarland 156
Sahm, H. 191
Salewski, M. 114–15
sanctions 8, 12–13, 16–17
  criticisms 198
  reparations 73, 87, 91, 198
  Rhineland 28–31, 34, 61, 63–4
Sarreguemines (Saargemünd) 156, 160, 163

Saxony 61
Scandinavia 136
Scandinavians 145
Scapa Flow 7
Schacht, H. 76–7
Schanzer, C. 141
Schledbusch 25
Schleswig-Holstein 185
Schneidemühl 191
Schneider-Creuzot 116
School of Political Sciences 59
Schubert, F. 47
Schuker, S. 70, 101
Schuman, R. 163
search engines 78
secession 6, 61
Second World War 44, 71, 77
   criticisms 197–8
   disarmament 146
   identity 172, 174
   Polish Corridor 185
   reparations 97, 99–106
   repatriation 165
Secret Service 47
Senate 7, 59, 146
separatists 32–3, 60, 62, 66, 177–9
sequestration 159
Seydoux, J. 66
Sharp, A. 1–20, 197–200
Shaw, - 50
shell shock 185
Siemens 114, 127
Sigwald, M. 163
Silesia 189, 193
Simon, - 15
Simons, W. 28
Skoda 116
slave trade 134
Smuts, J. 185, 192
social disarmament 119
socialism 24, 61
Sömmerda 128
South Africa 136, 185
South Africans 38
Soutou, G-H. 57
Soviet Union 24, 98–100, 121
   criticisms 199
   disarmament 126, 139, 144, 146
   Polish Corridor 191, 194
Spa 82, 122
Spain 106, 137
Special Branch 43

Special Repatriation Bureau 158
Spiegel 77
sport 47
starvation 45, 81, 86, 89–91, 198
Stasiak, M. 50
State Department 98, 101
Sterling Area 98
Sthamer, F. 15
Stinnes, - 15
Stranders, C. 125
Strasbourg 59, 159
Strauss, J. 47
Stresemann, G. 200
strikes 8
Stuart, H. 23–6
subsidies 90, 119
sugar 84–5
Summary Courts 39, 49, 51
Supreme Council 9, 23
Swabia 61
Swaboda, - 49
Sweden 106, 127, 135
Switzerland 106, 187

Tangiers 106
tariffs 29, 61, 64–5
taxation 62, 82, 86–7, 102, 159, 175, 177
Taylorism 86
technology 124, 127
Temporary Mixed Commission (TMC)
      136–7, 139–41, 143
Tenfelde, K. 113–31
Territorial Committee 188
terrorism 88
Teutonic knights 186
Thionville (Diedenhofen) 158–60
Third World 73
Thuringia 128
Tiegelstahl 116
The Times 42, 44, 50–1
Tirard, P. 23–4, 58–66
Tirpitz, A. von 7
totalitarianism 103
Trachtenberg, M. 57, 101
trade unions 83, 85, 88, 91, 124
transport 83, 86
travel permits 153, 155
*The Treaty of Versailles. A Reassessment
      after 75 Years* 69
tribunals 161–3
tricolour cards 154–6
Trier 33

Trotsky, L. 191
Truma, H. 106
Tsars 6
Tuohy, F. 40–1, 45, 49, 51–2
Turkey 6, 9, 139, 155
Tynan Hinkson, K. 44, 49

Umstellung 115
underdeveloped countries 78
unemployment 44, 70, 90, 158
unification 78
Union of Soviet Socialist Republics
    (USSR) *see* Soviet Union
United Kingdom *see* Britain
United Nations 98
United States 3, 6–7, 14, 23
    arms control 117, 139–40, 142, 145–6
    criticisms 199–200
    Flemish identity 176
    Polish Corridor 190, 192
    prohibition law 41
    reparations 73–4, 97, 99–101, 103–6
    Rhineland 57
Upper Silesia 6, 10, 189, 193

Vancauwenberghe, M. 177
Vatican 60
venereal disease (VD) 43–4
Venezuela 146
Vergennes, - 58
Versailles Treaty
    BAOR 38
    criticisms 197–200
    disarmament 113–14, 121, 124, 126–7,
        134–5, 142, 146
    enforcement 1–20
    Flanders 171–82
    France 59–60, 63, 65
    human price 81, 92
    implementation 133
    Lorraine 157, 165–6
    Polish Corridor 185, 190–2, 194
    reparations 69, 74, 83, 98–9, 101,
        104–5
    Rhineland 22, 24–5, 27, 31, 33–5
    Ruhr 57–8
Vienna Treaty 3
Vistula 191
Viviani, R. 136, 141
voluntary repatriation 153–66
Von der Heyt mine 91
voters 92, 165

Wagner, R. 47, 160
Wahl, A. 153
Wall Street Crash 200
Wanne 91
war crimes/criminals 3, 7, 15
war widows 101
Warburg Bank 74
Warburg, J. 74–5
The Watch on the Rhine 41
Waterlow, S. 13, 29
weaponry 114
websites 78
Webster, A. 133–51
Wehler, H-U. 114
Weimar Republic 15, 60–2 70
    criticisms 198, 200
    disarmament 114, 120, 128
    reparations 72, 77–8, 82
welfare benefits 90
Welsh Guards 38
West Flanders 182
West Germany 99
West Prussia 187, 193
West Yorkshire Regiment 50
Western front 1, 172
Westhoek 172–3, 175–82
Wetterlé, abbé 161
White House 100
Whitham, - 50
Wiesbaden 33, 51
Wiesdorf 25
Wilhelm, Kaiser 7, 40, 126, 163, 192
Williamson, D. 37
Wilson, C. 43
Wilson, H. 46
Wilson, W. 6, 22–3, 59, 101, 185, 187–8,
        190–2, 198–9
Wimberley, D. 44, 47
Wirth, - 86
witch-hunts 163–5
Witten 89
Wolf, G. 161
women 1, 38, 40–5, 155–6, 160, 165–6
World Disarmament Conference (WDC)
        133, 145
Worthington-Evans, L. 43
Wright, - 50

Young Plan 72–4, 76

Zeidler, - 126
Zind, P. 155

.

Lightning Source UK Ltd.
Milton Keynes UK
21 August 2009

142950UK00001B/61/P